SUN SPACE

SUN SPACE

Science at a Threshold of Spiritual Understanding

OLIVE WHICHER

With a Foreword by Ernst Schuberth

and a Preface by Owen Barfield

RUDOLF STEINER PRESS, LONDON

First Edition, Rudolf Steiner Press, London 1989
© Olive Whicher

Colour Plates
© Philosophisch-Antroposophischer Verlag am Goetheanum, 4143 Dornach, Switzerland

ISBN 85440 726 X

German translation by Thomas Meyer, Verlag am Goetheanum, Dornach CH 1989
Sonnenraum—Ein Übungsweg zum Verständnis des Lebendigen

All outstanding author's rights in regard to the works of Rudolf Steiner are with the Rudolf Steiner Nachlassverwaltung, Dornach, Switzerland

Cover design by Walther Roggenkamp
Typeset by Emset, London NW10 4EH
Printed in W. Germany by Freiburger Graphische Betriebe, Freiburg i.Br.,

Synthetic Geometry
and
Spiritual Science

Geometrical Models and Drawings
by
George Kaufmann and Olive Whicher

The modern school of Synthetic Geometry — among the less known of the great scientific achievements of the 19th Century — is a valuable aid to the understanding of the more cosmic forces which are at work in the living kingdoms of Nature. Rudolf Steiner frequently urged the scientists among his pupils to look for the further development of geometrical thinking and imagination along these lines, and he gave many definite indications for this research. Modern Geometry provides the key, above all, for a scientific theory of the "Etheric", celestial Forces, which the living plant receives from the wide reaches of the Universe. . . .

Facsimile of a poster, written by George Adams Kaufmann (later George Adams) at the entrance to an exhibition mounted in London, The Hague and the Goetheanum, Switzerland, on the occasion of the Goethe Bicentenary celebrations in 1949.

FOREWORD

When Rudolf Steiner drew attention to the idea of "counterspace", it was the young George Adams, who took it up and was able to give it substance through the use of Projective Geometry. The first seeds of this idea germinated and grew in the thirties and forties of this century, finding many fields of application relating to aspects of life. Much became illuminated in the light of this idea, as described in many publications. In the early days, Olive Whicher joined George Adams as collaborator and helped in various ways to demonstrate, widen and enliven the understanding of the polarity within which we human beings, the kingdoms of nature and the cosmos stand. For about a quarter of a century, Olive Whicher has furthered the work of George Adams, without having him physically at her side, thus revealing a deeply rooted loyalty to their common aim.

As everyone who can look back upon life knows, ideas live differently in a young person and in an older one. In the first half of life, we have the urge to penetrate the world with thoughts of a logical, conclusive nature, while in later life—according to our individuality—we seek to feel our way livingly into the thoughts of others and to make these thoughts socially fruitful, in the sense of Goethe's saying: "What is fruitful, that alone is true."

This book shows how someone, who has led a long life devoted to a work, has learned to see the manifold phenomena of the world in the light of a livingly ensouled idea. A younger person, to the extent that he seeks specialized systems of knowledge, will find this book less useful than some books on the same theme. But life itself, through its own inner necessity, leads us in later life to seek a widening out of thoughts and ideas into the social realm. In this sense, this book will be of inestimable value. What did Rudolf Steiner mean—what forces did he want to activate in us, when he spoke of Space and Counterspace? Towards what spiritual place was he pointing us? This must be read between the lines. The single themes dealt with in the book set signposts for our orientation.

Some who find the *mathematical* treatment of space and counterspace inaccessible, will be able to experience something of the "Sun Space" and will perhaps be motivated to undertake a study of the underlying thought-structure, as it is dealt with in other books. On the other hand, many a systematic treatment will here find the necessary growth and development towards realms of reality, which in fact, only the living quality of these ideas can really unfold.

Ernst Schuberth,
Independent College for Anthroposophical Pedagogy,
Mannheim. October 1988
(Translation: Olive Whicher)

CONTENTS

Foreword by Professor Dr. Ernst Schuberth vi
Description of Colour Plates ix
List of Illustrations x
Preface by Owen Barfield xiii
Introduction xix

Chapter I *An Individual Pathway* 1

Chapter II *Search for Lost Worlds* 4

Chapter III *Mathematics and the Freedom of the Human Spirit* 10

Chapter IV *From Euclid to Projective Synthetic Geometry* 15

Perspective Transformation—Concepts of Infinity 15
Line-woven Forms in the Projective Plane 17
Crystal Weaving in the Light of Space 19
Forms woven One within the Other 21
The Awakening in the 17th Century 23
Re-awakening in the 19th Century—Principle of Duality 25
Towards a deeper Understanding of Polarity—Polar Transformation 26

Chapter V *Rudolf Steiner on Polar Spaces* 32

Mysticism and Mathematics at the Dawn of the Modern Age 34
Mathematics at the Threshold 37
The "Negative Space" of the Body of Formative Forces 39
An Incisive Step in the Mathematics of the Twentieth Century 44

Chapter VI *Polarity and Trinity in Nature and the Human Being* 48

The Quality of Uprightness 48
Water, the Life-blood of the Earth 51

Towards a New Consciousness 54
Ethereal Spaces of the Plant World 56
The Plant and the Human Form 60
Metamorphosis 66

Chapter VII   *Science and Spiritual Understanding*   72

Research into Streaming Media 73
Path-curve Surfaces—Fact or Fancy? 76
Towards "Global Thinking" 79
Molecular Biology—The Living Environment of Organisms 79
Plate Tectonics and the Shape of the Earth 83

Chapter VIII   *Christianity and Sun Space*   85

The Being of the Sun 85
Wisdom and Love 88
The Mystery of the Sun Being revealed by Artists 93
The World-embracing Problem of Economics 97

Chapter IX   *Past and Future*   100

Cromlech, Dolmen and Tumulus 100
Goetheanum Forms 105

Epilogue   113

The Foundation Stone   115

Notes   119

Bibliography   125

Acknowledgements   131

Index   133

Black & White Illustrations 1-82

Colour Plates I-XVI

PLATES

I   Ethereal Space of Plant Growth (From *The Plant between Sun and Earth*)
     The planar cones reveal the gesture at the growing point

II   Lemniscatory Space (From *The Plant between Sun and Earth* first edition)
     The curves illustrate the interpenetration of cosmic and earthly spaces

III   Ethereal Space of Path-curve Surfaces (George Adams and Lawrence Edwards)
     Path-curve surfaces are of a higher mathematical order than lemniscatory surfaces; they solve more elegently the mathematical problem of depicting the nature of an ethereal space

IV   Germination in an Ethereal Space (Photographs by W. Schaumann)
     In the hidden, "empty" realms of the growing-points, substance is born anew

V   Descent of the Sun-Being (Ecole Perceval, Chatou, Paris)
     A child's Imagination: the Sun is not just a fiery ball in the sky, but an all-embracing presence

VI   Adoration of the Shepherds and Kings (Mural at Sion, in the Alps; unknown master, probably about the end of the 15th century)
     The two Families; one in the snowy cold of winter, the other in the sunlit world of the eastern potentates

VII   Adoration of the Shepherds, Adoration of the Kings (Flemish School, early 16th century)
     The two Families; one Child, erect and active, is revered by the Kings, while the other lies on the ground and the wingéd angels hover over him and sing

VIII   Betrothal of St. Catherine. (Lukas Cranach the Elder, 1472—1553)
     The Child, intensely aware, observes natural phenomena

IX   Nativity (Geertgen tot sint Jans, about 1465—1495)
     Descended to the three dimensions of the earth.

X   Presentation of the Jesus-Child in the Temple (Stephan Lochner, about 1410—1451)
     In a Human Circle there appears the Seed of New Life

XI   The Adoration of the Shepherds (Rembrandt van Rijn, 1606—1669)
     Human beings form a Sun Space on earth

XII   The Pilgrims at Emmaus (Rembrandt van Rijn)
     Conversation between Heaven and Earth

XIII   "Nole me tangere" (Liane Collot d'Herbois, born in Tintagel in 1907)
     The Resurrection-Body, still standing on the Earth

XIV   "Easter" (Beppe Assensa, 1805—1987)
     Redemption of the Cross of Matter

XV   "Light and Darkness"—Goethe's Theory—The morning after the Deluge—Moses writing the Book of Genesis (J.M.W. Turner, 1775—1851.)
     Space for the birth of new matter

XVI   "Plant Growth" (Gerard Wagner, born in 1906)

BLACK AND WHITE ILLUSTRATIONS

INTRODUCTION
Photographs (a) Rudolf Steiner   (b) George Adams Kaufmann   (c) Louis Locher-Ernst   (d) Blake's "Newton"

CHAPTER IV
Figure
1. Theorem of Pappos
2. Line of Points and Line of Planes
3. Plane of Lines and Points
4. Point of Lines and Planes
5. Finite Euclidean Forms
6. Triangle in a Projective Plane
7. Lines of a Point in relation to Points of a Line
8. The Harmonic Quadrangle
9. Transformation of the Quadrangle through the Infinite
10. Projective Net of Quadrangles in Step-Measure
11. Hobbema's Avenue
12. Regular Net of Quadrangles in Step-Measure
13. Planes in a Line and Planes and Lines in a Point
14a. Cubic Form projected from a "Vanishing Plane"
14b. Cubic Forms woven side-by-side (Step-Measure)
15. Quartz Crystal light-woven from a Projective Plane
16. Projective Transformation of Circle into Ellipse
17. Projective Transformation of Circle into Parabola
18. Projective Transformation of Circle into Hyperbola
19. Forms convex and concave
20. Step-Measure and Growth-Measure
21. Projective Net of Quadrangles in Growth-Measure
22. Regular Net of Quadrangles in Growth-Measure
23. Logarithmic Spirals (Growth-Measure and Circling Measure)
24. Projective Net of Cube and Octahedron giving Growth-Measure
25. Circle-Curves in Growth Measure
26. Circle-Curves in oblique perspective
27. Family of Circle-Curves touching two fixed points and two fixed lines
28. Theorem of Pappos showing the Principle of Duality
29. The Dual Theorems of Pascal and Brianchon
30. Points and Lines and the Circle-curve
31. Pole and Polar with respect to

32. As the Pole moves out, the Polar moves in, and vice versa
33. Pointwise and Linewise Circles
34a. Poles within answer to Polars without
34b. Polar Families of Circles in Growth-Measure
35. Creation of Lemniscate and Cassini Curves
36. Polar reciprocal Curves
37. Polar Reciprocation between Centre and Infinite Periphery
38. Pole and Polar with respect to the Sphere
39. Polar Transformation (Metamorphosis) Cube and Octahedron
40. Cube Contracting, Octahedron Expanding
41. Self-polar Tetrahedron
42. Icosahedron and Pentagon-Dodecahedron

CHAPTER VI
Figure
43. Eurythmists
44. Polarity of Circles in a Plane and Cones in a Point
45. Flowing Movement in Water and Plant (Schwenk)
46. Cosmic Space for the Development of a Life (Nilsson)
47. Field Hamster feeling towards Human Verticality
48. Sketch: Plant between Earth and Cosmos (Steiner)
49. The tiny Hollow in the Heart of a Seed
50. Germinating Seeds—Polarity of Centric and Peripheral Gestures
51. The Well, an inner, living space
52. The Tree's Unfolding Growth and Plastic Outline
53. Two kinds of Force and the Horizontal Plane
54. The Sheath of Muscles (Vesalius)
55. The Man of Bone (Vesalius)—Finished Form
56. Heart and Lung (Rauber Kopsch)—Leaf and Bud
57. Study of a Nude Youth (Michelangelo)
58a. Growth-measure revealed in the Human Hand (Rauber Kopsch)
58b. The Spinal Column (Vesalius) pictures a projective Growth Measure
59. Bones of the Vertebral Column (Rauber Kopsch)—Lemniscatory Formation
60. Experiment on Foot
61. Plant and Insect Metamorphosis

CHAPTER VII
Figure
62. Christ in the Mandala (Veselay, France)
63. Path-Curves (Edwards)
64. Models of parts of Path-curve Surfaces
65. Path-curves in Plant Buds (Edwards)
66. The Tetrahedral Structure of the Earth

CHAPTER VIII
Figure
67. Twelve-year-old Jesus in the Temple
68. The Virgin and the Child (Leonardo da Vinci, 1452—1519)
69. Madonna di Terranova (Raphael, 1483—1520)
70. Mestre de Sant Joan de Boi (End of the 11th century)
71. The Annunciation (Lukas van Leyden, 15th century)
72. The Nativity (Meister Francke 14th—15th century)

73. The Baptism (Gerhard David, around 1460—1523)
74. The Enthronement of the Virgin (Jean Fouquet, around 1415—1460)
75. The Last Supper (Meister des Hausbuches, end of the 15th century)
76. The Resurrection (Fra Beato Angelico, 1387—1455)

CHAPTER IX
Figure
77. Irish Sun Cross
78. A Dolmen (south of Penmaenmawr, Caernarvon, N. Wales)
79. The First Goetheanum (drawing by Axel Ewald, from a photograph)
80. Freely drawn symmetry exercises for children (after Steiner)
81. Polar curves with respect to an imaginary circle
82. Sun Seal (after Steiner)

Unnumbered—
Dodecahedron in the Sun Space (sketch by Karl Kemper 1881—1957)

PREFACE

Anyone who has interested himself historically in the nature of human consciousness and the changes it has undergone in the sequence of the ages can hardly fail to be struck by one outstanding feature that marks the most recent of those changes. I mean the one that most distinguishes our own age from all those that have preceded it; and I am referring to a change in what had been called the 'reality principle'. The whole way in which human beings look at, feel about and act upon the world around them depends, more than anything else, on what they assume to be real and what they assume to be unreal.

Present day humanity, at all events in the West, believes, or rather it takes for granted, that anything it can perceive through the senses, and especially solid objects, is real and that the rest is unreal. If this emphasis on the importance of sense-perception is the outstanding characteristic of the age we live in, there is still something else that distinguishes this last from all preceding changes. Whereas those were wholly evolutionary and non-intentional, this latest change has been partly intentional. It is by no means the case that contemporary man never has an "inner" experience as influential as a sense-perception. If he nevertheless regards only the latter as real, it is partly because he has been led to do so by the development during the last three or four hundred years of a natural science whose method of enquiry, and therefore its conclusions, are founded, for good and ill, on that very assumption.

It is true that modern science also assumes the real existence of "forces", which are not perceptible by the senses, so that there is a certain inconsistency there—an inconsistency that was underlined by Auguste Comte, the father of positivism, when he maintained that the concept of a disembodied force is a survival of primitive animism. But since the only forces with which science has so far concerned itself (gravity for instance) can be exactly measured by their perceptible effects the challenge could be safely ignored. So common sense about the world, which is another name for everyman's 'reality principle', takes it for granted today that that world consists of solid objects in space and the forces that move them to and fro there. It is true, there is also a something called 'consciousness', or 'mind', but that is merely a rather anomalous attribute of the objects, a flicker hovering over the physical brains to be found in a few of them. It is common sense to experience the world in that way, because that is the way all sensible men experience it.

And yet that is an overstatement. Latterly, and especially in the last few decades, the validity of the common sense outlook has been called in question by a small but steadily increasing number of thoughtful minds. It is still a very small number and its very existence, let alone its significance, is virtually unknown to the public at large. The same could be said of the scientific establishment; for though it is true that the thoughtful minds include among them one or two speculative physicists, this has so far had no effect on the presuppositions limiting the method by which scientific research in general is ruled. I emphasize the last few decades, because it seems to me that the questioning minds of the immediate present differ from earlier ones whereof we have any record in two respects. Firstly they are more numerous, and secondly they tend no longer to see their own questioning merely as an interesting academic exerdise but rather as voicing a desperate need. If what everyone takes for granted is indeed largely based on illusion, that drawback must be rather more than amusing. So much of what is amiss with contemporary humanity, and now with the planet it inhabits and exploits, can be shown to originate in the reductionism or materialism, call it what you will, on which its common sense is based. Or is "amiss" a strong enough word? "Menacing" would perhaps be more adequate.

Maybe the number of these questioning minds will continue to increase. I believe it will. Perhaps the argument that reductionism begets illusion will in time be aired in public. If so, will that suffice to remove the menace? I fear not. Because what we are talking about when we speak of a reality principle is not a system of ideas but a mode of experience; and it is not the less so when it is founded (as to a considerable extent it is today) on *superseded* ideas. The reign of King Reductionism, and the laws by which he governs behaviour, will not be overthrown by convincing arguments alone, though it will not be overthrown without them. For what would have to be changed is not a system of ideas but an inveterate outlook. And that will have happened only when it has become a matter of everyday experience that the inner world of consciousness is on the same footing of reality was the world of things—that the former is not an attribute of the latter but correlative to it. Or, putting it another way, that the relation between them is not one of categorical severance between a real and an unreal, between a substantial and an unsubstantial, but of a polarity between reals.

It has perhaps come true by now that to *conceive* of a polar relation between the phenomenal and the noumenal, or (more crudely) between matter and mind, is not all that difficult, though it is difficult enough. Nor is the further step—becoming convinced of it—a very long one. But how to convert the conviction from mere acquiscence in a metaphysical proposition to actual experience? How to *realise* it? Samuel Johnson had an acquaintance who once told him that he had tried hard to be a philosopher, but "cheerfulness kept on breaking in." In the same way contemporary common sense keeps on breaking in on attempts to realise the polarity. Samuel Taylor Coleridge, who devoted the main energies of his life to arguing for polarity, saw this corollary clearly enough. "It is not enough", he wrote, "that we have once swallowed it—the *Heart* should have *fed* upon the *truth* as insects on a leaf—till it be tinged with its colour and show its food even in the minutest fibre" (Collected Works, Vol.4, p.338. Princeton).

It is that indispensable second step forward that this book is designed to facilitate. More particularly its aim is to help its readers to overcome one special stumbling-block that plays a prominent part in that "breaking-in" of common sense and the illusion it fortifies. And here a brief digression may be serviceable. The English language has a significant idiom for expressing doubt about the reality of some phenomenon by which the speaker is confronted. "*Is it really there?*" he asks. That way of putting it is significant because it implies an automatic assumption that reality depends on position—not a specified position, but *some* fixed position—in space. Incidentally the German word for existence, *Dasein*, carries the same implication. Reality is felt to depend, not alone on sense-perception, but also on "thereness". In other words the post-renaissance consciousness that has led to our absolute Cartesian dichotomy between matter and mind is closely connected with our way of experiencing space. It is above all that way—"the predominantly spatial thinking of today", as the author calls it—with which the book is deeply concerned. The polarity it particularly expounds therefore is, not that general one between matter and mind, or between macrocosm and microcosm, but the polarity between point and plane, between periphery and centre—indeed, a polarity between conceptions of space.

How do we habitually imagine space, if we stop to imagine it at all? Surely as something like the inside of a room that isn't there, consisting of a number of places where we can put articles of furniture etc. We cannot really distinguish the idea of space from that of place; and flowing from this disability comes the habit of imagining space itself as a kind of something that is still present even when it is empty. Certainly (we feel) space may not exist to the same extent as the furniture—but still, it is a lot more real than mind. Einstein's relativity has no doubt attracted much attention, but it has had no effect on our *experience* of space. It could be tempting to go on from here to consider how far this curious reification of emptiness is responsible for those generously quantified and slenderly evidenced speculations of contemporary astronomy and astrophysics concerning billions of 'light years' of untravelled and untravellable distance; but this is not the place for it.

Certainly the spatial thinking of today is not the spatial thinking of all time. It is not that of a period even as recent as the middle ages. We are frequently informed, by those who have never looked into it, that the philosophy of those days enjoyed discussing how many angels can stand on the point of a needle. But what Thomas Aquinas, for instance, in fact maintained was, that the angelic consciousness occupies space, not by filling but by *containing* it. What was so different in the past may, it seems, again become different in the future.

I have thought it best to use most of the space available to a Preface to place the book, so to speak, in the broad commonwealth of ideas, rather than to attempt any prospective summary of its contents. Its more immediate connections are sufficiently mapped by names and acknowledgments to be found in the text. For the rest, the reader will discover for himself that its backbone is mathematics; mathematics considered both historically and epistemologically. Historically it traces the crucial part played by precisely mathematics, and particularly Euclidean geometry, in what may be called the descent from an older, living link between man and nature—a link that amounted to conscious participation in nature's process—and it goes on to show how once again it is mathematics, and particularly projective geometry, which is adapted to lead human consciousness out of its present severance from the life of nature and upward to a participation therein that is at once old and new. Old because it is participation, new because it is a kind of participation that no longer entails (as was the case with the older, atavistic one) an absence of controlling self-consciousness.

Projective (Synthetic)[2] geometry flowered early in the nineteenth century; but the synthetic geometry with which the author is concerned goes beyond the merely formal, geometrical realm. It contains a new mode of perceiving or way of thinking, which was initiated by Rudolf Steiner and then developed above all by George Adams. The reader will soon discover that he is not merely being informed of the place occupied by that discipline in the history of ideas but is, with the help of some practical exercises, being intensively educated in it. So that if he is to get from the book anything like the whole of what it has to offer, he will need a good deal of patient application.

There are two features in it which some may find disturbing. Directly and indirectly the exposition in based, not quite exclusively but nearly so, on the work of Rudolf Steiner. This causes the present writer no difficulty since he has long been convinced that historians of the future will find Steiner's mind at least as central to the present and coming age as Aristotle's was to the pre-renaissance world. But in any case the objection is one fit only for a dryasdust. In assessing their validity serious thinkers ignore the provenance of ideas and concentrate on their substance. Others may be puzzled by a text that alternates in an unusual way between acute and sometimes highly technical exposition and appeals to feeling. It would take too long to go into this. It is not an accident of the author's personality. The relation between thinking and feeling is here part of the *res gestae*. Or, in the Coleridgean metaphor, encouraging the insect to feed, as well as crawling, on the leaf is integral to her subject. The kind of imaginal thinking Olive Whicher inculcates is a kind wherein feeling, and indeed a measure of willing, is incorporated and absorbed. This is something altogether different from logical, or would-be logical, thinking, distorted by emotion. Anyone acquainted with her earlier book, written in collaboration with George Adams, *The Plant between Sun and Earth*, will, I think, see what I mean. Projective geometry in all its austerity is there too; but such a reader will have found it impossible to re-open that book without being reminded, for instance by its beautiful coloured plates, of the tenderness of feeling towards even some common wild flower that is inseparable from imaginal thinking about its growth and structure, and the enhanced perception that that entails. He will find it equally impossible not to welcome as warmly as I do another book from the same source.

Owen Barfield
Forest Row, Sussex.
March 1987

Rudolf Steiner 1915

INTRODUCTION

Two main aims have inspired the writing of this book. The first is to help those who do not find easy access to ideas clothed in mathematical or geometrical thinking, who therefore find the idea of polar spaces and polar forces abstract and difficult, perhaps setting it aside as an intellectual and unrealistic pursuit. In describing something of my own pathway, first to Rudolf Steiner and Anthroposophy,[1] and then to the modern science which is at the heart of it, I hope to show that for a general approach to what is admittedly quite a difficult subject, an advanced training in mathematics and physics is not the only way of access (it may even prove a hindrance). Nevertheless, it goes without saying that to establish a strict method of approach to the fields at the gateway of which modern science itself now stands, a rigorous mathematical treatment, with proper regard for the tenets of a true science, is essential. This is however already available in a number of publications so that I feel justified in writing, in an elementary and simple way, a companion volume to *The Plant between Sun and Earth*.

The second aim is to call attention to a theme at the heart of Rudolf Steiner's lifework, which gives it, I believe, its unique character; namely that it is in relation to modern *materialistic thinking* that the time has now come for mankind to go forward towards a renewed understanding of fundamental spiritual issues. Steiner showed that the scientific materialism of the west is a right and inevitable phase in mankind's evolution. We should be grateful for it and for the opportunity to transmute it, because the emptiness of materialism is the very ground into which that freedom of thought is born, which will allow the science of the future to blossom and grow.

Science, in its materialism, has temporarily lost sight of the human being and of the living aspect of nature, but it has freed itself from mysticism and from the influence of traditional beliefs. Steiner saw the non-Euclidean geometries of the 19th century, and above all modern Synthetic or Projective Geometry[2], as significant evidence of a new and free activity of modern thinkers. He called for the further development of Synthetic Geometry to provide the necessary mathematical forms of thought to counterbalance the one-sidedly analytical nature of materialistic science.

It is with complete confidence that I place Rudolf Steiner in the centre of my life and work. I have yet to find a figure of such stature in present-day culture. This book addresses itself to those who have already met Anthroposophy[1] but find its relation to science difficult, and also to others who recognise that science today, notwithstanding its great achievements, is one-sided, often leading up dark alleys in its dealings with realms of life—human life and living nature.

For example, people coming from the medical schools are often full of questions, for they realize that, in all the years of study, they have not acquired the facility to diagnose, and that apart from the wonderful achievements of surgery, modern medicine has not taught them the art of healing. In agriculture, too, the question is urgent—how to understand living nature and grow real food.

Anthroposophical practice in these two fields has progressed a very long way since the first men and women listened to Rudolf Steiner and spent their lives using these indications and growing towards a fuller understanding and achievement. Both anthroposophical medicine and bio-dynamic agriculture, though thinly spread, are now world-wide. In the field of education the Steiner schools form the largest group of non-affiliated schools in the world.[1]

It is characteristic of the way Steiner worked that it was only when questions were put to him in the various practical fields did he feel free to answer and thus to open up new avenues of research in so many aspects of life. Thus it was in the arts and the sciences and even in the creating of a modern Way of Initiation.

In 1919, only six years before his death, the specific question was put to Rudolf Steiner concerning the possibility of establishing a counter-balance to the prevailing one-sidedly atomistic theories of science through the further development of the concepts to be found in projective synthetic geometry. He at once confirmed this possibility and began to indicate the direction in which mathematical research should go, towards the further development of this field. He began to awaken the idea of polar spaces where forces work in an opposite way to the forces known to mechanical science. To the familiar idea of Earth-space he began to add the idea of a cosmic type of space according to the laws of which the forces of life work. He used such terms as 'etheric space', 'sun space', 'negative space' and 'counterspace' (Gegenraum), and he called for the mathematical formulation of such a type of 'polar reciprocal space' with the forces inherent in it. (Today he might be better understood by the use of other words, but our task here will be to rise beyond terminology and theory and to reach towards a realm of actuality, which will include not only abstract mathematical thoughts, but also fundamental and intuitive experience.)

First in this field of mathematical research were George Adams Kaufmann, M.A. Cantab. (1894—1963) and, some years later, the Swiss mathematician, Professor Louis Locher Ernst (1906—1962). Others have followed these two pioneers, the most stalwart friend among them being Dr. Georg Unger, who, following Dr. Locher-Ernst, has for many years led the Mathematical-Astronomical Section at the Goetheanum in Dornach, Switzerland.

A scientist well known in the modern world, once his thesis has been to some extent accepted, can afford to write—or let others write—in a popular style about work not always easily accessible to his readers. In a science arising out of Anthroposophy, very great care must be taken, because the borderline between it and what might be termed "pseudo-science" may become confused, and false impressions may arise. Anthroposophy is based on clear thinking and not on any vague mysticism or outworn dogma; it is in this sense that it is modern.

Reductionism is a necessary phase in science, but only a phase; it is a way of thinking which deals efficiently with what has *already been created*, especially in the field of inanimate nature. Today, however, research into the living organism reveals problems, such as "organisation" in biology—and in other spheres of life—calling forth questions concerning the *creative process* and the origin of life. Where are the boundaries of Science today? With this question, science is at a threshold.

Rudolf Steiner points the way across this threshold, in terms of modern and future ways of thinking. He does not negate materialism, but shows how to transcend it, while preserving the exactness and clarity of thought upon which the purely materialistic way of thinking is based. This, in itself, belongs to the evolution of human consciousness. It has provided mankind with great power, in the observation of natural phenomena through the microscope and the telescope in the laboratory, the clinic and in the field.

Mathematics is the handmaiden of science, but it is an art, and like all arts, it relates to deep truths of existence. It is a mode of expression which is born of sense-free thinking; among its many aspects is geometry and herein lies its kinship with imagination.

The reader will find various fields of art and science merely touched upon in this book, but brought together in order to reveal the width of application inherent in the new forms of so-called 'geometrical' imagination and to inspire further research. To this end, attention is drawn to the other relevant publications.

A deep and truly spiritual understanding of the Idea of Polarity complements a one-sidedly analytical and mechanistic world conception.

* * *

My thanks are due to many friends for their indispensable help, both spiritual and practical, and not least to all those, who so generously contributed financially, in order to bring an otherwise expensive book into a price-range accessible to students. I owe a debt of gratitude to Thomas Meyer, who enthusiastically began the translation into German, before the English text was finally completed, and to the Goetheanum publisher for his support and understanding in the making of the book.

Olive Whicher

Easter 1989

George Adams Kaufmann
(1894–1963)

Louis Locher-Ernst (1906–1962)

Georg Unger (geb. 1909)

Chapter I

A PATHWAY

> "I am the way, the truth and the life".
> St. John, Chapter 14, verse 6.

The search for a way on beyond materialism has become very urgent and more vocal in recent decades. In the words of Christopher Fry, events have become 'soul size' and the cry to awake 'for pities' sake' begins to reach deeper into human hearts, with the question, whether modern science is leading in the right direction. Individual biographies recount in ever more dramatic colours the human struggles to transcend the emptiness of modern life; for some it becomes a matter of life and death, even in youth and childhood.

My own experience, in a happy and sheltered childhood and adolescence, was far less dramatic, though nonetheless incisive. In beautiful English countryside, the fairies were surely very near, and Orpheus with his lute was always close at hand. Once, walking alone, listening to my footsteps ringing on the granite pavement, stars shining in the evening sky, I knew for certain that they and I and the Earth belonged together—that all was one.

Then, when the time for questioning came, it came like a bolt from the blue: What if there is nothing behind the beautiful cows in a green field? What if my atheist friend is right after all and there *really is no God*! Simply to believe what others tell me will not do; there must be some way of *knowing*!

Life gave abundant opportunity for exploration and my search led in many directions and into several countries. Then one day, on a beautiful Sunday evening in springtime, I walked almost inadvertently into a house I had not noticed before, although I had passed it often enough on the top of the bus, while visiting, ever since I was a small child. It was Rudolf Steiner House in London.[1] Soon after I entered, one of Steiner's early pioneers, Dr. Walther Johannes Stein began a series of four weekly lectures; the first was on the mineral kingdom—then came plant, animal and man. I listened enthralled. Why had I not heard things like this before? It all seemed so familiar, so obvious, and yet it was all quite new. Here for the first time were thoughts about realms I had hitherto met only in the form either of religious teaching or scientific questioning. Here was nothing vague or mystical; religion and science merged here in a way which was clothed in clear thought.

At last I had found what I had been looking for, and the large hall turned into a great gateway, through which I could pass into a quite new phase of my life.

Reading the book *Occult Science* and continuing to attend lectures felt like rediscovering a world I knew and nevertheless had still to discover. Here indeed was the beginning of the path to which my search had led. Many were there then, besides Dr. Stein, who had known and worked with Rudolf Steiner, until his death ten years previously; among them was D.N. Dunlop, one of his closest friends.

Some two months later, in May 1935, I met George Adams Kaufmann, who was later to become a lifelong friend and colleague. It befell that Mr. Dunlop, who was then Chairman of the Anthroposophical Society in Great Britain[1], died, and the first occasion I experienced in this Society was his cremation. It was an unforgettable occasion, at which two of his friends spoke, Dr. Willem Zeylmans von Emmichhoven from Holland and George Adams Kaufmann on behalf of the movement in England.

In the years which followed, until war broke out at the end of the decade, there was a rich and active time of work in London and on the continent and opportunity for introduction to the new art of Eurythmy, to painting, sculpture, woodcarving, drama. Some who had worked with Rudolf Steiner came to live in England, and many visited. Frau Dr. med. Ita Wegman, founder of the pioneer medical work, and Dr. Elisabeth Vreede, leader of the Mathematical Astronomical Section at the Goetheanum, were often with us.

Among all the lectures and courses were those in projective (synthetic) geometry given by George Kaufmann. At school I had loved Euclidean geometry, the feeling of certainty it gave, and the opportunity to tackle proofs. Now geometry began to reveal itself in quite a new guise and the mobility of thinking and quality of inner thought-pictures to which I was now introduced helped me greatly to begin to understand Rudolf Steiner's immense work.

Beginning to study Anthroposophy and learning at the same time about the scientific tasks and indications Steiner had given, I realized that these new geometrical concepts served as clear guidelines into a new way of thinking. Just as the old, well-tried Euclidean concepts I had so much enjoyed had given me such a firm foundation, so now here was an equally sure pathway; old and familiar thoughts and pictures could be entertained in the mind and transformed into entirely new ones. Also, in practice, beautiful drawings could be made, which helped me to understand and take hold of new and difficult ideas,—ideas I met and tried to compass in anthroposophy as a whole. The way led clearly beyond the realm of mere outer form or inner theorising. Here indeed lay a life's task and I lost no time in taking it up.

Although at school I had enjoyed algebra, I had not gone very far with it; now I quite consciously avoided it. I was encouraged in so doing by my teacher, whose gift it was to surmount the abstract methods of science and mathematics and to create the picture-quality of the new "geometry." As he himself put it, the task was to disenchant the beautiful princess, hidden as she was—and in part still is—in a thicket of abstraction difficult to penetrate and bring to life.

In George Adams' first book *Strahlende Weltgestaltung** and in the later work *The Plant*

---

* *As the author was English, he left off the Kaufmann during the Second World War.*

between Sun and Earth there appear for the first time full illustrations of what in the classical textbooks is described with few diagrams and most often expressed only algebraically. Algebra is indeed a most useful and necessary tool, and many a mathematician experiences beauty in it. Adams, however, if he was unable to solve a problem geometrically in his imagination, would say jokingly that he would have to "put it through the sausage-machine" and solve the problem algebraically. It was, however, always a last resort to which he turned reluctantly. It is, indeed, a shortcoming, not to be able to work the sausage-machine, but the training in mobile, yet exact pictorial thinking is far more important and is indeed essential, if the princess is to reveal herself in all her beauty.

During the years following Rudolf Steiner's death, artists and scientists in the various fields who had heard and worked with him began to take their work further. These were the years which saw especially the medical work grow and develop in the hands of Dr. Ita Wegman. In the year 1934, Adams published the large, fully illustrated volume in German *Strahlende Weltgestaltung*, revealing the beauty of synthetic geometry, its relationship to the historical development of art and of modern, thought-permeated consciousness, seen from the point of view of Anthroposophy. A second volume was to have been added, which would have dealt in further depth with the ideas of polarity and of polar reciprocal spaces and forces. In fact, the destiny of the Anthroposophical Movement after the death of Rudolf Steiner made the writing and publishing of this second volume impossible. The conception was however published in 1933, though in smaller compass than intended. It came out in companion articles in German and in English in the two anthroposophical journals in existence at that time. This work appeared again in the two small books published shortly after the death of George Adams, entitled *Physical and Ethereal Spaces* and *Von dem Aetherischen Raume*.

Working independently, Professor Louis Locher-Ernst came later also to the same mathematical solution of Steiner's conception of counterspace. In 1940, he published his *Projektive Geometrie* and in 1951 *Raum und Gegenraum*. George Adams amplified his first statement of *Physical and Ethereal Spaces* in the work we produced together *The Plant between Sun and Earth*, which he considered took the place of the second volume of *Strahlende Weltgestaltung*.

In the elementary approach to this whole realm, which the present book is attempting, I have not introduced all the concepts of higher mathematics which are essential to the scientific treatment of the subject. For instance, we should need to include the realm of the imaginary numbers in mathematics,[4] which, even in the books on the plant had to be contained to a minimum. The interested reader should turn to other subsequent works, also of other authors.

My attempt is to remove still more of the thorny hedge surrounding the beautiful princess and to allow her to speak through the world of picture and of ordinary human experience. The pathway of mathematics has led humanity away down into the bowels of the Earth in search of life, but it has begun to lead upward again. The art of mathematics, which built the downward steps, sheds light on our upward path.

Chapter II

SEARCH FOR LOST WORLDS

> "It is no exaggeration to say that the future of civilization depends on the degree to which we can balance the forces of science and religion."
> A.N. Whitehead in 1925:

One day a child was playing beside a mountain stream. The little four year old boy was with his parents as they sat resting by the stream. He played with flowers which grew in the grass; far away in a world of his own, he picked the flowers and then planted them again in the soft, damp earth by the water, to make a 'garden'. All the while, the sunshine entered through the trees and the water sang its song as it frolicked by.

There grew in this place many Forget-me-nots and the little boy kept looking at them. He felt their soft, green stems and leaves and saw the ring of beautiful, blue petals, the little yellow circle within, and within that, in the very centre of the flower, the little hole, black and dark inside.

The child was deeply fascinated by the little round, black hole in the heart of the Forget-me-not flowers. He held one in his hand and peered into the little hole. Suddenly, he was inside! He had slipped through the tiny opening into another world! All about him was light and colour and he felt very happy, full of joy and peace. After a while, he slipped out again, into the world where his parents were sitting quietly on the banks of the stream. And then, for what seemed a long time, he went on playing with the Forget-me-nots, slipping in through the little hole to the wonderful world within and coming out again at will, back and forth between the two worlds, until his parents called him and they went on their way.

It was a never-to-be-forgotten experience, the wonder and brightness of which did not fade in later life, but could always be recalled, bringing with it the inexpressible feeling of joy and happiness, even when life had become difficult—very dark and cheerless.

The story is a true one. At the end of the Second World War, some twenty-five years later, the boy, now a young man, married, whose career had been delayed by the war, was back at University, taking a degree in Mathematics. During a vacation he had attended a course given by George Adams in Stuttgart, on "*Projective Geometry and the Science of Physical and Ethereal Spaces*," during which time reference was made to the plant world and to Goethe's *Metamorphosis of Plants* and Rudolf Steiner's descriptions of the etheric worlds, in the light of synthetic projective geometry, which gives a new approach to morphology.

After the course, the young man told me the story as an expression of his gratitude, that here in clear and objective mathematical thinking, he had found confirmation of the spiritual—even scientific—reality of a world of subjective experience, which, however vital it had seemed, had had to be regarded as a mere phantasy of childhood. "Now I know", he said "that my experience in childhood corresponds to a scientific truth."

How many a childhood experience goes beyond the prosaic reality of everyday, dipping into another world, which seems to be just beyond or hidden within this one... Poetry, fairytales and dreams tell of it—another realm, which reveals itself from time to time, filled with something alive or magical, different from the ordinary world.

Just as it is when looking back into memories of childhood, so also into our time there shines the light of a Golden Age, a time which *was*, before mankind had descended into the dust and turmoil of the present materialistic civilisation. Just as the child in growing up gradually comes out of a dream world to meet the glare of everyday "normality", so in the scientific age men throw away poetry and religion and concentrate hard on external, material sides of existence.

This is really as it should be, if all that is left of religion is an empty phrase, depending only on belief. For it is indeed the task of our time to go beyond mere belief and begin to *know* again. We must regain access to those lost worlds of experience, *without losing* the hard won footholds of an earthly consciousness. It is an adult, day-waking consciousness which the modern world provides, based as it is on the clear thinking which sustains mechanics and physics.

To turn away from science, however materialistic, seeking consolation and relief only in the beautiful pictures and sayings of the past, is to go to sleep again and will be of little avail. The task is to struggle through, until the pictures and the words come alive again, to be experienced not only as beauty but as truth by the individual. Then it is the individual who *knows*, and it will not be a question of relying on faith or belief. This will be future science.

The paths to such experiences have always been there in the past and they are still to be found. What is different today is that the search takes its start from the bricks and mortar, the rubble of a fallen citadel. To materialistic science—to the honest thinker in this field—the spirit cannot exist and the soul is a rather puzzling attribute of the body, and yet no-one can deny the presence of life. But what is it, and where does it originate?

The search goes on amid the rubble. Histology began in the third and fourth decades of the nineteenth century and received its greatest impetus from Schwann's conclusion that cells are the basis of the formation of all animals and plants. We are taught that the cells are the 'building bricks' of all living forms, but despite the intensive investigations in the study of minute anatomy a clear answer as to how life originates in the first place and then how the ordering of the cells in so miraculous a way comes about is not yet forthcoming.

The question is whether the search is going in the right direction and one can meet with leading biologists who say privately, and increasingly in public that biology is in need of quite new ideas.

Rudolf Steiner likens the way the materialistic physiologist works who limits his study to what goes on in the substances of the body, to a being who, seeing footprints on the surface of the earth, sets about burrowing under the surface to find out what caused them. He studies the events taking place in matter, without realising that the origin might be found in quite another area (Dornach 21.XI.1914).

Today, research with the help of ultra-modern equipment in, for instance, the study of the processes which take place in the formation and maturation of the human ovum is epoch-making. Phenomena are revealed in this minute area of physiology as never before in human history. The work is stupendous, yet the question of the origin of definitive cells within the organism itself remains a matter of dispute, let alone, the origin of life as a whole.

The German scientist Johann Wolfgang von Goethe, whose study of forms in nature—he coined the word *morphology*—took its start from the whole, rather than the part. In his botanical studies, Goethe looked at the entire sequence of development of plants, from seed to seed, and he also included the environment. He came, as he saw it, to the perception of a higher principle ruling or guiding the various outer manifestations of plant form and life, which he called the Archetypal Plant (Ur-Pflanze). He saw it as an Idea, hovering above or pervading individual plants and the whole plant kingdom.

While the other great botanist, Linnaeus, was ordering and classifying the plants according to the spatial structures and patterns shown by their flowers—the *created forms*, Goethe, who was also deeply interested in Linnaeus's work, looked in a different way and saw something of the *creative process*. "Everything is leaf, and through this simplicity the greatest diversity becomes possible." Goethe means leaf as a *type* or *Idea*. Perhaps one might call it the principle through whose potential, or capacity for transformation, the various plants and plant organs come to visible manifestation.

Taking his start from the phenomena. Goethe struggled to grasp the formative principle as such. He reached a certain degree of understanding; what he inaugurated has to be taken further (Dornach 6.IV.1921). Rudolf Steiner's conception of the world of formative forces has indeed taken Goethe's steps further, and this must in its turn be developed still further to meet the questions of modern biology.

The etheric or ethereal[2] world (Aetherwelt)—a realm through which cosmic, formative forces work—has been known since time immemorial in the old instinctive ways of the past. It needs now to become a guiding idea and recognised principle in science. The physical, material body of a living form, which can be studied by means of the physical senses, is permeated by supersensible members, named variously by Eastern teachings.

Rudolf Steiner describes them as the etheric or life-body, the astral body, which is the seat of feeling and sensation, and the ego, or spiritual individuality. Plants are permeated by an etheric world, animals by an ether and an astral body and the human being by both ether body and astral body and also by the individual ego or spirit.

The inhibitions of the materialistic scientist towards ideas of this sort are fully justified, for admittedly, science is based on its analytical and quantitative method of approach to substance, however refined the substance in question may be. The analytical method has led to the concept of the infinitesimal worlds of the atom and its particles, the cell and its minute parts. Every particle of substance, qua substance, is subject in a greater or lesser degree to the law of gravity and other laws of physics.

In fact, however, it is the *material body*, the so-called physical body, which is subject to the known laws of physics. The corpse lies inert when life and soul and spirit have departed from it. The ether body is subject to laws of an opposite kind, and it is only by virtue of the laws of the ether-body that the astral and ego forces can work into the physical body, for they too are supersensible and not bound to the laws of the material world.

These are unfamiliar thoughts. The most formidable obstacle to be overcome is, however, the predominantly spatial thinking of today. It has been with us ever since the days of Euclid, whose geometry makes conscious in abstract thought, the laws of the space in which all material bodies are to be found. It is a deeply engrained and important mode of experience, giving one the feeling of being well and truly grounded on the Earth. Yet the ebullient feelings of vitality, the sheer joy we can feel at being alive, is an equally common experience. We do, after all, when healthy, experience daily, whether it is fully explained by science or not, that one can carry one's heavy body through the door; an experience for which one may feel deeply thankful.

It is not yet a very widely known fact that just as ancient geometry gives the mathematical basis by means of which to conceptualise the laws of space and the laws of classical mechanics, so projective or synthetic geometry provides equally clear conceptual access to their polar counterpart, the laws of a world of processes which permeate and take hold of substance.

Rudolf Steiner called on the scientists and particularly the mathematicians in his audiences to think clearly about the forces working in and through what he called ethereal, or negative space (Gegenraum); he described these forces as being polar opposite to the known mechanical forces. He saw the transition from the analytical aspect of mathematics to that which introduces synthesis, as significant for science in that it provides "an inner way of thinking which leads towards the reality present in an outer realm of nature." It does this in such a way that "the same inner experience is reached as when one rises from the ordinary grasp of a concept to a spiritual imagination." At the same time he warns of the danger of taking hold of this realm of mathematics in "the narrow way in which it is still often understood today" (5 IV.21).

Goethe held back from the abstract and quantitative aspect of mathematics because it was *qualities* he was seeking. Rudolf Steiner, too, was concerned with qualities and he took this view also; it is as an art that the new mathematical approach to morphology inspires ways of thinking and conceiving which are new.

Just as a long and devoted training—or a genius—gives birth to art, so it is with the transformation of natural science and its further development beyond the present materialistic phase.

Since the time of Descartes, modern physics has continued in the Euclidean tradition and based itself on the concept of the *point*. It has, as it were, delved into the point and reached the infinitesimal worlds! Now it is time to balance things out and bring to bear the polar concepts, the *plane* and the peripheral aspect of forms. The task is not to contradict, but to complement the findings of science and to begin to look at all the amazing data provided by modern techniques, in ways that will raise science to other dimensions. Not that the answers will be just round the corner, but perhaps the right questions will be asked.

In the study of morphology provided by synthetic geometry in this more complete way, the eye gradually learns to perceive nature's forms and colours differently, and the understanding dawns that nature speaks two languages. Nature speaks the language of all created form and at the same time she speaks the language of their creation. This is easiest to understand in the plant, for there the planar world speaks more simply, without the complicated tones brought in by the astral and the ego. If you have the thoughts with which to perceive it (and thoughts perceive in the supersensible, as eyes see in the sense-world), then the plant is as Rudolf Steiner describes it; "an ethereal form filled out with material substance" (28.VII.22).

Besides the material forms, great and small, which reveal the grandeur or the delicacy of the dimensions of earth, there are the hollow spaces, *where matter is not*—where matter has held back, perhaps sacrificing itself to form expectant areas, enveloped and created by sheathes and surfaces and delicate membranes, within which to cradle and sustain new, young life. These are the ethereal spaces—silent, receptive, matriarchal; matter already created waits to receive creative forces and to bring forth new forms. There is a constant rhythm of dying and becoming, between the world of created forms and another world indwelling them. Soul-forces also need these ethereal spaces and so, indeed, does the spirit, in order to permeate substance. The human being, in the spiritual activity of thinking and meditation, learns to find the silent, inner spaces, where, not sleep, but a vital and intense awareness prevails in the emptiness, where all worldly wisdom must be sacrificed to make way for illumination, which will come if the heart is pure enough. It is the search for the "Not I" in our time of awakened ego-consciousness.

Rudolf Steiner formulated the notion of *counterspace* (*Gegenraum*). It will be our task here to try to understand why he went as far as to describe the sun itself as being in polar relationship to the earth. In lectures to scientists and mathematicians, he would often describe the surprise a modern scientist would have, were he actually to get inside the sun!

The Mysteries of the Sun are the mysteries of healing and of life; they are mysteries of the future. The Sun is the macrocosmic heart of our universe, receiving into itself the spiritual, creative forces of stars and planets, not for itself, but to pour such forces forth in bounty upon the living beings of the Earth. All forms of life come about in the interplay of these great cosmic poles, of which modern science knows only one. We in due course will learn to know these mysteries, if we would heal the earth with new ways in medicine and agriculture, heal the sickness of the waters of the earth, the sickness of mankind.

It is not in substance that life begins; the truth is that life is primary and from its processes substance arises. The plant, like the human being, is a microcosm growing between sun and earth, and *while we see it spreading upward from the earth, we may learn also to see it unfolding downward into three-dimensional earth-space from its inner, intensive organs, the "sun-spaces"*—growing-point, eye and seed.

In its selflessness the plant gives of its bounty as nourishment to man and animal and to the whole planet Earth. To quote Schiller: "If thou art seeking the highest, the best, the plants can teach it thee." Scientific thinking, clear and objective, can reach an understanding of realms, which are the well-springs of life, received by the plant and thus by the living planet, Mother Earth.

This is no sentimental dream; it is a modern exercise to unite clear and active thinking with a great love of the world of phenomena. It is also a social exercise.

There may seem a long way to go; yet in realising that thoughts, too, are not mere products of the physical brain, but powers able to move mountains, we should take courage, knowing that the task is an individual one. In the future mankind will learn to know that the Mystery of the Sun and its relation to the Earth is in fact the Mystery of Christianity.

Speaking at Cologne on 27th February 1910, Rudolf Steiner said: "How, in effect, do we think of a planet nowadays? Science describes the planet earth in terms of physics, chemistry and mechanics... Yet we are at the threshold of a profound change in this respect. In the now coming phase of science, the planets will no longer be explained by the mere play of dead, inorganic forces, but by plant-like forces—in other words, etheric forces.

"While the root of the plant points to the centre of the earth, the shoot is related to the Sun, and it is here that we shall find the forces which really make a planet what it is. The force of gravity is secondary... In fact it is the living plants which first form the planet and then provide the substance of which the mineral ground consists. Goethe was setting out in this new direction with his Morphology of Plants, but he was not understood.

"The time is coming now, when men will begin to *see* the etheric realm because it is the realm, which is characteristic of plant life. Moreover in perceiving the living force of growth in the plant kingdom, man will be freed from the forces which now hinder him from seeing the Risen Christ... An ever growing number of people will presently behold the Christ in His etheric form; they will behold the ethereal Earth from which in truth the plant-world springs."

Such words, spoken in 1910, reveal the profundity of Rudolf Steiner's spiritual science and at the same time his confidence in humanity. The objective quality of pure thinking must prevail and become strong and alive enough to go beyond earth-bound thoughts and reach life's deeper mysteries, about which otherwise only religions and beliefs speak today. In the coming phase of science, humanity already turns towards the distant goal, when through free human initiative and striving, the lost worlds will be rediscovered and science, art and religion reunited.

To Marie Steiner, his companion in the creation of a modern pathway towards the Mysteries of the Future, Rudolf Steiner wrote:

Sterne sprachen einst zu Menschen,	The Stars spake once to Man.
Ihr Verstummen ist Weltenschicksal;	It is World-destiny
Des Verstummens Wahrnehmung	That they are silent now.
Kann Leid sein des Erdenmenschen;	To be aware of the silence
In der stummen Stille aber reift	Can become pain for earthly Man.
Was Menschen sprechen zu Sternen;	But in the deepening silence
Ihres Sprechens Wahrnehmung	There grows and ripens
Kann Kraft werden des Geistesmenschen.	What Man speaks to the Stars.
	To be aware of the speaking
	Can become strength for Spirit-Man.

Rudolf Steiner: Wahrspruchworte
Translated by George and Mary Adams in *Verses and Meditations*.

Chapter III

MATHEMATICS AND THE FREEDOM OF THE HUMAN SPIRIT

> "The righteous man serves neither God nor the creatures, for he is free, and the closer he is to righteousness, the more he is freedom itself." Meister Eckhart.

Rudolf Steiner (1861—1925), in his autobiography, describes two incisive moments in his life that relate to geometry. The first came when, at the age of nine, his teacher put a geometry book into his hands and for days and weeks he thought about circles, triangles, squares and the like, realising that it was possible to have clear inner thoughts about the shapes he could see around him. In a childlike way, he realised through this experience that it might be possible in the future to describe in equally clear thoughts a world he already experienced within himself, an experience which he had already understood that other people did not share. He writes of the happiness that this geometry brought to him.

Then, at the age of nineteen, Rudolf Steiner learned in a university lecture on projective synthetic geometry, that mathematicians were thinking of a straight line as continuing out to the infinite and returning upon itself from the opposite direction, involving a a kind of circling property, yet keeping its quality of straightness. He writes that he left the lecture hall feeling as though a load had fallen from his shoulders; for the second time he experienced happiness. It was no longer necessary to contemplate the difficult idea of space continuing on and on 'into the void,' (He adds here, however, that the problem of time still presented him with difficulty.)

Throughout his work, Rudolf Steiner calls for the transformation of present day consciousness in the experience of space and time. In about 30 books and over 6,000 lectures, he renewed, through the spiritual activity of thinking, the great perennial truths of existence, expressing them in a form suitable to modern consciousness. More than is sometimes realised, Rudolf Steiner's thinking is permeated with the quality of mathematics.

In a lecture given in the Hague (10.IV.22) entitled *The Anthroposophical Method of Research*, Rudolf Steiner describes his *Philosophy of Spiritual Activity*[2] in these terms: "Whoever reads my Philosophy of Spiritual Activity will, I believe, find that in it there rules a kind of thinking, which is akin to mathematical thinking. It is strange, but true; it is a mathematical thinking by means of which this Philosophy of Spiritual Activity aims to find the origin of the human impulse towards freedom and morality. The manner in which this book attempts to deal with moral and ideal questions is qualitatively no different from the manner in which the soul is active in mathematics."...

"There are few people in the world" he says, "who have the right respect for the true mathematical process," and by this he means a condition of soul into which one can come, through the *inner experiencing of space* in the activity of mathematical thinking. Rudolf Steiner describes how it is possible to grasp and experience inner questions with the same clarity and certainty with which one can prove the theorem of Pythagoras and that, if one can achieve this, one knows oneself to be active in a supersensible world of Imagination, Inspiration and Intuition. (For the reader unfamiliar with these terms, one might translate them as meaning a higher spiritual form of thinking, feeling and willing). One knows then, he says, that however long and accurately one observes and experiments, if one takes only into account the world of the senses, one will not reach the full truth.

In the past, men were guided by religion and belief; ways of access to universal truth were always there. But just as in adolescence the hard light of the external world grows more dominant and the urge grows more urgent to find one's way alone, so too in the development of mankind, when the link with divine worlds has become dim and unsure, it is the intellect alone which seems reliable and sheds its beams of light onward. At first it is a cold light, but our task is not to let it falter but to learn to warm it through with warmth of objective feeling and the fire of individual will.

In the past, the path of inner training was guided by the Guru, on the basis of the Yoga of Breathing; for us today there has been opened up the path of the "Yoga of the Light." We must ourselves learn to live actively and rhythmically between observation and thinking, between percept and concept. Thinking and willing must find their true balance as we gradually learn to recognize (re-cognize) and see through the outer veil of sense-perception, and at the same time to draw aside the inner veil of the sanctuary. This is Rudolf Steiner's way into the future.

We are at the beginning of this path in its modern form, which inevitably leads through materialism, for it is here that the all important question of human freedom is involved—complete freedom from forms and controls which belong to the past. It is in the modern era, when thought alone becomes a conscious tool, that the possibility of the freedom of the soul arises. The soul can experience thought-pictures, and pictures leave one free. But *where* is freedom? The answer already began to sound in the words of the French Revolution: Freedom, Equality, Fraternity.

Rudolf Steiner's printed works are vast and deep and may to some be daunting; also the numbers of those still with us, are dwindling who knew and worked with him and who can tell of the uniqueness of his personality, so balanced between wisdom and love. Those of us who can still hear first-hand stories and who seem almost to see and to feel the sternness and the warmth that shone from his eyes are grateful for this, indeed. But through all the humour, fun and friendliness, the humility, there must have shone also the deepest pain and loneliness; for in truth, humanity today is very hard of hearing.

Besides Rudolf Steiner's renewal of the ancient path of meditative training and the path revealed in his *Philosophy of Spiritual Activity*[2] (which should not be taken as a philosophical work in the ordinary way, *but* as a path of spiritual training), he also drew attention, particularly in the years after the First World War, to the historical development of mathematical and spatial thinking in relation to the tasks of science and to spiritual development. The references to mathematics and geometry in Rudolf Steiner's more scientifically oriented lectures describe a path of training in thinking, which is of fundamental significance, for it leads modern science—and the individual human being who pursues it—beyond the confines of materialism. These lectures are less generally accessible, partly because of their scientific and mathematical nature, but partly also because Rudolf Steiner, as he himself very often says, was not intending and did not have the time to give final and detailed formulations. He was answering questions put to him and, particularly in the fields of mathematics and physics, was only indicating the tasks to be undertaken by those with the necessary training and competence.

It was on such an occasion, in a small group of people, that George Adams heard Rudolf Steiner say, concerning his conception of cosmic spaces and cosmic forces: "I am only giving you indications. It is for the mathematicians in my audience to sit down and work out the idea mathematically." Adams had asked the question and he was the first to formulate mathematically the conception of what Rudolf Steiner called "Sonnenraum"—a counterspace or Gegenraum—and the forces working through it.

In the second lecture (5.IV.21) of a course given in Dornach, entitled *The Fertilizing Effect of Anthroposophy on the Sciences*, Rudolf Steiner spoke a great deal about the part played by mathematics in scientific research and the part it should play in the future. He describes how the meaning of the term 'mathematics' has changed since ancient times from being identical with the word 'science'—Mathesis, 'the science of knowing'—to 'the science of quantities or sizes.' Even in the time of Descartes and Spinoza, both of whom strove to build their philosophies according to the reliable pattern of mathematics, philosophers did not conceive of the term in its narrow connotation as the science of mere measurement.

Using a simple Euclidean example, Steiner shows the obvious need to use mathematical reasoning, because of the transparent certainty of its thought-forms, and then he continues to show that this very quality of certainty and completeness was greatly enhanced when, in the nineteenth century, the old Euclidean thought-forms were superceded by the non-Euclidean geometries—he uses the word "Metageometrie"—of Lobatschewski, Bolyai and Gauss. "All the imaginations—thought-pictures—which have entered into modern thought, are a sure proof of the feeling of certainty given by the transparency of the mathematical process."

Continuing, Steiner emphasizes the importance of the fact that mathematics lives within us, not as outer reality, but as inner picture. Though with mathematics we may approach outer reality, inner pictures leave us free. In contemplating outer nature we feel satisfied, if at least we can enter into her manifestations with an experience of the same transparency that we have met with first in the mathematical, geometrical pictures. He then completes the lecture by extolling the great virtues of the modern transformation of Euclidean geometry into projective or synthetic geometry, using the example of the theorem of Pappos. This is a fundamental theorem, discovered from the Euclidean point of view by Pappos of Alexandria and then centuries later, in modern time, completed and given its synthetic character. This theorem is a first illustration of the Principle of Duality so important in synthetic geometry. It paves the way for the proper idea of Polarity, without which the concept of polar spaces would not be possible.

After going through this theorem in all detail on the blackboard and insisting that all one needed was a ruler and pencil, (see Chapter IV of this book), Rudolf Steiner says: "If with real inner forces of soul one follows the path which leads from analytical geometry into synthetic geometry—if one sees how, if I may put it so, one is caught up by something which comes near reality in the way that reality is present in the outer existence of nature, then one has the same inner experience—exactly the same inner experience—which one has when one rises from ordinary logical thinking to Imaginative thinking. One must then only go further in this way of thinking; but one has made a beginning when one progresses from analytical to synthetic geometry" (5.IV.21).

The path of knowledge is paved with exercises; mathematics—the Being Mathematica—inspires and guides the souls of men on the path of developing consciousness. "God geometrizes," Plato wrote above the portal of his academy.

Blake pictures Newton actively engaged in a geometrical pursuit. It is one concerning measurement, in the quantitative field of mathematical thinking, which deals with the laws of measure, number and weight. These are the laws man needs to know in order to deal with the things of the earth,—quantities and substances. We have become chained to this world, as Prometheus was chained to the rock.

But mathematics shows other universal laws and Rudolf Steiner was pointing in this direction when he said that, if with real inner forces of soul one follows the path which leads from analytical into synthetic geometry, one has the same inner experience which one has when one rises from ordinary logical thinking to imaginative thinking.

This mode of cultivation of mathematical thinking which includes the qualitative as well as the quantitative realms, reaches beyond substance into the realm of qualities, such as light and colour.

It was this kind of mathematical reasoning that occupied the minds of thinkers and philosophers during the nineteenth and on into the twentieth century. G.H. Hardy, the famous English mathematician, as well as A.N. Whitehead and Bertrand Russell, among others, were influential in Cambridge when George Adams studied and graduated there. He, as a physicist intent on going beyond the one-sided monism of atomic theories, was introduced by them to this new field of projective-synthetic geometry with its concepts of polarity and the transformation of spaces. They were working with the non-Euclidean geometries, seeking, on the basis of them to develop further the philosophy of science. For Whitehead, it was impossible to 'confine mathematics to being the science of number or quantity.'[3]

Alfred North Whitehead was born in the same year as Rudolf Steiner; he too spent a lifetime concerned about the future of education, the meaning and future of learning, and was also one of the greatest of 20th century philosophers. Confirmed in what Cayley had said before him, concerning the all-relating properties of projective geometry, Whitehead described the relationship of ordinary space to the various conceptions of metrical projective spaces. The expression "Anti-space" is attributed to Whitehead, but in his time no importance was attached to it in relation to physics. Adams was deeply interested in it and in the fact that the detailed formulation of a "polar Euclidean space" was not to be found in the mathematical literature of his own time.

In the following chapters we will attempt in a rudimentary way to experience something of the transition from ancient to modern geometrical thinking and then to enter into some thoughts about polar Euclidean space and the polar forces. Science has long out-grown the idea that all processes in the universe conform to the known laws of classical mechanics in a cartesian space. That the sun and the elements sustain life on the earth, is also a familiar fact. The idea of a "Sun-space," polar to "Earth-space," in which the forces of life function in an opposite way to the forces of death and destruction, would seem to be a quite straight-forward mode of approach to the understanding of life.

«Newton» von William Blake

Chapter IV

FROM EUCLIDEAN TO PROJECTIVE-SYNTHETIC GEOMETRY

> "It is necessary to point to the transition from the analytical treatment of geometry to the synthetic, and to the fact that a further development along this path will lead to imaginative contemplation, so long as one does not stop short at formalism, but progresses to a living grasp of the phenomena"
> Rudolf Steiner. (6.IV.21)

Perspective Transformation—Concepts of Infinity

Let us take pencil and ruler to experience and illustrate the theorem as Rudolf Steiner showed it in the lecture mentioned in the previous chapter. First we will do it in the form in which Pappos discovered and proved it. (Proofs may be found in all the classical textbooks.)

Draw two lines a and c and choose on each of them any three points; number the points in order, as you choose them, so that the points on one line are paired with the points on the other. Now join up all points, *except the pairs*, and see how this results in three points which will fall in line. You will *always* find, however you arrange the drawing, that the meeting points of the corresponding line-pairs will lie in a straight line!

Euclid taught that a straight line is described as the shortest distance between two points; that is to say, it is of finite length and is determined by the concept of measure. In this theorem, once we have chosen the three pairs of points, however freely, the various distances between them are then fixed. Then the unexpected happens; a third line arises, *which does not* depend *on the chosen measurements, but on relationships between them.*

Here is a theorem which does not rest entirely on measure, as is otherwise characteristic of Euclidean geometry; it rests on the idea of relationships, an idea which, as we shall see, is characteristic of modern geometry. In its complete form, which was not discovered until centuries later, the theorem of Pappos is basic to projective or synthetic geometry, through which runs the important new *Principle of Duality*. It was, in fact, this principle which Rudolf Steiner was intent on demonstrating in the lecture.

Before continuing this theorem, however, we will undertake a few more elementary drawing exercises in order to experience the first fundamental difference between the ancient and the new geometry: namely, *the transition from finite forms and their fixed measures to forms containing the concept of the infinite and involving the principles of movement and transformation.*

A fundamental qualitative difference is revealed here, which renders the continued use of the word *geometry* quite inappropriate and invites to use a much freer word in relation to the study of such mobile forms. I prefer to use the word *morphology* : the study of form and form-creating principles.

The three elements basic to geometry are *point*, *line* and *plane*. In projective morphology, a line is simply a picture of *straightness* it can be called forth by any two points, wherever they are, or by any two planes interpenetrating one another (Figure 2). The plane is a picture of immeasurable *flatness* (it needs *three* points, not in a straight line, to determine it (Figure 3). Then there is the point, which could be called a picture of *sharpness*; it arises between any *two* lines or any *three* planes, not in a line (Figure 4). We find complete and beautiful forms arising simply through the interplay of these three elements, plane, line and point—but *only* when the idea of *elements at infinity* is included.

Here we are invited to think with Descartes, Kepler, Galileo and others, in a way which was at that time quite new, a first step in overcoming the dominance of Euclidean thinking.

Given the thought that the straight line is not just the shortest distance between two points, the familiar figures of triangles, squares etc., take on a very different guise and pose other questions. Is for example, the space of points inside a triangle all there is to it, when each line stretches away to infinity and returns on itself again? Do we not have to begin to think differently about all the familiar geometrical forms?

In projective morphology, the triangle as we commonly think of it is only a *part* of the entire triangle, which is stretched out in the plane. Gone is the simple thought of an inside, separated off and having nothing to do with an outside; there are other areas involved here (Figure 6).

Three lines interpenetrating in three points determine a triangle, which can take on a myriad shapes, and lies as though embedded in a vast plane. The difficult question is: what happens at the 'ends' of the three lines? The correct answer to this question is all important and involves our first step into the unknown.

Mathematicians since the time of Descartes in the seventeenth century have considered that the point in the one direction is the *same* as the one in the other direction, but that it is at "infinity."

A useful way to get hold of this idea is to draw a line and put a point somewhere outside it. Then think of lines turning in the point, as on a pivot (Figure 7).

Simple observation tells one that each line, as it pivots on the fixed point, has a point in common with the fixed line. This point moves along the line as the turning movement continues, until, of necessity, the moment comes, when the two lines are parallel. At this moment the question arises, "Where must I look to find the common point of the two endlessly long straight lines?" Euclid would answer "When the two lines are parallel, there *is no* common point," but the moderns created the idea of *an infinitely distant point*. With the further turn of the pivoting line, this point will come moving in from the opposite direction and return to its starting-place. The simple circling of lines in the fixed point involves what is called the *"ideal" point at infinity* of the fixed line.

We watch this moving point disappear out into the distance (in either direction, according to the direction in which we imagine the line in the fixed point to be turning). At just one moment the moving point will disappear into the invisible—it has gone beyond mere distance—it is in the infinite. Contrary to what we first learned at school, a line is not only the shortest distance between two fixed points; in projective geometry, there is a single point at infinity belonging to *any* line we like to think of, pointing in any direction. In other words, a point at infinity is an idea, a *thought*! Though at infinity, it has not ceased to exist and it is still a *single* point, but it is immeasurably far away, and invisible to the finite eye. The mathematicians call it an *ideal* point, which is a true name for it.

In teaching, I think it is important here at this first step to use terminology which overcomes the spatial connotations which prevail in the classical textbooks of projective geometry to this day. Some progressive mathematicians are still content to use the old terminology, such, for instance, as that parallel lines "*cut* at infinity", which is manifestly absurd. We prefer to avoid such terms where possible. Just as two people can have something in common—a common point of view—so can parallel lines have a point in common in the infinite. It is interesting to think that any two lines which have a point in common, will also always have a common plane; (it can also be stated the other way round: any two lines which have a plane in common, will also have a common point). So, too, parallel lines, which always lie in a plane, will also always have a point in common, —the ideal point at infinity, indicated by the direction in which they are pointing. I believe the quality of such terms (and there are others) to be pedagogically important, for it is the very task of the new morphology to provide an exact way of thinking, which shall lead beyond materialism, even beyond our ordinary conception of space. One only needs the experience of teaching this "geometry" to realise how stubbornly spacebound we still are today.

The very laws of projective geometry express a social quality; *the thought-forms are essentially social*, based on relationships rather than on measurable quantities. Why should lines or planes which intersect be described as *cutting* one another? Moreover, it is the essence of our task to be concerned with thoughts and not only with things. Mathematics teaches the reality of thought, and this realm of mathematics provides exercises which take our thoughts beyond the realm of finite things. Thoughts which are sociable will also be creative, just as unsocial thoughts can be so destructive.

Line-woven forms in the Projective Plane

In drawing all the projective constructions, the experience will be brought home to us that these infinitely distant elements do actually function, just as ordinary points and lines and planes do; in fact, without them the forms will not be complete! The ellipse in Figure 31, for example (see page 27), would not be complete if, in the drawing, a point at infinity had not been used. One can admire the ingenuity and courage of the men of the seventeenth century, who were explorers in all aspects of life on earth. It is fascinating to think that without these thoughts, reaching beyond Euclidean conceptions, our technical culture could not have arisen!

Returning to the drawings—and it is good wherever possible to do the simple constructions:-
Draw any straight line, such as the bottom one in Figure 8; choose freely any point on it, say A' and draw any two lines from A', into the empty space above (it could also be below). Now choose freely any other point on the bottom line. It matters not where, except that some choices might take the drawing off the page; so choose, say, a point in the region of B. Then draw a line from B which crosses the two from A'.

This will result in two new points, like 1 and 3. Now choose a point somewhere in the region of the point A and draw from it lines to the two new points 1 and 3. With this, two more points come into being 2 and 4. Now draw the common line between these two new points and see where a fourth point arises—the point B' on the bottom line (Figure 8).

This is what is called a Harmonic Quadrangle, and the wonderful thing is that if you draw another one, choosing lines quite freely in the same order as before (first from A', then from B, then from A), the last line will *always* lead back to the *same* fourth point B'! In this process there are no fixed measures to start with; the points and lines become fixed one after the other and play their part according to a law of relationships, which, as though with an inner necessity, embraces them all.

This law does not depend on the size or shape of the quadrangles but on a special relationship between the four points. (This is called a harmonic range of points.) Keeping these four points as they are, the figure can be moved and transformed in an infinite number of ways. Imagine, for example, moving a corner (4 in Figure 9), letting it pass through the infinite and return again from above. As the point moves, the three other corners and the four sides of the quadrangle change their positions accordingly. The quadrangle undergoes a continuous *transformation*, in this case stretching through the infinite and returning back, to become almost unrecognisable.

Through such a continuous transformation, the form changes its shape but it nevertheless remains true to itself; it still functions as a complete whole. These are important imaginations in the new geometry, which literally open up the limited horizons of our commonplace spatial pictures and forms of thought.

If now we let the first line play the part of a horizon-line and set one quadrangle side-by-side with another (Figure 10), we get a picture very reminiscent of a perspective picture, like a set of squares in a Euclidean field. (You start off by drawing a line from one of the two points which give diagonals of the first quadrangle, to one of its corners, thus establishing the proper sequence of points to continue the net. It becomes clear that simply *through the relationships* inherent in the lines and points of the first form, *the whole plane* becomes penetrated by a net of quadrangles. In it we see that no form has the same shape or size as any other, but that all are in harmony with one another, following a principle which is beyond the realm of ordinary measure. At once, the relation of this picture with what the artist does in perspective drawing is evident; it is only necessary to bring in an element of symmetry to see this. The line with which we started functions as does the "vanishing line" in the artist's perspective picture (Figure 11).

What we have done in drawing, is to experience the forms *created from the periphery (the "vanishing line") inward*; the lines, like rays of light streaming in from the periphery, create first one quadrangle and then all the others. Each quadrangle, different in shape, retains its identity, while at the same time maintaining and making possible the creation of all the further ones. This is a principle which belongs to creative life processes: it preceeds all *created* form. The true understanding of any form depends on knowing the *process* whereby it came into being; the process comes first, then the form.

Pausing to think of these related forms, it is wonderful to realise that once the first quadrangle is there, the whole plane is already penetrated through and through with sister forms belonging as though to a family. They are already invisibly there, waiting to be picked out in the drawing! I am reminded of an occasion in New England, U.S.A. when a young mother was sitting under a Sugar Maple tree with some children; a little boy of about six years old came running, excitedly, with a bunch of beautifully coloured leaves he had gathered from the ground. "Look! Look! he cried, "*All* the leaves on this tree are the same shape!"

The exercise should help us to see that individual shapes in nature, for instance in crystal and plant, are expressions of an archetypal, invisible form-type which the human being is capable of thinking.

Such thought-principles come to meet the way Rudolf Steiner describes the working of living, formative processes. We shall see that again and again he evoked the idea of *planes and surfaces* when describing the characteristics of living processes.

Watching a spider spinning a web, that glistens with many coloured dewdrops in the early morning sunshine, one might ask: How come, that such a wonderfully wisely woven surface arises by means of such a little creature? He moves across from one point of attachment to another. But surely the web spread out around him is an integral part of the tiny living organism?

The exercise involving the weaving of harmonic nets can be carried out with other shapes; particularly fascinating is the harmonic web of hexagons. Above all, we experience the nature of an *entire* plane, a limitless field or surface, stretching away on all hands into the distances below; it would return from beyond the vanishing line! (This process is pictured for a single quadrangle in Figure 9.) It is important to realise that this 'vanishing line' pictures a line at infinity—*but it is only a picture*. Take it really to infinity and parallelism will invade the plane. Surely we can then see that the pairs of parallel lines have their **common points** in the line now deemed to be at infinity! (Figure 12).

As the mathematicians say: *The line at infinity of a plane is the locus of all the points at infinity of all the lines which lie in the plane.* This line must be thought of as *straight*; it can be shown to satisfy all the laws of any straight line. There is nothing in this thought to imply the idea of curvature.

Crystal-weaving in the Light of Space

It is helpful here to modify the first picture we drew of a moving line in relation to a fixed line and try to imagine a *plane* pivoting in a point outside a fixed *plane* (Figure 13). This is more difficult, for we are unused to bringing a *whole* plane into our thought and imagination. With practice, though, it is possible to see the common line of the two planes moving all over the fixed plane, reaching the infinite when the parallel situation is reached and flashing in from it from one side or another, according to the way the pivoting plane moves. In any direction at any moment, the common line of the two places can disappear from the world of measure, but this does not mean that it then ceases to exist; it is still attainable in thought! Rudolf Steiner uses the word "Umkreis" for this invisible line, a term George Adams translates as "the Encircling Round."

Just as we can think of a quadrangle or square woven from lines raying in from points on a "vanishing line", so now we can imagine a cubical form woven from a *plane*, in a similar way. Then we must think not only of its lines (edges), but also of its planes (surfaces), raying in from the periphery, thus forming it from *outside*.

Instead of just one vanishing line, we now need three, to form a triangle and thus determine the plane (Figure 14a). Imagine the top line of the triangle to be the vanishing line for the top surface of the cubical form, and draw it in as a harmonic quadrangle, as in Figure 8. Drawing on a large enough scale and very accurately, it will be found that the "uprights" may then be drawn from the bottom corner of the large triangle, and that the harmonic law allows that a base for this cubical form may be drawn in at any level, always fitting perfectly! The base will already be fully determined by the first line of it you freely choose to draw.

Figure 14b shows how it is possible to draw a cubic net in a similar way to the harmonic net of quadrangles. In this case the bottom point of the triangle has been taken to the infinite (the "vertical" lines are here actually vertical—and parallel. It allows of a less extreme perspective distortion, so that the drawing stays more easily on the page. The forms can be drawn above and below one another also, and one can begin to imagine the cubic forms filling the whole of this projective space, just as, ideally, ordinary space can be thought of as filled with cubes—like a giant grid.

It is a geometrical picture conforming to our idea of earth space, but we have seen it come into manifestation from the periphery inward, woven through by planes and lines, with the points coming last, not first. Instead of creating by measurement between points, the ordered measure in these forms is a *result* of the process.

The whole is presided over by the special relationships between the harmonic ranges of points on each of the three sides of the "archetypal triangle," which are expressed numerically by a certain "anharmonic" ratio or cross-ratio. In stating a proportion, two *lengths* are brought into relationship with one another; in the cross-ratio, it is two *proportions*, which are brought into a relationship. In this process, our thought is raised beyond the realm of additive measure, into one in which relationships prevail. The concept of a harmonic range of points in a line (also of lines in a point) is fundamental to this "geometry," which brings static forms into movement.

This geometry was developed by mankind as from the fifteenth century. It is important in education—and indeed in self-education—to practice such thinking in quite simple exercises such as these, to experience the freedom from the domination of measure, the inner activity required to think the exercise through and make it work, and then the *wonder*, when it does work and forms the basis of a beautiful drawing! As someone once said in a class: the feeling comes that 'God is in his heaven, all's well with the world.'

This is the type of mathematical process, which led George Adams to give his first work the title *Strahlende Weltgestaltung* (a work he never intended should be translated into English). One might use the words *Raying Formation of Worlds*. The projective, creative process reveals what might be called the crystal-weaving of the light, creating forms in space.

We should realise and picture clearly in our minds that in our drawings we have seen the crystal forms arising *linewise and planewise from the periphery inward*. We did not build them, point for point from a centre outward, in the way all material construction requires. We learned that measurement can be secondary rather than primary. First comes the *creative process; the created form is secondary*. The exercise is a healthy one, involving only clear and mobile thinking, a sense for beauty of form and accuracy in drawing, (look, for instance, at Figure 15).

So far we have thought only of forms with straight lines and flat surfaces, but by the same process of 'strahlende Weltgestaltung'—light-radiant weaving of forms in space—all manner of curves and surfaces may be created, as for example the conics, (known in Greek times as sections of a cone) in a plane. With practice it is possible to see pure and complicated metrical relationships of mathematical curves and surfaces come about before your very eyes as you draw. Measure arises as the forms come into being, as in the process of development of an organism. In this way, the ellipse, parabola and hyperbola in Figures 16—18 were drawn.

Forms woven one within the other.

We have so far also only thought of forms set *side by side,* a situation which is natural to forms once created and set in earth space; even in the living kingdoms, the finished forms as such maintain an existence side by side (Figure 19). It is however also possible to carry out the harmonic weaving in the light of perspective transformation by setting the forms *one inside the other*. In doing this, it is as though we step into another world and immediately come closer to living things. It is not without reason that Rudolf Steiner drew attention to the Russian Doll type of toy for children, a toy, which as I have seen, is much beloved by little girls.

Here, instead of working with *one* infinitude (the line or plane at infinity), when the resulting forms relate to the "grid" system, maintaining equal steps in space (*step-measure*), we now find that the forms are spanned between *two infinitudes*, the line or plane without and a point within, between which the perspective process or 'échelle fuiant' leads (Figure 20). The measure here is a simple logarithmic progression (*growth-measure*) and we find ourselves in the realm of the type of spirals which are to be found in living organisms (*not* to be confused with the Spiral of Archemedes, which is set in step measure). We touch here on a most important theme, which will serve us well in our later attempts to understand the true nature of living morphology. Life is spanned *between two infinitudes*. The Archemedian spiral is held in the centre by one fixed point in the finite. It pictures the descent to earth, where forms are side by side, *but* does not speak of worlds within worlds, which is characteristic of all life.

In Figure 21, we see the quadrangles of Figure 10, but now set one within the other, in ordered measure, drawn from the "vanishing line", as before. When, as in Figure 22, this vanishing line has really vanished into the infinite, the matrix arises upon which the logarithmic spirals may be drawn, as in Figure 23. It becomes clear that in this type of spiral, which is the type revealed in plants and shells of all kinds (Figure 19), the ideal form runs between nought and infinity; it would go on and on, in towards the innermost point, which it would never reach! Mathematically, this innermost point is *thinkable*, but with the lead of our pencil we reach it all too soon! The being in nature, who creates its home according to such a principle of proportions, has to make a compromise, and must fill the centre in, as for instance, in a snail's shell.

Figure 24 shows a first step, in three-dimensional projective space, beginning with a cubical form and drawing the form, which would arise within: an octahedron (compare Figure 14). Looking ahead to Figure 39, we may be helped to see that according to this process it would be the octahedron, which would arise within the cube. (Compare also the process shown in Figure 21.)

Ideally, the process shows (though it would not be easy to draw in many more of the alternating forms), that deep within, there is a point functioning like a point at infinity; *and* also outward, a plane would function as an infinitude, into which the forms would flatten, on the principle shown in Figure 9 for the quadrangle.

When not only square (or hexagon), but also the circle is transformed in this way, a world of flowing forms arises, awakening a feeling of life and movement. To draw these curves in all their mobile balance is, indeed, a healing activity. Guided by clarity of thought, we learn to love the art of the moving, yet quite exact form, and not only the hand and the eye, but a true feeling for form, as it lives throughout the whole body, provides the necessary dexterity. Thinking, feeling and willing are all engaged, and one learns to experience what might be called *the dynamic of form* (Figures 25, 26).

Colour, used according to the objective laws of colour—the colour circle and the way colours arise between light and darkness—reveals the movement from one curve to the next. No longer fixed in step-measure, but arising through the laws of proportions, these forms release the soul from the over-burdening dominance of step-measure and beat and speak to it of the musical harmonies of our universe, out of which the material world is born.

In Figure 25, the curves are moving in towards an inner point at infinity, and outward to the line, which pictures the line at infinity of a family of *concentric* circles (cf. Figure 22). Some of the curves go through the real infinite, changing into a parabola and then into hyperbolae. We are helped in this picture to understand what would happen in the further development of Figure 24.

Figure 26 shows a family of conics—or circle-curves, as we prefer to call them, in an unsymetrical projection. At once they become still more alive. The harmonic net of quadrangles, which form a kind of skeleton or scaffolding for them, has here been left out, and there is no circle among them.

In Figure 27, yet another aspect of a family of circle-curves has been brought to expression. Here another projective process has been used, resulting in a different relationship of this transformed family of circle-curves. This time they have a different kind of intimacy, for they all (considered pointwise) run through two fixed points and (considered linewise) touch two fixed lines. George Adams, who brought these 19th century thoughts out of their abstract algebric form into pictures, also called them by less scholastic names. The "Breathing Involution," which is here made visible in the flowing forms is reminiscent of forms revealed by water, for instance, on the sea-shore in the ebb and flow of the tides. They awaken us, not only to form as such, but to the "*gesture*" of form. *Forms speak*, and we must learn to see (and hear) their gesture.

Euclidean geometry has taught us to perceive the monumental grandeur of dead forms, fixed and immobile. What timeless wonder of a life—or lifetimes—speaks in the gesture of the countenance of a dead person? It is what went before, —living processes and experiences—which carved that immobility and lets it speak.

Projective "Geometry" is no longer *geometry* (earth-measurement), as it was taught in ancient times. Nevertheless it is concerned with the study of form (morphology). Adams used the untranslatable words "Strahlende Weltgestaltung" (Light-radiant Creation of Worlds). One could call it *Projective Morphology*. The cube speaks to us of the Earth and reveals the three dimensions of the cross of the world. Projective Morphology shows the cube to be created from an archetypal *Three* in the plane at infinity—a triangle of lines and points. What for ordinary geometry is invisible and unthinkable, is made visible in Projective Morphology, and is accurately attainable in clear thinking. We have but to awaken our corpse-like way of thinking and get it moving—warmed by Art.

The illustrations show that whether by setting forms side-by-side or one within the other, they may be created quite freely, from the periphery inward, by means of lines and planes, which ray in, as light does, from the periphery of space—from the plane-at-infinity.

In the forms projectively created, it is however the *line-woven, planar, surface-aspect* of the forms, in all their plasticity, which is paramount (see, for example, Plate III); points *result* from the interplay of lines and planes, rather than being put there in the first place as starting points from which to measure.

In Egypt and in Greece, in bygone days, we were taught the laws of earthly measurement, to build enduringly upon the Earth.

Since the time of the break-through into the Copernican, Cartesian, Galilean way of thinking, the ease with which points can be handled algebraically has led the way in science; analysis of this kind prevails to this day. We are reminded by the new morphology of something which these methods have largely left out of account; namely, that we *can* learn to allow the planes and surfaces of the worlds of colour and light, which shine into our world, to light up in our imagination, not only in art, but also in science.

Forms are not born of substance; rather is substance moulded and lifted into form by a process we yet have to learn to understand. In modern optics we study the corpse of light and quite rightly so. Now is the time to begin to know light in its creative aspect. The words from Rudolf Steiner's *Portal of Initiation* may ring in our ears!

> "The weaving essence of the Light rays forth
> Through realms of Space
> To fill the World with Being."

The Awakening in the Seventeenth Century

All that we have so far contemplated and pictured derives from the steps taken by the mathematicians who first broke with Euclid and overcame the static and rigid nature of Greek geometry. The steps were introduced to geometry by Girard Desargues (1593—1662) and Blaise Pascal (1623—1662). They conceived the treatment of the conic sections as perspective transformations of circles, which was made possible by Desargues' idea that the two extremities of a straight line may be considered as meeting at infinity and that parallels (in a plane or in space) differ from other pairs of lines only in having their common points at infinity. To the Greek idea of the curves resulting from sections or *cuts* through finite cones, a conception related closely to the sense of touch in the physical world, they added another idea, investing the same curves with laws relating to the sense of movement and the sense of sight.

This was a dramatic time in the history of mathematics and science. Desargues was a friend of René Descartes (1596—1650),[4] the giant figure in the further development of science. Numerous other famous French mathematicians were colleagues of Desargues, Pascal and Descartes; the lifetime of Galileo (1564—1642) stretched almost throughout the lifetimes of the three, and Newton (1642—1727) followed immediately afterwards.

It is since this time that for mathematicians and physicists, "earth space" is the space you can conceive of by starting from any point-centre and reaching out towards the points on the plane-at-infinity. It is according to this way of thinking that the basic concept is reached of the three axes at right-angles to one another—the famous Cartesian axial system—on which our conception of space and also classical mechanics is based. This is the mathematical picture, or imagination, of three-dimensional space; it is Newton's idea of absolute space.

Desargues is often called the father of projective geometry. He and Pascal, having left the beaten track, uncovered new and beautiful facts in the new geometry, but owing to the direction taken by Descartes, who was inspired by analytical geometry, their work became overlaid and ignored. Desargues' writings were lost until the beginning of the 19th century and then only partially recovered.

Descartes was supportive of his friend and held him in very high esteem, but he decided for himself (in his own words), "to quit...abstract mathematics, that is to say, the consideration of questions which *serve only to exercise the mind*, and this in order to study another kind of geometry which has for its object the explanation of the phenomena of nature..."[4]

The destiny of this moment in history is expressed in the almost legendary pictures of Galileo Galilei sitting in the cathedral, watching the swinging lamp and Newton seeing the apple fall. Descartes was attracted by the science of mechanics and it is towards this aspect of the understanding of nature that his co-ordinate geometry has led. His new step was to introduce into geometry an analytical method which enabled him to represent curves by algebraic equations. (The question might be asked whether the term 'abstract,' used by Descartes, *is* really the distinguishing factor between the two geometries).

It is a time of paradoxes, into details of which it is not our task to enter here, except to point to the fact that the very step taken by mathematics in reaching beyond the finite to the conception of points, lines and a plane at infinity, was a step which also led deeper into the material realm. As a philosopher of his time, René Descartes, seeking the spirit with the powers of the intellect, was reduced to the one guiding fact of his own inner consciousness of self: "I think, therefore, I am." This was all that his honest intellectual striving could reveal to him. Yet, he was one who re-introduced the concept of infinity into mathematics, undoing, one might say, the deed of Euclid and freeing the development of mathematics for vast new fields. Through the powers of the intellect, the way is open to a higher, more spiritual aspect of the soul of man.

Steiner calls attention to the great change in the quality of thinking around the time from the fifteenth century onward, the time of development of the spiritual aspect of the soul of man—the Spiritual Soul (Consciousness Soul).[2] With this is connected the question of freedom; with growing consciousness in thought, the human being takes on a greater individual responsibility, leading into realms of darkness as well as realms of light.

It is understandable that Descartes played such a prominent part on the scene of modern science. History tells that he was obstinate and aggressive; he often played a controversial part and on occasion, his work was sharply criticised by his colleagues. Desargues, on the other hand, is a shadowy figure, of whom hardly a picture exists and whose work was lost for two centuries. He was an architect and engineer in Lyon, whose aim was to help craftsmen and artists in their work. The famous theorem which bears his name is a fundamental pillar in the new edifice of geometrical and mathematical thinking, and there is no doubt that his and Pascal's contributions to geometry are impressive and illuminate the minds of scientists far into the future, far from being exhausted, as is generally assumed.

Returning now to our exercises in synthetic geometry, we shall experience the leap across two centuries to the time when the work of Desargues and his young pupil, the genius Pascal, was taken up again.

Reawakening in the Nineteenth Century—the Principle of Duality.

So far, we have here dealt only with one aspect of the Theorem of Pappos, as it opened the way to *Perspective Transformation* in the seventeenth century. The Principle of Duality, which Rudolf Steiner describes in this lecture, involves a much deeper change and activity of will in thinking. It forms a first step in the understanding of what is called *polar-reciprocal transformation*. (see below). This belongs to the thinking of the first third of the nineteenth century and leads us to a new aspect of synthesis.

The type of thinking required by this exercise is not easy, partly because we are led away from ordinary, habitual, spatial ways of thinking. In this, however, lies the significance of the exercise, and it is perhaps for this very reason that polar reciprocation, as a mathematical process, is still a pioneer field. We are such earthly-minded mortals, chained to the cross of the three dimensions, however infinitesimal or infinite and seemingly non-spatial our imagination may be in science today. Descartes analytical mind still dominates.

So, let us repeat the exercise with which we began (Chapter IV, page 15), and now enter into the process Rudolf Steiner was at pains to show, the *dual* of the Pappos theorem. *This means that points and lines change places.* Whereas we began with two lines, a and c, we now begin with two points A and C. Instead of choosing any three points in each line, we draw any three lines through each of the two points. Now, instead of looking for the lines common to points, we have to seek points common to the lines. Once more it is not the paired ones which come into question, but all the remaining alternatives.

The strange and remarkable thing then happens—and will always happen! The point pairs will give rise to three lines, which will always meet in a *common point*, (whereas before we found three points, which always lie on a *common line*).

Taking together the Theorem of Pappos and its dual, as Rudolf Steiner was doing in his example of the significance of projective geometry, we experience a qualitative turning inside-out of thought, between pointwise and linewise relationships in mathematics (Figure 28). Another example of the principle of duality is given by the two theorems of Pascal, and Brianchon. (Figure 29).

Pascal's Theorem (1660)
The points common to corresponding lines of a hexagon inscribed in a conic are collinear.

Brianchon's Theorem (1806)
The lines common to corresponding points of a hexagon circumsribed about a conic are concurrent.

Charles Brianchon (1785—1864) discovered the dual of Pascal's famous theorem, concerning the *hexagrammum mysticum*, as it was called. Pascal's theorem departed from the quantitative aspect of the metrical geometry of the Greeks and his projective method introduced the concept of invariance: metrical properties are not invariant, whereas the morphological *qualities* remain invariant in perspective transformation. So, too, the principle of invariance rules in the theorem of Brianchon: but as between the two famous theorems a quite new idea arises: the *Principle of Duality*. Moreover, it is not until this time in history that the dual of the ancient theorem of Pappos dawned in the minds of mathematicians!

Rudolf Steiner, in teaching the theorem of Pappos in its ancient *and* its modern forms, is concerned precisely with this principle of Duality, which paves the way to a true understanding of Polarity.

Towards a deeper understanding of Polarity—Polar-reciprocal Transformation

Many famous mathematicians from various western countries were active in the first half of the nineteenth century, contributing to the development of mathematics, both in its analytical aspect and according to the discipline of synthesis. Synthetic geometry became very popular and came to a certain culmination at this time.

It was another Frenchman, Jean Victor Poncelet (1788—1867), who, with Charles Brianchon, caused a surge of interest and industry in the subject, giving it a strong new impulse. Poncelet is often called the father of projective geometry. A graduate of the École Polytechnique, and as a young man of twenty-four, officer of engineers in the French Army, he was left for dead on the frozen battlefield of Krasnoi in the retreat from Moscow in November 1812. Restored to vitality in the April sunshine in a prison on the banks of the Volga, he turned to mathematics as a mental exercise, resolving to reproduce what he could of all he had learned—this without books and with only scanty materials. In September 1814, he returned to Paris with manuscripts, which contained the germ of projective synthetic geometry in its classical form.

Taking up Brianchon's discovery of the principle of duality, Poncelet introduced the method of polar-reciprocation and initiated the geometrical interpretation of the "ideal" elements of space and the "imaginary" numbers.[4]

The Principle of Duality and the closely related theorem of Poncelet's: *Pole and Polar with relation to a conic or circle-curve*, which introduces the idea of polar reciprocation, leads to a much deeper understanding of *polarity* than the idea of opposites, such, for instance as north and south poles, high and low, or simply inside and outside. Our approach to the understanding of polarity is a conceptual and at the same time a morphological one. Taken deeply into one's meditative thought, it becomes an invaluable key to life.

Let us continue our elementary excursion into this new realm of "geometry". Take a circle (or an ellipse or any other conic) and draw a line in its plane; we will first choose to draw the line outside the curve. Choose any point on the line and draw the two lines this point sends forth, to touch the curve from the outside (tangents). The two points of contact of the tangents on the curve will give rise to a new line, which in turn will create a second point on the line with which we started. If now we draw the tangents to the curve from this second point, we shall always find, surprisingly, that the line common to the points of contact of the second pair of tangents will also contain the point with which we started! Here again is a figure with a very satisfactory quality of completeness.

We began with a *line outside* the curve and now find that there is a corresponding *point within* it. The point is called the Pole of the Polar Line, with respect to this particular conic. If the polar is outside, the pole will lie within, if the polar is within, the pole will be found outside the curve (Figure 30).

For each point on the line outside the curve, there will be a polar line passing through the pole within. The movement of one point or line in the picture will result in the ordered movement of all the others, for they are, as it were, organically related, according to the harmonic law through which they have been brought into being.

See how, as a corollary to the movement of the lines, which you can picture moving in a point, the points will move along a line, circling away into the infinite in one direction and returning from it again in the other (Figure 31).

Now bring the picture into movement in another way, by moving *either* the polar line or its pole in towards the centre of the curve or out to the periphery. It will then be found that moving the polar line out will result in the pole moving in towards the centre of the curve. It is the curve itself, which calls forth this reciprocating movement. This is the basis of what is called *Polar Reciprocation*. It becomes clear that *the line at infinity of the plane in which the curve lies is the polar line of its central point*, and also that *for a tangent to the curve, the pole will be its point of contact*.

Thus, to the centre of a circle there is related a peripheral line-at-infinity and, also, together with any point of a curve, we must think of its tangent line. (Figure 32). It is very one-sided to think of curves only in terms of their points.

We are here led to a more complete picture of what a circle is (or any other of the conics—circle-curves, as we prefer to call them). Euclid defined a circle as a curve formed by all the *points* which are equidistant from a fixed *point*. We now see that there is a polar form to Euclid's circle, namely, an envelope of lines which *also* form a circle. (Figure 33).

Take a Euclidean circle and polarize it, for instance, with respect to a larger circle, which is concentric with it. The polar form will be a circle enveloped by lines encircling the whole. (Once you have found the polar line of one of the inner points, the measures of the reciprocal radii will be determined. It is then a simple matter to draw in any number of lines to complete the envelope.)

This simple picture (Figure 34a, when completed) raises interesting questions. Let the inner circle of points expand, until it reaches the circumference of the "unit" circle, and you will see that the envelope comes in to meet it. The further expansion of the pointwise circle, beyond the boundary of the unit circle will result in the *inward penetration* of the envelope towards the centre, into which it would only merge entirely, if the pointwise circle were really to expand to the infinite! Conversely, were we to imagine the envelope growing so vast that all its lines merge with the infinitely distant line of the plane, then only would the points of the inner circle actually converge on the central point! The polar circle-families in Figure 34b are helpful here.

This picture of inward and outward polar-reciprocal movements calls into question the use of the words *expansion* and *contraction*. These words suit the quality of the pointwise movement, but it is misleading to use the same words in regard to the envelope, as we shall see all the more readily later on. It is better to use the word *intensive*, when the linewise circles close in towards their innermost infinity, which would be a *point of lines*. Older mathematicians actually called this a "star" (Figure 34b).

These exercises lead to the understanding of the nature of a "*lemniscatory space*"—a space in which two archetypal worlds are united. In Figure 35, the fusion of these two worlds is demonstrated, using the crossing-points of the polar circle-families to find the points of the so-called Cassini curves and the Bernoulli Lemniscate. In Plate II, we see a perspective transformation of such a space. (See notes 9 and 10, and page 46.)

It now requires rather a greater effort of imagination to picture the circle in the form of a sphere (or the ellipse as an ellipsoid) and to imagine the similar reciprocal process taking place as between points and *planes* with respect to this unit sphere. Just as a circle is only complete in our thought when the tangential aspect unites with the pointwise one, so is our usual conception of a sphere also miserably onesided. It cannot be drawn in a geometrical picture and it takes a power of imagination to picture it in the mind; but conceptually, in synthetic geometry, a hollow sphere made of infinite planes is an indisputable phenomenon of mathematical imagination.

Perhaps it is because of the overwhelmingly formative effect of the predominantly pointwise, Euclidean thought-forms, which are taught—often exclusively—in schools and universities today, not only in physics, but also in biology, that the light-filled imaginations of projective geometry do not so easily penetrate the mind. They require a more energetic and quite different way of thinking than does the simple accumulating of outer, pointwise facts and phenomena, however wonderful and thought-inspiring these may be.

It must be repeated that in our excursions here into the elements of modern mathematics, a great deal has had to be left out. Contemplation of the few illustrations which follow will however reveal to the observant thinker that given the magic of the sphere, every form can be compared to a sister form with polar characteristics.

Flat surfaces may be transformed into pointed forms. convexities into concavities, qualities transposed. We meet here with the laws of metamorphosis. The study of form—

morphology—takes on exciting and quite unexpected aspects. The language of the living forms of nature will speak with a new eloquence, in the light of polar metamorphosis.

The steps taken by the mathematicians of the early nineteenth century were as epoch-making as the transition made by Desargues, Pascal and Descartes from the earth-geometry of the Greeks. They reflect the evolution of human thinking, which sets out to compass both earth and universe. Moving from perspective transformation to polar reciprocation (from collineations to correlations) is a tremendous morphological experience. It could be compared with walking along the poplar avenue, which involves movement and change of scene, but no great change of forms, and then, in some way, to slip through that infinitely distant point and find oneself on the other side—like Alice, disappearing down the rabbit-hole or melting through the looking-glass into a wonderland beyond!

Perhaps this is not so very far-fetched; be that as it may, the change which comes about through a polar-reciprocal process is deep and radical, involving complicated qualities of turning inside-out, transposing perhaps from right to left and going through the infinite. Unexpected things happen and to carry out such exercises requires presence of mind and freedom from preconceived ideas.

The plant and the insect both reveal this radical type of transformation, when, after continuing to produce only leaves or appearing again and again as a caterpillar, they reach a quiescent stage, like the flower-bud, and then, miraculously, an entirely different form appears.

Polar reciprocation teaches us to expect such miracles and get to know the type of law prevailing here. In the plane, not only circles, but every kind of curve can be made to metamorphose into something radically different and yet closely related. In Figure 36, for instance, the inner lemniscatory curve was drawn inside the polarising circle—and see what became of it! To explain in detail would take us too long, Suffice it to say that all the *qualities* of one curve (sharpness or flatness, for instance) are to be found *transposed into their opposite* in the sister curve. Pure reciprocity, like question and answer, comes to expression in these forms. The two curves balance one another out completely, pointwise and linewise; when one takes an interest in the central point, the other seeks out the line-at-infinity. It is a realm of laws relating to relationships, even the dynamic ones between people and between their discarnate and incarnate lives.

To explore in more detail polar reciprocation with respect to spherical forms, would be necessary here. The three dimensional drawings show how to follow this, on the basis of what we have done with the circle. The same laws apply, only now the reciprocation is between *plane* and *point*, and this is shown in Figures 37 and 38. Figure 37 shows the polar plane moving out, resulting in the pole moving in, and vice versa; the two merge at the sphere's surface. Just as we recognise that a circle can be created by all the lines which envelop it, so now we can learn to imagine *a sphere enveloped from without by planes*, which would inter-weave in the outer space, right out to the plane at infinity. The sphere is then an *inward hollow*—not easy to imagine and impossible to draw! *Here we must abandon the habit of picturing three dimensions.*

Figure 38 shows again the polarity between point and plane with respect to the sphere. To the plane outside, there is a pole marked within the sphere. Move the point about freely, *keeping it in the plane*, and see how its polar plane (which is shown by the elliptical plane inside the sphere) will move, so that it *pivots* on the inner pole. One must imagine both planes extended on all sides and inter-penetrating in a line, which moves too. To take hold of all the possibilities for mobility provided in this Figure is an important and very rewarding exercise.

Figure 39 shows the sphere surrounded by a cube, which just touches it from outside. The points at which the planes of the cube touch the sphere, mark the corners of the polar form inside it. This form, too, completely balances out the cube, its polar opposite. It is the octahedron, which has six points instead of six planes and eight planes instead of eight corners, like the cube. And one can find further reciprocal characteristics between these two.

In Figure 40, we see the pair again; this time the octahedron is outside and the cube within. Furthermore, the picture shows the octahedron growing, which causes the cube to shrink! Try to imagine what happens, when the eight planes of the octahedron are so far away that they have disappeared, melted *all of them at once*, into the plane-at-infinity! When this happens, the cube points would have to melt together into the central point of the sphere. (But don't forget that the cube *lines and planes* would still exist, for we must not think of these forms as though they were finite, Euclidean forms, although we have to draw them that way.) In the last resort, the shrinking cube would turn into the three lines and three planes, which give it its three dimensionality in the centre of the sphere.

Cube and Octahedron are two of the five regular forms known to the Greeks, —the only simple regular forms that can be thought out. It is, however, only in modern time that we recognise their polar relationships with respect to the sphere. The other two are the Tetrahedron, pictured in Figure 41, which is self-polar, and in Figure 42, the Pentagon-dodecahedron is drawn surrounding the sphere. Its polar form, the Icosahedron, is called forth by the points of contact of the twelve dodecahedron planes with the sphere. The icosahedron therefore has twelve points; it has twenty planes, whereas the pentagon-dodecahedron has twenty points.

This theme, concerned with the polar reciprocal relationships involved in these classical forms is undoubtedly of significance as material for meditation in our time. Unfortunately, the *Platonic Forms* are more usually referred to as *solids*, and this shows how only too easily we fall back on the innate habit of thinking in ordinary, three-dimensional space—the space of earth-substance. In fact, in making the drawings, we have to do this, for it is impossible to make a fully true picture of a cube in projective geometry, which would show that in this way of thinking, *each plane must be pictured as of infinite extent*, with resulting interpenetrations in the infinite! It is easy for the intellect, and perhaps especially for the mathematician armed with the facility of algebraic thinking, to say to himself "Oh yes! This is all quite understandable," and yet to fail to reach the *experience* and the deeper meaning of polar reciprocation.

The theme of polar reciprocation in modern synthetic, projective geometry not only involves the practice of sense-free thinking, which is the task of all geometrical thinking (mathematics), but a further step is here involved. In this exercise we are practising a way of thinking in imaginations, which accords with and reveals the laws of polar concepts of space and the way they can be seen to relate. As we shall attempt to show, this path of mathematical thinking leads also to an understanding of the polar types of *force*, which relate to these types of space.

It must not be forgotten that the analytical mode of mathematical thinking is all-important and must not be denied, but redeemed. It is, however, understandable why Steiner based his teachings, particularly in education, on the development of *Art*, involving pictorial imagination and sense-free thinking.

With all the beauty of form and freedom of movement which come to expression in projective space through the processes of perspective transformation and polar reciprocation, the culmination of the development of synthetic geometry lies in the concept: *polar to a central point is the plane at infinity*. This describes the modern conception of earth-space. But the question remained open: What, then, is polar to this concept? *What is polar to the conception of earth-space?*

No-one appeared to be interested; Adams never found the answer fully formulated in any mathematical literature.

In what follows, we shall be concerned with the answer to this question, which has taken projective geometry further, from where it rested in the first half of the nineteenth century into the twentieth century.

Polar to a central point is the plane at infinity, with the myriad points and lines within it; it pictures the idea of space, as one stands at a point and looks out and up to the starry sky. The picture which is polar to that one would be to look inward from the starry sky to some innermost infinitude—a point within, which, however, in contrast, would "contain" its myriad planes and lines, (see p. V.44).

Considerations such as this, arising from the questions Adams saw Steiner approaching in scientific lectures, as well as from the promptings he himself had already received as a research graduate in Cambridge University, resulted in the publication in 1933 of the mathematical conception of Polar Euclidean Space, which Adams entitled *Physical and Ethereal Spaces*.

It was a first-time publication of the theory, but related as it was so closely to Rudolf Steiner's spiritual science, it found at that time no echo in academic circles. Significantly, it was just in these years, when physicists—among them former colleagues of Adams in Cambridge—were deeply engaged in what might *seem* a more practical aspect of science, namely, atomic fission. Looking back through half a century, it is clear to see that the seed sown by the theory of physical and ethereal spaces and forces is a polar counterpart to the theories which resulted in the atomic bomb.

A few years later, Louis Locher published his thoughts on the subject of polar euclidean spaces. He came independently to the same conclusions as Adams, working out the basic thoughts in his textbook *Projektive Geometrie* (1940), which was followed (1970) by *Raum und Gegenraum*.

Chapter V

RUDOLF STEINER: POLAR SPACES

> "As long, my friend, as you have space
> and time in mind, you shall not grasp
> what God and Eternity are." Angelus Silesius

High in a mountain garden, in brilliant autumn sunshine, the mauve flower spikes of a huge Michaelmas Daisy move in the soft breeze in the midday sun, as though bowing to the majestic mountains. Through the rhythmic passing of the days and nights, the plant changes its colours with the changing moods of the mountains—sometimes shining, pale and almost white, in the moonlight, sometimes revealing a deep saturated purple hue as though it were glowing from within.

Clearly manifest here is the truth declared by Goethe, that colours arise with the 'deeds and sufferings of the light', interplaying with the darkness. This does not contradict what Newton saw, when he defracted the beam of light with a prism in his darkened room and also saw the colours. These are two aspects of a whole, just as we have seen that there can be more than one aspect to the study of forms.

Now, at midday, the hot sunlight has drawn a humming world of bees around the plant, collecting the last nectar of summer. Red Admiral butterflies, too, are gathering there, gracing the plant with their peculiar wing-movements, outspread above the mauve flowers. All is movement; one has the impression of contented movement; a fulfilment is taking place, both for plant and insects. It is a *whole* world,—a small universe.

How impossible, even absurd it seems at this moment to think that by looking into the substances of these tiny forms with however powerful a microscope we shall be able to find out how they come to life! Yet maybe even the microscopic pictures will one day be studied with less one-sided forms of thought. Mankind is in danger of being caught and literally suffocated by the results of analytical research into the chemistry of substance. No wonder that people are becoming restive—and the very Earth as well!

May not a wider and quite different—a complementary approach to the understanding of the creation and transformation of living *forms* have a bearing in the realm of *chemistry* also? This was indeed the question which had prompted Adams, arising out of his researches with others in Cambridge at that time, to look into the thought-forms of modern projective synthetic geometry.

In his writings, for example, in articles[5] entitled *Science at the Crossroads* (1927) and *Physics and the Light of the World (1930)*, Adams was at pains to describe the then prevailing

state of science and to draw attention to the overcoming of scientific materialism—
"Scientific materialism has been transcended by the advance of science itself"—but
also to the fact that precisely in this process the scientist himself, moving in a world
of pure forms of thought, has lost touch with *reality*. He quotes Professor Eddington:
"The farther physics goes, the emptier the world becomes."

In this article, written in 1930, Adams says:

"Physics, as everybody knows, is undergoing undreamt-of changes. It is already several stages removed from the secure materialism which gave or seemed to give it stable foundation during the 19th century.

For a short while, the electric theory of matter might provide a passing refuge for the materialistic conception. Though the 'electron'' were in name not a particle of "matter" but of "electricity", still it would be conceived—at any rate by the majority of scientists and laymen—in a materialistic fashion. It is not the *name*, it is the *quality* of the idea, that matters. But as I said, this was no more than a passing refuge. The discoveries and forms of thought that underlay the "electron" theory led very quickly to a still further resolution. The "particle of electricity" (naïvely so conceived, in the popular imagination)—this in its turn was submerged beneath the waves of thought. Physical science has to-day become, in its fundamental ideas, a pure structure of thought. There is no longer any *thing*, any *substratum, about* which the scientist is thinking, in the theories of modern physics. He moves in a world of pure forms of thought: these are the "laws" which he expresses in his mathematical equations, in calculi whose intricacy seems to know no limit. He knows the "laws," we may say, but he has no idea of who or what it is obeys them.

Long, long ago, it was a *Who*—it was the living being, Goddess Natura. The laws of Science were the thoughts of God; Nature His handmaid. Science was born as Natural Philosophy. Then it became no longer Who, but *What*? Science grew atheist, in substance if not in sentiment. Matter obeyed the laws of motion; these, in their essence and effect, were the sum-total of the 'laws of Nature." Now, even the *What* is taken away. Now have the "laws"—that is, the empty *forms* of thought—completely swallowed up the *being*, or the *thing*, that obeyed them. (The "laws of motion," wherein we deal in modern theory—"quantum" and "relativity" and "wave-mechanics" and the rest—refer no more to spatial conditions in which the human imagination can picture any "material" existence. Therefore, for science, there is no longer any content in the old idea of matter— or of any quasi-matter, as electricity or ether—as at the basis of all things.) Physical science itself approaches dangerously near to the condition which the humorous rationalist, Bertrand Russell—that 18th century philosopher, transplanted by some quip of Fate into our time—assigned to mathematics: it is the science in which we do not know what we are talking about, nor whether, what we are saying is true."

Ironically enough, it was, in particular, Bertrand Russell, who steered George Adams towards synthetic geometry!

"Small wonder, if in this state of things the scientist himself—I refer to Professor Eddington in his recent Swarthmore lecture—declares that for *Reality* man must turn again into his inner life: to the poetic and the religious experience. *The farther Physics goes, the emptier the world becomes.* That is the essence of the situation. Increase of knowledge fans into thin air the secure reality of all things, which the untutored mind calls "matter." The outer world, that seemed to us so full, is empty. Wouldst thou find fulness, oh man, then thou must look within!" Such is the verdict of a scientist—a physicist and an astronomer—to-day.

Mysticism and Mathematics at the Dawn of the Modern Age

In the Middle Ages in Europe, the outer material world had still, for the human being, been to some extent ensouled, but at that time the inner life of the human soul had not attained to spiritual freedom. In the development of science through the 17th and 18th centuries matter was disensouled by degrees, until, of necessity, the nature beings, servants of the hierarchies, were banished to the dusty shelves of libraries and the Goddess Natura hid her face.

At the turn of the century, in 1900, Rudolf Steiner gave a series of lectures in Berlin, which he later summarized in the book he entitled: *Mysticism at the Dawn of the Modern Age.* By means of the ideas of the mystics from Meister Eckhart to Jacob Boehme, I found expression for the spiritual perceptions, which I decided to put forth." (This book was no more intended to be a history of mysticism, than the *Philosophy of Spiritual Activity* is a book on philosophy in the usual sense of the word. We are being shown a pathway, which is being trodden in our time.)

Rudolf Steiner, going back even as far as the thirteenth century is concerned to reveal essential phases in the awakening of European culture towards a freedom and intensity of individual thinking, which then led over into modern science. In the American edition of this book, *Mysticism at the Dawn of the Modern Age*, (also entitled *Eleven European Mystics*), there is a fine introduction by the historian Paul M. Allen, giving short but colourful life-histories of the men in question.

There is a possibility, indeed, a necessity, Dr Steiner insists, of finding in the present-day knowledge of nature, seen in its true character, a way "which could so incline the soul as to find in mystical contemplation, the light of the spirit." . . . "Why do mystically inclined souls" he asks "find satisfaction in Meister Eckhart, in Jacob Boehme etc. but not in the book of nature, in so far as, opened by knowledge, it lies before man today?" The intention of the book is to show that out of the disposition of soul of the old mysticism there developed a way of thinking, which would be able to incorporate the newer knowledge into itself. This was, for example, particularly the case with Cardinal Nicolas of Cusa.

> "In such personalities it becomes apparent that present-day natural science too is capable of a mystical intensification. For a Nicolas of Cusa would be able to lead his thinking over into this science. In his time one could have discarded the old way of inquiry, retained the mystical disposition, and accepted modern natural science, had it already existed."

Nicolas of Cusa (1401—1464) was an expert mathematician, who opened men's minds once more to the concept of a universe which is infinite. In learning to understand what the concept "mystical intensification" means here, we are helped by understanding the step from the quantitative to the qualitative—from the calculable to the incalculable—even as expressed in mathematics. In the ancient civilization of Greece and Rome, mankind's thinking was directed down into the quantitative aspect of the fixed and finite world of created things. This was world destiny. The New Age has the task of uniting the experience gained from the methods of earthly reckoning with the other equally real, spiritual aspect of the universe, which is infinite.

The mathematical concept of infinity was slowly to dawn in men's minds. Already in the thirteenth century, Thomas Aquinas (1225—1274), while not disagreeing with Aristotle's statement that there is no such thing as the infinite (in an outward direction), conceded that a continuum cannot consist of indivisible entities. He pointed to infinity in his inner search for God, with the thought that it would be possible to divide a fixed continuum ad infinitum, thus reaching towards the idea of the infinitesimal within. This was an abstract thought with which it was possible to relate in the soul to the idea of the Divine within,—the thought that God dwells within each human soul.

Two centuries later, when the age of the "sentient soul"—the feeling soul of mankind—was beginning to give way to the dawning of the new age, the time when men would receive into themselves the forces of the thinking soul (the "consciousness" or "spiritual soul"),[2] Nicolas of Cusa opened men's minds again to the concept of a universe which is infinite. Paul Allen writes:

> "Today Nicolas of Cusa is remembered for his cosmological conceptions, his originality and breadth of thought, and his courage as a thinker. As the famous French mathematician and philosopher, René Descartes was to write nearly two hundred years after Nicolas' death, 'The Cardinal of Cusa and several other theologians have supposed the world to be infinite, and the Church has never condemned them for it. On the contrary, it is thought that to make His works appear very great is one way to honor God.' Nicolas of Cusa's work was appreciated by such men as Giordano Bruno, philosopher, poet, and martyr, Johannes Kepler, the astronomer, and Descartes, to name but a few. The courage necessary for a thinker to grasp the implications of the new age was present in Nicolas of Cusa, and the scope of his investigations in the world of thought is evidence of his importance and stature."

Courage and the love of God inspired these early thinkers. Their stories tell no easy tale; troubles and tribulations faced them on all sides, through which they upheld the courage of their convictions, sometimes in face of the inquisition and the stake.

The story of the development of mathematics and of the Copernican world-conception is rooted in these human experiences. Men sought an inner path towards enlightenment and at the same time an outer path began to open up towards nature and the understanding of life. Some of these "mystics" were professors of theology, some were practising professors of mathematics and of medicine. The last three about whom Rudolf Steiner writes were contemporary with Desargues, Pascal and Descartes; these were

Jacob Boehme (1575—1624), Giordano Bruno (1548—1600) and Angelus Silesius (1624—1677). Among the eleven described is Paracelsus also, who lived in the 16th century.

The complicated weaving of the tapestry of human destiny became evident to the seer of the twentieth century. Rudolf Steiner's book *The Threshold of the Spiritual World*, written in 1913, sets the modern thinker very concisely on the path towards the recovery—now in the light of modern thought—of the understanding concerning the *Who* and the *What* and the unveiling of the Goddess Natura. We are taught how to find our way through thinking to perceive once more the world of Being, which is hidden and lost in the present-day picture of the world of atoms. In truth, just as mathematics has laws, which should not be misused, so the Spiritual World sets a Guardian at the Threshold.

Here is where courage is needed; materialism is a "psychic phenomenon of fear". Fear certainly is abroad in the world today. Courage has always been demanded of those who would cross from the world of the senses to that world, which is hidden by the veil of *maya*. Today the path leads within, as in the old mysticism, and *at the same time* it leads to the unveiling of the mysteries of the world of nature—the world of outer phenomena. The call can be heard today: Man! Know thyself! Man! Know the world!

Courage is indeed required, and courage, surely, is also abroad today, called forth by men, women and children all over the world, in the very course of daily life, as the result of conditions and situations prevailing in our time.

We may choose to go around with our eyes shut; or to play our part. I believe that in modern time, the Mystery Temple is not hidden away, accessible only to the few; the *whole world* is the Mystery Temple today, and all are free to choose, whether or not to enter.

> "The spiritual being, hidden in man, which is man himself, but which he can as little see with ordinary consciousness as the eye can see itself, is the Guardian of the Threshold of the Spiritual World."

The extreme cleverness of the cold intellect has created the infinite intricacies of our modern materialistic world. What has happened in the last few decades, based on the ingenious use of mathematical physics, has changed the world as it has not been changed in thousands of years. But face to face with materialism, human beings are looking in other directions for survival, and other forces are becoming strong, and will grow stronger—a readiness to work together across all boundaries. "Where love and fellow-feeling are stirring in life, we sense the magic breath of the spirit, interpenetrating the physical world." (The Threshold of the Spiritual World)

Once again, the words sound forth from *The Portal of Initiation*, this time transformed:

> "The weaving essence of the Light rays forth
> From Man to Man
> To fill the World with Truth."

Mathematics at the Threshold

Mathematics, in its further development, is both a guide and a tool, both spiritually and quite practically. The certainty given by the clarity of mathematical thinking can penetrate the veils of uncertainty, which prevail today in all manner of realms. It rests with human beings to learn to use the sword of the Archangel Michael, a clear thinking warmed through with fiery will.

Riding the horse of the intellect, we need courage to face the dragon. This Archangel of the Sun, who is the guiding spirit of our time, can show the way, *provided that human beings so will it*; for freedom prevails in the world of thinking. Mankind, in the grip of materialism, must find the way onward. Materialism has begun to give way, but confidence and discrimination are nevertheless more than ever necessary. Mathematics is a vast and wide field; it contains very many answers. The essential thing is to ask of it the right question for today.

The events and beings and the created things of the physical world are the outward expression of the realm beyond the world of the senses spread around us in space and time. The first realm beyond is the etheric or ethereal world; to learn to understand its laws is the first step across the threshold of the world of the senses.

How did Rudolf Steiner attempt to awaken in his hearers an appreciation of the necessity to formulate a *conception of space* on the basis of synthetic geometry *which accords with the realities of the etheric world?*

To quote from the lecture of 8.IV.22, entitled *The Position of Anthroposophy among the Sciences*: Remarking that "Anthroposophy encounters difficulties when it enters the fields of the various sciences", Steiner maintains that the fundamental attitude of consciousness in Anthroposophy has been drawn from that branch of present-day science, namely, mathematics, which is least of all attacked in respect to its scientific character and importance. Regretting that in order to come to terms with the idea of etheric space he will have to inflict on his audience "somewhat remote ideas—things which in ordinary life may be called difficult but which are necessary", he goes on to discuss the mental attitude a man assumes, when actively engaged in mathematical thinking, which, he says: "when practised, leads to supersensible perception." He takes an example from geometry,— the science of space, as he calls it—going into great detail concerning the way we learn, as children first to *experience* by means of our body and then to *think* in an abstract way about the three dimensions of space.

Rudolf Steiner would have us see that our conception of ordinary Euclidean three-dimensional space comes about through having objectified into abstract thoughts the actual experience of the three dimensions which we feel bodily, when we learn to lift ourselves into the upright position, to orient ourselves between left and right and to gauge the third dimension by focusing in depth with our two eyes. In thus objectifying a physical experience into abstract thinking, he says:

> "We lift out of our body what we have first experienced within it"... "We actually go out of ourselves when in thought we construct space in this way"... "In thus objectifying space we are able to study the external movements and relative positions of objects, with the help of ideas formed geometrically within space; we feel thereby that we are on scientific ground..."

Having first, in a less conscious way, experienced the physical reality of the upright posture, the left-right dimension and the forward-backward dimension, we are able later in life to think about it abstractly, thus, by putting ourselves outside of the body, as it were, we are able to look back on it and recognise in it also the three geometrical dimensions of space. *A deeply intuitive experience is brought to consciousness.*

The fact that the single individuality finds itself incarnated in a three-dimensional physical body is a repetition or reflection of what took place historically in the whole development of mankind. Throughout history, art has depicted this process; scenes appear, gradually coming out of the gold background as it were, into the three dimensions of space through the development of the laws of perspective. It was not until the early fifteenth century that painters and draughtsmen began to introduce the third dimension in a systematic way.

Just as in each single incarnation the individuality goes through the stages through which humanity as a whole has passed in evolution and the time comes when the child can enjoy being taught to think abstractly about geometrical facts, so in the time of Euclid, geometry as we know it in terms of the laws of parallelism and the right angle was thought out and written down. Then, not until the seventeenth century came the actual conception of cartesian space and the laws of perspective.

Thus the historical development of mathematics went hand in hand with the development of the modern scientific way of thinking, which relies on the sure support of mathematical thinking.

Steiner is saying in the lecture to which we are referring, that the mathematical experience of three-dimensional space *is already a supersensible perception*, although we do not think of it as such. As spiritual, thinking beings, we experience the world around us, learning to understand the laws of the things to be met with in space,—the forms and the substances.

> "If we approach mathematics in the right frame of mind, we come to see precisely in the mathematician's attitude when 'mathematising' the pattern for all that one requires for supersensible perception. For mathematics is simply the first stage of supersensible perception." The mathematical structures we 'perceive' in space *are* supersensible perceptions—though we, "accustomed to perceive them, do not admit this".

Having thus described how our familiar conception of physical space arose, Rudolf Steiner puts forward a new proposition: *What if the human being could do with other experiences what he has done in transforming his bodily experience of space into a mathematical conception?*

> "Suppose we could shape other experiences—our mode of perceiving the qualities of colours and tones, for example—in the same way that we create and shape our experience of space from out of ourselves! When we look at a cube of salt we bring the cubical shape with us from our geometry, knowing that its shape is identical with the spatial concept we have formed. If we could create from out of ourselves, let us say, the world of colour, and then confront external coloured objects, we should then in the same way, project, as it were, into the outer world what we first build up in ourselves"...

Rudolf Steiner is now saying that there is an aspect of mathematics with which to approach the realm of *qualities*, a realm hitherto regarded as being outside the realm of science.

"Just as we have unconsciously constructed for ourselves the form of space and created things out of our human constitution, so we can train ourselves, this time by a conscious effort, to draw from out of ourselves the whole gamut of *qualities* contained in the world, so as to find them again in things, and then again in looking back upon ourselves. What I am here describing is the ascent to so-called *Imaginative perception*".

The "Negative Space" of the Body of Formative Forces.

Rudolf Steiner then refers to the possibility in modern mathematics of extending algebraic calculations to postulate a fourth and even higher dimensions, thus conceiving of other spaces and other geometries well known today.

"These operations are logical in the mathematical sense and quite correct, but anyone who knows the genesis of our idea of space, as I have described it, will detect something quite special here". Referring to the to and fro movement of a pendulum, he says that just as it does not swing further and further out, but turns back, so too, in reality," one cannot pass on into an indefinite fourth dimension; one must turn back at a certain point and the fourth dimension becomes simply the third with a minus sign before it... Our perception of space must return into itself". In turning back through the third, second and first dimensions, we annihilate them one after another and reach to a point in "*negative space*"..."then space is filled with spirit, whereas three-dimensional space is filled with matter."

On very many occasions, when trying to make clear what he means, by a negative space in contrast to earth-space, and when describing how the scientist should think about the true nature of the sun—a realm, which is emptier than empty, more than a vacuum—Rudolf Steiner gives an interesting example taken from the realm of economics. You know, he says, that you can have a pocket full of money, then you can spend it, until the pocket is empty. But your pocket can be *more than empty*, for then you are in debt! In such fashion Rudolf Steiner often describes the "negative space" of the sun in comparison to the "positive space" of the earth. *This is based on a modern mathematical conception which is true to the spiritual scientific facts.*

In the following lecture (9.IV.22) entitled: *Anthroposophy and the Visual Arts*, Rudolf Steiner describes more fully what he means by a *negative space*, in which the three positive dimensions have been abolished. The pendulum was an example taken from physics, but now Rudolf Steiner takes the example of the sculptor, to describe the two kinds of space about which he is speaking. Here he describes this other space of negative dimensions as "the space into which the sculptor enters"... "The secret of this space is that one cannot set out from one point and relate all else to it" (as in the cartesian axial system). "One must set out from the counterpart of this point, nothing other than an infinitely remote sphere to which one might look up as at the blue vault of heaven."

Here it must be clear to the reader that the infinitely remote sphere (seen from its centre outward) is in fact the plane at infinity, with which we have now become familiar; for an infinitely large sphere, mathematically conceived, no longer has any curvature, but is flat. Go out into a field on a clear starry night, with a free view of the sky. Simply to look up, to map out and record the stars in a merely intellectual way is an earth-space activity,

> "But if you confront the starry heavens with your whole being, you experience them differently. We have lost the perceptive sense for this, but it can be reacquired." Experiencing the night sky in its different moods and conditions, with the different groupings of stars, perhaps with the moon shining there, or when it is invisible, one can learn to know one's cosmic environment in a deeper way, just as one can feel one's way into the human organism in order to experience space.
>
> "Then as one advances beyond ordinary perception, which suffices for geometry, one acquires the perception needed for these wide expanses: one advances to what I called...'imaginative cognition'... One receives an 'imagination' of the whole cosmos, One receives a counter-image of...the three geometrical space-dimensions. What one receives can take an infinite variety of shapes."...
>
> "If one intends to take in this way one's idea of space from the starry heavens, one cannot express it exhaustively using the idea of three dimensions. One receives the idea of a space which I can only indicate figuratively. If I indicate the ordinary space by three lines at right-angles to one another, I should indicate this space by drawing everywhere sets of figures or configurations, as if surface-forces, or forces in surfaces (Kräfte in Flächen) were approaching the earth from without, from all directions of the universe, and were working plastically on the forms upon its surface."
>
> "One comes to such an idea when, advancing beyond what living beings—above all, human beings—present to physical eyes, one attains to what I have been calling "Imagination". In this the cosmos, not the physical human being, reveals itself in images and brings us a new space. As soon as one gets so far, one perceives man's second body—what an older, prescient, instinctive clairvoyance called the "etheric body". A better name is "body of formative forces" (*Bildekräfteleib*). This is a supersensible body, consisting of subtle, etheric substantiality and permeating man's physical body. We can study this physical body if, within the space it occupies, we seek the forces that flow through it. But we cannot study the etheric body (body of formative forces) which flows through the human being if we set out from *this* space. We can study this only if we think of it as built up out of the whole cosmos: formed plastically from without by "planes of force" (*Kraftflächen*) converging on the earth from all sides and reaching man."

It is much easier to formulate in mathematical thought the experience of being point-centred in earth-space, than it is to describe accurately in thought the equally intuitive polar experience, of being outspread in the starry canopy and at one with the universe of stars. The former is an old and everyday experience, the latter an experience to which we now have to become more awake. Such an experience may be had in dreams or at the point of death or of birth; the experience is akin to being outspread in the plane at infinity and looking inward, as towards a tiny point far away within or below. It is, in fact, not an uncommon experience.

To have a conception of this kind of experience in clear thought is perhaps difficult, unless one has already worked at the mathematical formulation of a space which is polar to the earthly space of the body. Such work provides the necessary thoughts with which to imagine a space, which accords with one's experience of the etheric body. This intuitive experience—as well as the gravitational one—may also be translated into mathematical conceptions and thus objectified.

In so doing we awaken to the laws of the etheric body and can begin to think clearly about the forces we employ, when we stand upright and move. Here we meet with an equally intuitive experience, for which the word 'levity' is appropriate. (We are, however, now using the word *levity** in a strictly scientific sense.) On the basis of the new mathematical conception of polar-Euclidean space, in which *planes* are fundamental, rather than points, we are justified in postulating the idea of forces working from plane to plane, as well as those conceived of in classical mechanics as working between point-centres.

Rudolf Steiner's new art of Eurythmy[6] lives with these new imaginations, revealing to all who practice and to those who see these movements, the subtle Kräfteflächen (planes of force) of the supersensible ether-body, as it allows the physical body to move through space.

The space of this "body of formative forces" is the 'other kind of space' into which the sculptor enters (and the Eurythmist). One might say that the clay is in one kind of space, but that the hands of the sculptor work in this other kind of space (counterspace) and according to its laws. These are the laws according to which the formative forces of the life-processes take hold of substance and form it. In this "space" it is not a question of adding substance; *addition is an earthly process*, used in building houses in the ordinary way. The sculptor raises the form from out of the substance, as though to draw forth the living form within. Rudolf Steiner sculpted at the surfaces of huge masses of wood, which had to be cut away with smooth chisel cuts, laid side by side to create *surfaces*, thus to reveal forms in "negative space"—in this *other kind of space*.[7] His sculpture speaks through the quality of the *relief* in art.

Substance is subject to the downward pull of gravity; it is at home in the point-space of earth, subject to the forces of pressure and consolidation. The sculptor lifts the substance into another realm—into the world in which the forces work, which Rudolf Steiner calls "suctional", "levitational", "planar".

Using the mathematical thought-picture of polar reciprocation (Chapter IV) we can now begin to visualise in thought-pictures the planes coming in from the periphery,

---

* The word *levity* is used here simply to describe a process, which is polar opposite to gravity; it has no mediumistic connotation.

drawing their polar points out towards them, after which the two worlds interpenetrate.

Plane upon plane comes in from the periphery of cosmic space (that is, in the 'other kind of space') and as they do so, they draw up or 'suck' up the points—the living substances—away from the centre of gravity.

This is a mathematical interpretation of what happens in the process of growth. Rudolf Steiner and Ita Wegman, for example, describe it also in the book *Fundamentals of Therapy:*

> "Observation shows, after all, that the phenomena of life have an altogether different orientation from those that run their course within the lifeless realm. Of the latter we shall be able to say, they reveal that they are subject to forces radiating outward from the essence of material substance. These forces radiate from the—relative—centre to the periphery. But in the phenomena of life, the material substance appears subject to forces working from without inward—towards the relative centre. Passing on into the sphere of life, the substance must withdraw itself from the forces raying outward and subject itself to those that radiate inward.
>
> Now it is to the Earth that every earthly substance, or earthly process, owes its forces of the kind that radiate outward. It has these forces in common with the Earth. It is, indeed, only as a constituent of the Earth-body that any substance has the nature which Chemistry discovers in it. And when it comes to life, it must cease to be a mere portion of the Earth; it leaves its community with the Earth and is gathered up into the forces that ray inward to the Earth from all sides—from beyond the earthly realm. Whenever we see a substance or process unfold in forms of life, we must conceive it to be withdrawing from the forces that work upon it as from the centre of the Earth, and entering the domain of others, which have, not a centre, but a periphery."

In planar or etheric space, the forces *do not press down and in* by means of gravity; they *hover* inward, but their effect is *to draw living substances upward and outward* by means of *'levity'*. True, the planes come inward, and there is a tendency to slip back in thought to ordinary space concepts and imagine them pressing in physically. They are in fact *levitational in quality* and their creative, moulding force is characteristic of the etheric formative realms; they mould and form with forces which belong to light and not to the darkness and weight of matter.

> Describing the Venus of Milo, Rudolf Steiner says in the lecture of 9.IV.22, "It was not created after a study of anatomy, in respectful reliance on forces which are merely to be understood as proceeding from the space of the physical body. It was created with a knowledge, possessed in ancient times, of the body of formative forces which permeates the physical body and is formed from out of the cosmos—*formed from out of a space as peripheral as earthly space is centric* (my italics). A being that is formed from the periphery of the universe has beauty impressed upon it—"beauty" in the original meaning of the word. Beauty is indeed the imprint of the cosmos, made with the help of the etheric body, on a physical, earthly being.". . .

We have thus described the step envisaged by Rudolf Steiner on the basis of projective synthetic geometry; it is a step leading towards the faculty of supersensible perception.

> "Natural science applies mathematics as it has been elaborated to date. But anyone who wishes to understand clairvoyant supersensible activity must seek it where it is present in its most primitive form: in the construction of mathematical forms. If he can then raise this activity to higher domains, he will be developing something related to elementary, primitive 'mathematising'' as the more developed branches of mathematics are related to their axioms. The primary axioms of clairvoyance are living ones and if we succeed in developing our "mathematising" by exercises, we shall not only see spatial relationships in the world around us, but learn to know spiritual beings when,...in this way, we raise to higher domains what we develop by "mathematising." (8.IV.22).

The spiritual beings of whom the spiritual seer speaks are firstly elemental and angel beings of the ethereal worlds, which are just beyond our normal vision today, but which in special moments, do sometimes flash in upon our consciousness, or allow us to hear the rustling of their wings.

It is helpful to learn to think and imagine forms in terms of *planes* and *surfaces*; for these are the *type* of form in which the beings of the elements of water, air and fire reveal themselves. Like a memory of by-gone days, the artist's imagination shows the angels and the hierarchies with wings and haloes. Such beings are up-borne by cosmic planes and surfaces, even as we ourselves are bound to the earth, yet nevertheless upheld in all our movements. When we move, these are the forces brought into play, and we experience them quite intuitively as part of our way of being on the earth. We take them for granted.

It is also important to realise that the rhythms experienced in living movement can only arise as the result of a harmonious interplay between the polar realms. Such, indeed, is the true nature of rhythm; it swings between two poles and is not tied to the hammerbeat of matter as in earthly mechanics. It is wise here to give a thought to the phenomenon of the Foucault pendulum, when seeking to understand Steiner's picture of a swinging pendulum in his advice to think more in terms of three negative dimensions, rather than to postulate a fourth and more positive dimensions, as is usual in physics. (Adams loved this phenomenon, and in contemplating it, he would say: "That pendulum is hitched to a star!!)

Natural science is certainly not minded to see fairies with wings like fireflies. But in pressing through to further mathematical and morphological formulations, we may perhaps give wings to our thoughts and begin to see more in natural phenomena than at first meets the eye.

Art speaks in the words of colours, tones and surfaces, out of a deeper and more spiritual understanding of form. The ethereal, invisible aspect of form becomes visible and audible in art. In learning to see forms not only from their pointwise aspect, according to the laws of the Cartesian space in which they appear as *created shapes*, but also by experiencing the planar gesture of form, which reveals something of the *creative process*, one begins to see beyond the material form; qualities otherwise hidden, invisible, begin to light up in the imagination and in clear thought. They are the qualities of life, of soul and of the in-dwelling spirit. It is a path of training leading to a new way of perceiving.

The new path for science, which was opened up by Goethe's morphological studies and taken further by Rudolf Steiner,[8] involves the bringing together of percept and concept, for instance, in the contemplation of the world of plants. We learn to observe and think in such a way that *the true Idea belonging to the phenomenon* is born in the soul. "Just as we have eyes to see the physical, material world, so we must find the thoughts with which to perceive the invisible, the spiritual world". Then, with our own eyes we shall see that it is true to say that "the whole form of the plant is spiritual reality, is supersensible reality, only this spiritual form is filled out with material substance!" (7.1.24).

A Step in the History of Mathematics in the Twentieth Century.

For the future scientist, the support and objectivity of mathematical thinking is as important as it ever was to give integrity to his ideas. The new science of morphology, laced through with the ideas of projective geometry and then taken further, will provide a sure path. A clear mathematical formulation of *Raum and Gegenraum (Space and Counterspace)* is a first step.

To sum up this formulation, in the words of George Adams in *"Physical and Ethereal Spaces"* in 1933, we may say:

Physical Space is pointwise in character and it is centric. It has as its infinitude the infinitely distant plane, the Absolute of physical measure, with its imaginary circle.	*Ethereal Space is planewise in character and it is "spherical." It has as its infinitude a "star-point" within, the Absolute of polar "measure", with its imaginary cone.*[4]

Once it had been realised by the earlier mathematicians that underlying the rigid space of the earth with its Euclidean principles of measurement, there was the more mobile, metamorphic space of projective geometry with all its point-planar symmetry, it was felt to be unsatisfactory that there was no polar equivalent to the plane at infinity itself, and the specialised metric arising from it. Other non-Euclidean spaces are derivable from modern geometry. Professor A. N. Whitehead called one of them Anti-space, and there are occasional references in the earlier literature to the kind of space we are now describing, among all the other possibilities, only to be left aside as seemingly of no particular interest or use.

It is important to realise that for physical, Euclidean space the Absolute is permanently given (it is the plane at infinity), and that any point in this space may be regarded as a centre or point—an origin from which to establish a Cartesian system, such as the three-dimensional axes with their planes at right-angles to one another. *The Absolute point of ethereal space, however, may be situated anywhere in physical space*, for ethereal spaces permeate physical space, wherever life is to be found; and these ethereal spaces all share the same planar origin—the plane at infinity of physical space. It is a magnificent reciprocity.

Within physical space, which is fixed under the firmament of the plane at infinity, the mobile ethereal spaces come and go in space and time, wherever life flourishes or decays. *The ethereal or sun-spaces have the infinitude of physical space as their origin and source, and a particular "star-point", embedded somewhere within this space as their Absolute—the infinitude into which they spend their living forces.*

In physical space:

One Absolute cosmic plane with which many points (earth-centres) are related. Point-centred forces radiate outward towards a peripheral infinitude.

In ethereal space:

Many Absolute "star-points" with which one cosmic plane (ground of worlds) is related. Peripheral, *planar* forces are received inward by an infinitude within.

This is a wonderful concept; it is true to life. In physical space, which is spanned as it were beneath the cosmic canopy of the star-strewn heavens, the ether-spaces come and go in constant flow. They are present wherever life flourishes; they disappear when life ebbs away; they might be called *Time-Spaces*. The infinitude of physical space is the origin or foundation of ether-spaces. Some particular "star-point" which becomes embedded in physical space is the Absolute of an ether-space and the infinitude into which it pours its living ethereal forces.

The reader will understand the word "star-point" as referring to the "innermost infinitude" of a polar Euclidean space. In our work on the plant, we refer to it sometimes as "star-centre" and sometimes as "sun-centre"; ethereal or sun-centre in the realm of the shoot, star-centre more often in the realm of the flower.

Cayley (1821—1895) and von Standt (1798—1867) use the mathematical term "Absolute", referring to that element—point, line, plane, or actual form—in mobile "projective space" which, if held constant, determines a particular type of metric space. Earth-Space is determined when the plane at infinity is constant (invariant). Ethereal or Sun-Space is determined by an inner functional infinitude,—an invariant, which is a *point at infinity within*.

For earth-space, which we experience through our physical bodies, there is one outer infinitude; it is in the periphery—the *plane at infinity*. Standing on the earth in the physical space of a point-centred body, perhaps in the dark, at night, looking up to the points of light in the starry sky, we look out as though to that infinitude.

Ethereal space (sun space) has two infinitudes; here we live between two infinitudes—an outer plane at infinity and a functional, inner infinitude within. If we would experience being spread out in the infinite plane (as we actually do in the first three days after death, when the physical body has fallen away and we awaken to the consciousness of the etheric body) we might try to imagine being all over the plane at one time, looking inward with planar vision, towards a *planar point* of light—a "star-point"—which is the *inner infinitude* of an ethereal space. It is in this kind of space that the living, universal forces work. It is possible to form an imagination of this space and look from the "canopy" of our universe inward to the star-point within—the functional inner infinitude. To know and experience *both spaces at once*, interwoven one with the other, is to awaken to the *wholeness* of the human body and the universe of Sun and Earth.

This inner point is quite different from an ordinary point, such as the point we think of as the centre of the earth. Mathematically, we conceive of it as being *woven of planes and lines. This point has a planar quality*; it is the world in which the lines and planes meet; the point 'contains' them. *These lines and planes are parts of this new kind of point, just as lines and points are parts of the plane in the ordinary way, in ordinary space.* The earlier mathematicians who first thought of this kind of point, and who were not so distant from the imaginative world, called it a "star". Later on, as the cloud of materialism grew denser, the mathematicians resorted to words drawn from more material pictures such as "bundle" and "sheaf".

While we are in a material body on the earth, it is an unfamiliar experience to be spread out in a cosmic plane and looking *inward* to a star! To a trained mathematician this is a perfectly clear thought. The mathematical concept of the polar Euclidean spaces, the life-filled spaces through which the ethereal forces weave inward to the living, seedlike points on the earth, which are like focal points of invisible light, is for the modern mathematician quite easy to attain (unless his vision has been totally darkened by the analytical aspect of mathematics alone).

What does this new development of projective, or synthetic geometry signify for the development of consciousness and the future of natural science?

As we have seen, the thought-pictures of Euclidean geometry accompanied mankind into the depths of the dark world of Earth. We live in the limbs, which bear us through the world of space. We can lose touch with the divine worlds and die into matter, deep into the realm of earthly space and earthly time.

In the dawning age of awakening to the perspectives of the wide horizons and the search for a balance between "inner" and "outer", mathematics brought the awareness of the "encircling round" and the innermost point, between which, in the beat of heart and lung, there lives the rhythmic pulse of life. This is the realm of the Soul of Man.

Now, in the twentieth century, mathematics, in the quietness of thought, leads towards a deeper understanding of the worlds of darkness and light, and the knowledge that these worlds of the "Depths" and the "Heights" may become united, through the free will of man. The universe becomes a Whole once more, through the will of the individual to find the light in the darkness and rise with it again.

The mathematical curve which comes very close to picturing the interpenetration of centric and peripheral worlds, which Steiner was in the habit of using to illustrate his descriptions of the relationships of earthly and spiritual worlds and processes, is the lemniscate[9] (figure-of-eight). To understand his meaning, it is, however, insufficient and often very misleading to think of the curve as a sequence of points only, with both loops of equal value. The picturing of polar processes is almost always what he has in mind in using this geometrical form or symbol. A Lemniscate of Bernoulli, together with the Curves of Cassini, which belong to it, may be created by the interpenetration of polar families of circle-curves, as shown in Plate II and Figure 35. These pictures, although actually created pointwise, give an archetypal picture of polar processes, working together from a positive focus and a negative, or "star" focus (page 45). The complementary colours, as Goethe saw them, of green and "peach-blossom" are used here, to help in picturing the qualitative difference between the two foci.

This lemniscatory picture is capable of great variation; one such, simple and beautiful, is shown in Plate II. It is a valuable exercise to move in thought back and forth between the polar realms, the concave and the convex spaces, which involves passing through a point of nothingness to make a complete polar transformation from one space to the other. One is the peripheral space of the body of formative forces; the other the centric space of the physical body. It forms as a whole a picture of what Rudolf Steiner called a *lemniscatory space*—the space, in which, in fact, realms of centric and peripheral processes are united. He saw the relation of Sun and Earth in terms of a space-formation of this kind, and the creation of the human form also.[10]

To conclude this chapter, we will quote Rudolf Steiner again. After having described the space of the plastic, planar forces, the creative world of the sculptor, he said:

"Only some sketchy hints that require to be thought out could be given here. But you will have seen from these brief indications that the sculptor requires more than a knowledge of man gained from imitating a human model; he must actually be able to experience inwardly the forces that work through the cosmos when they build the human form. The sculptor must be able to grasp what takes place when a human being is plastically formed from the fertilised ovum in the mother's body—not merely by forces in the mother's body, but by cosmic forces working through the mother. He must be able to create in such a way that, at the same time, he can understand what the individual human being reveals of himself, more and more, as the sculptor approaches the lower limbs. He must, above all, be able to understand how man's wonderful outer covering—the form of his skin—results from two sets of forces: the peripheral forces working inwards, from all directions, out of the cosmos, and the centrifugal forces working outwards and opposing the former. Man in his external form must be, for the sculptor, a result of cosmic forces and inner forces. One must have such a feeling towards all details." (9.IV.22).

Chapter VI

POLARITY AND TRINITY—NATURE AND THE HUMAN BEING

> "As the Earth-forces live, by means of its formation, in the physical body, so in the ether-body there live those forces. which from all sides, from the circumference of the cosmos, stream in towards the Earth"
> Rudolf Steiner. 25.I.25
> Anthroposophical Leading Thoughts.

The Quality of Uprightness

How do we experience our human posture? How is it that we stand and walk on the earth, upright and free, in a way in which no animal can do (though some come very near it)? We take it so much for granted. Yet, to stand and walk, as we do, on two small surfaces—the soles of our feet—is a phenomenon beyond the capacity of present-day science to explain in a satisfactory way to a physicist, or a biologist.

Quite often, in a normal transition from different states of consciousness, as, for instance, between sleeping and waking, things happen, which give one food for thought. For example, in a waking dream, I was once poised, high up above the earth, which was far below me. Vertical, arms at my sides and toes pointing earthwards, I was slowly descending. Far away in the blue distance, at shoulder level, there was an "infinitely" large ring of light, which appeared to belong to me. The horizontal ring of light grew smaller as I descended, coming closer and closer on a level with my shoulders, the nearer I came to the earth below; until, at the moment when it merged into, and closed around my shoulders, my feet touched the earth—as though to caress it—and I awoke!

Everyone knows that dreams—expecially dreams on awakening—can take on a special quality, which does not fade, as dreams mostly do; one knows, when they are worth taking note of and when not. This dream was clearly related to the new geometrical thoughts, but also to experiences, while learning Eurythmy at that time, and at the same time, while studying singing with the Swedish singer, Valborg Werbeck-Svärdström.[11]

While practising and learning Eurythmy (Figure 43)[12] and a new form of gymnastic movement,[20] a direct experience can come about of an inner column of light, which, as it were, inwardly sustains the outer movements. Similarly, in singing, one can be aware of an inner region—a column of "silent" sound, which, when "contacted", results in quite a different quality of outer tone. It is as though the tone, instead of being thrown out like a ball, from a centre to the confines of the hall, can be experienced as though all-pervading; it resounds in the innermost "column of tone", and is at the same time "out there", without being in any way forced. This is an experience to be striven for, perhaps with long practice; it has been confirmed many times over by artists, both

Eurythmists and famous singers. The difference in the quality of both movement and tone is perceived by the experienced performer and onlooker or listener alike.

Plate I and Figure 44 picture the archetypal polarity, between a central axis and the line at infinity at right-angles to it. In Cartesian space, the central axis passes through the physical body and the line polar to it is a line at infinity, as, for instance, in the case of the earth,—its axis and the ecliptic (although, of course, the axis of the earth is inclined). If one asks *what is polar to this physical space polarity*, the answer is: the outer line at infinity and an *inner* line at infinity at right-angles to it, functioning as an infinitude within. This is the relationship between the two (linear) extremes *in ethereal space*.

It is a clear imagination in thought to which one comes, after working at the law of the reciprocating movements of the circles in the tangent plane of the polarizing sphere and the cones in its point of contact with the sphere (Figure 44).

As the circles expand from their mid-point, so the cones close in from their "median plane", becoming slimmer and slimmer, until their planes merge all at once into the inner line, which is functioning as an inner infinitude. Moving in step-measure on the plane, from mid-point to a line of points at infinity would mean in the reciprocal, planar world of the cones, to begin in the horizontal plane and close in towards the functional infinitude within (and vice versa). *Moving in growth-measure implies moving between infinitudes in both cases*; then the horizontal plane becomes a functional infinitude, as well as the inner most line.

In the ordinary space of the circles in the plane, the words "expansion" and "contraction" mean just what they say; in describing events in the ethereal space of the cones, to avoid a misconception, we prefer the words "extensive" and "intensive". To understand the laws of the etheric, one must learn "to think the *extensive* intensively and the *intensive* extensively."

Standing on a mountain peak and looking out towards the distant horizon, however far away I may think it to be, I am, myself, in the centre of what I conceive earth-space to be. I am in the centre, at a physical point on the earth, and my centre is determined by the calculable centre of gravity of my body, which, when standing, is oriented around a vertical axis, considered as a *line of points*. Just as I have been taught to think of the earth as a ball, with a centre of gravity, so too I have a conceptual understanding of the albeit more configured form of my body. I think of it as situated in three-dimensional space—a point-centred, Cartesian space.

Polar to this picture is the one in which my horizon becomes the infinitely distant ring of light from which I come, and the innermost line of light—*my ethereal axis*, is a line of planes, in relation to which I hold myself upright as an ego-being. It is important to realize that I must now think of this inner line as a *line of planes*; it is polar to the vertical line of points of my physical body.

If the planar cones become infinitely slim, their planes would at last merge into the innermost infinitude. This innermost line of my stature, as I descend and touch the earth, passes through the earth's centre, which, in the space in which we are now thinking, is a "star" point!

It is possible, guided by the exact mathematical laws (positive-negative point-plane and positive-negative line-line) to move freely in thought from one space to the other, to see how the pictures can fuse, yet keep their clarity. The material world is a world of points; planes and lines are determined by them. The ethereal world is planar; in it, points and lines are determined by planes.

This line-line polarity is most fundamental; it contains the Thought out of which worlds are made in the creative weaving of the light (*Strahlende Weltgestaltung*). The word "ray" (Strahl) may mean not a line of points, but a *line of planes*!

The Archangel's sword is not so much meant to pierce and kill as to picture a ray of transforming light—like the light of thought. In Philadelphia, (U.S.A.) in the city museum, there is a remarkable stone figure of St. Michael, brought there from Middle Europe, in which the sword is plunged vertically down *inside* the body, parallel with the spine!

It is this world of the creative weaving of the light, which we see, when the Eurythmist[12] lets flash forth planes and surfaces of colour and movement, in an art which has never been seen before, until this century. This art speaks to the human being of a world from which he has come and the world towards which he must find the strength to go, through the forces of metamorphosis.

Have we wandered too far from the domain of science? I do not think so, for these are the truths to which science in the future will come. It is not through my physical body that I experience being in reality a body of light, living in a body of darkness; I experience this with another member of my being, of which I can learn to become aware. It is the ether-body, or body of formative forces, which forms, in its relationship to the nerves-senses system, the rhythmic system and the metabolic-limb-system, the basis for the soul forces, which are also of a threefold nature—thinking, feeling and willing.[13]

Standing on the earth, I am so structured that my physical body may well be described as a pillar of substance, bone set upon bone, limb upon limb, from foot to head, like a building, stone upon stone, with lower and upper stories, undifferentiated. This is the modern-day picture; and it would seem nowadays not to matter whether, as in some modern sports, the head, the hands or the feet are used according to the centric, earthly forces, to punch or to kick.

True, the skeleton holds firm in a healthy body, but the forces of life which buoy me up are *not* the gravitational forces to which the substances of my body will be given over at death. I am, however, also a column of water; a very high proportion of the growing human organism is fluid! Water—the fluid element in the organism—is the bearer of the etheric body.

Rudolf Steiner refers to the etheric body as the second man within us; then the third man, a column of air, bearer of the astral or sentient body, the soul, by which we are also permeated; then the fourth man, the organism of warmth, the column of fire of the Ego. We each have our own warmth body, differentiated in each organ and held in balance in the healthy body by the ego, in relation to outer heat or freezing cold. This is the fourfold being of man, physical body, ethereal body, astral body and ego. (Occult Science, Chapter II or, for example, the lecture of 5.VI. 09 in Budapest.) The four ethers, in which the ethereal body lives, are manifest in the four elements, earth, water, air and fire, which permeate the physical body of the human being.

Only the three-dimensional body of physical substances accords with the laws of centric, pointwise space (Euclidean space). This body when left alone, is subject to the laws of gravity.

The other three bodies are related to the polar forces—peripheral, anti-gravitational and cosmic. Here the geometrical imaginations related to *planes* and mobile *surfaces* will be helpful, and the thought that in the new morphology the planes are primary and points secondary.

Rudolf Steiner often describes as a polarity, the physical and ethereal on the one hand and the astral and ego on the other. The ether-body is closely tied to the spatial body; it stays with us all through life, even in deep sleep; whereas soul and spirit depart, until, on awakening, we become conscious of them again in the morning. It is through the peripheral forces of the ether-body, that the soul and spirit can cause the heavy substance-body to arise and stand upright. Once the ether-body has departed, the substances begin to disintegrate.

Water, the Life-Blood of the Earth

As water is the life-blood of the earth, bearing the forces of life into substance, so the second man in us, the watery body, mediates between the cosmic and the earthly. Only via the formative forces of the ethereal body can the cosmic forces of soul and spirit work into physical substance.

Water behaves in two ways. Obeying the force of gravity it flows downhill, thus manifesting the laws which the science of hydro-dynamics—looking at the phenomena from one point of view only—sees in it. The other way in which water behaves is, however, not fully accessible to that one-sided way of thinking. For this we must contemplate not only the moving, changing forms which flowing water reveals, but also the clear mathematical thoughts, which lead directly to a scientific understanding that water has cosmic as well as earthly attributes.

In its downward flow, water generates the kind of force, which drives turbines, a phenomenon made possible by means of the mathematics applied in technology. Water has, however other qualities and is the bearer of other forces, towards the understanding of which mathematics is equally capable of leading the scientist and technician. Quite another aspect of mathematics is here applicable (cf. Chapter VII).

In his book *Sensitive Chaos*, which has appeared since 1960 in six editions and been translated into numerous languages, Theodor Schwenk has revealed, through laboratory experiments and in observation of nature, that the *surface*-quality of water is paramount; as it flows, it is permeated through and through with sensitive, membrane-like surfaces (Figure 45). Volumes of water move in circling paths and spiralling surfaces; typically, water is always being drawn downward, seeking a lower level, while equally typically, it tends towards the rounded form of the drop and rises upward. It is always striving to create a sphere, be it the spheroidal form of the separate drops—which both fall and rise upward—or be it the vaste sphere, created by the waters of the whole earth.

Water obeys the gravitational, downward pull, but we see it also obeying a law, which must be called anti-gravitational, even levitational (provided the word is not misunderstood). How is capillary action explained—or surface tension in a droplet of water?

Here the modern mathematical concept of a sphere *in its full sense* comes to meet the phenomenon; we have learned to see the sphere, and can learn to see the water-drop also, as an organic whole. We have seen the sphere poised between two poles, seen also its all-relating nature (which makes it akin to water!).

The spherical form may also be revealed in a rounded piece of granite rock created, as indeed, it often is, by flowing water. A sphere may be embodied as a heavy boulder, left behind in the bed of the stream, or it may appear in the form of a droplet.

The sphere created in the form of drops or droplets—a dewdrop, for instance—even to the outer eye, is quite different; it is an organ of the earth's etheric organism, in truth, an ether-sphere. Such drops are formed by the sensitive surface-tension within the water; they are capable of allowing the colours of the rainbow to shine out into the eye of the beholder. Like the rainbow, they speak of other worlds, which an awakened thinking can actually *see* before it, in earthly space. *Without such focal, ethereal sun-spaces in the world around and within us, there would be no life on earth, nor in earthly organisms.*

Such living, enveloping and enfolding fluid surfaces are like the membranes which permeate a living body. Every organ is sheathed around with a non-cellular living tissue or skin, the so-called "connective tissue" known to biology today. It is remarkable, in that it is not made up of separate cells, but forms an entire continuum.

The delicate skins and surfaces inter-penetrating an organism are organs of the etheric body, permeable membranes and epithelia. Even the entire skin can be compared to the surface of tension of a water-drop; it closes off what is within from what is without, and yet the inner and outer worlds breath through it. Like the sphere, with respect to which the mathematical process of reciprocation takes place (page 29)—which we learn to raise into the realm of Imagination—the ethereal body *mediates* between the cosmic and the earthly worlds.

Think of Mother Earth herself, surrounded in mantles of moving water, air and warmth. May we not perhaps recognise her to be a physical globe, moving round the sun in Copernican space, while at the same time, she is like a water-drop. She is sustained in her physical body through the elements of water, air and fire by the spiritual forces of the sun, which work through the ethers, of which the elements are the outer manifestation.[14]

Plato classified the four basic elements—Earth, Water, Air and Fire and he added a fifth, calling it "Quinta-essentia." In this light he considered the four regular forms: cube, icosahedron. octahedron and tetrahedron (see Chapter IV); the fifth he related to the *essence of life*. Rudolf Steiner encompasses this classical picture, taking the fifth form—the Pentagon Dodecahedron—as the spiritual Imagination of the Goetheanum Building.

Steiner classifies what he calls the four ethers: Warmth-ether, Light-ether, Chemical-ether and Life-Ether, thus relating the elements to the ethereal realm. Here, again we touch on a fundamental aspect of Anthroposophy, relating also to the four members of the human being, Ego, Astral-body, Etheric body and Physical-body.

We are primarily concerned here with the realm of the ethereal formative forces—the etheric body of man and earth—and thus it is that the planar world speaks first in the pictures of flowing water. It speaks also in the shafts of light flooding the skies and in tongues of fiery flame.

The Imagination of the Pentagon-Dodecahedron speaks with a powerful voice; it contains all the other four forms. Once, in conversation, Rudolf Steiner said that there are in reality seven forms, for to the five should be added "the sphere from within and the sphere from without." By this is meant, the sphere created of points from the centre outward, and of planes from the periphery inward.

As the dewdrop shines out into the sunlit air, it reveals the manifold colours of the light-ether. Perhaps this was the truth which shone into the souls of those astronants who looked towards the Earth from the vantage-point (or plane!) of the Moon. The simplest of the five Platonic forms, and the one which is self-polar with respect to the sphere, is the Tetrahedron, which is no doubt of significance in relation to the tetrahedral structure of the Earth (p.VII.83).

Colours and tones are qualities belonging to water; sound moves fast and easily through water and colours shine and reflect from its moving surfaces. As well as seeing only one side of the being of water, we learn to see it—and warmth also—in terms of ethereal space, which is a realm in which the *negative* of gravity prevails.[14]

Think of the human being, developing from a tiny ovum in the warmth of the Mother's body and look with clear, imaginative vision at the marvellous pictures revealed by the achievements of the new technology. Contemplating such pictures as, for example, Figure 46,[15] we may well be reminded of the words of Goethe, that the laboratory bench should become an altar! It is as though embryological research has opened a little window to heaven, without knowing it (or does it know it!). The whole subject is being so earnestly and widely considered today.

How perfect a form is revealed by the Amnion sack, which is indeed like a cosmic space into which, at first on the periphery, the tiny, fertilized ovum settles itself. The very early forms arise as infolding *surfaces*, within this enveloping sheath. Compare it with the space in which the plant forms develop in the germination and further development of the shoot (Plate IV).[16] Although incomparably more complicated than in the plant, the processes of embryological formation are also basically planar and peripheral at first.

The plant will open out and reveal its ethereal forms to the light and air; into the human form will work also the forces of soul and spirit, and very soon, this will show itself, and then the human seedling will take its own time in developing, for this is a cosmic space, in which cosmic time prevails. As long as it is upheld by the waters, the little human being is not yet on earth, but still in a Sun-space.

To medical doctors, Rudolf Steiner once said:

"Embryology today makes the mistake of looking at the human ovum only as it develops in the mother's body. All the forces that form the human embryo are supposed to be therein. In reality, the whole cosmos works through the mother's body upon the configuration of the embryo. The plastic forces of the whole cosmos are there, just as the magnet needle is directed by the forces of the earth". (9.IV.22).

Fritz Wilmar,[17] points out that Rudolf Steiner, sixty years ago, described phenomena, which now, since the forties and fifties are more and more becoming a part of modern knowledge. He refers for instance to the sudden change in the forms, which comes about at the end of the third week of embryological development.

It is important to bring new concepts to bear in the contemplation of the developing forms in these seemingly tiny spaces, enveloped by their sheathing membranes. It is not a question of size, but of learning to read the gesture of the forms, without falling back into ordinary spatial concepts. The task is urgent, in face of the dangers connected with some aspects of genetics and genetic engineering.

Towards a New Consciousness

Just as the Sun receives into itself the cosmic forces of stars and planets, not for itself, but to pour these spiritual forces forth upon the living beings on Earth, so the ethereal body of the human being (like the dew drop) receives the cosmic forces into its sun-space and bestows them upon the organism of earth-substances.

In Chapter III of *The Threshold of the Spiritual World*, referred to here in Chapter V, Rudolf Steiner describes this second principle of human nature in the following words:

> "This etheric body is the second principle of human nature. It forms the basis of the life of the physical body. But as regards his etheric body man is not cut off from its corresponding outer world to the same extent to which his physical body is detached from the physical outer world. When we speak of an outer world in connection with the etheric body, it is not the physical outer world, perceived by the senses, that is meant, but a spiritual environment which is as supersensible in relation to the physical world as man's etheric body is in relation to his physical body. Man, as an etheric being, stands in an etheric, or elemental world.
>
> Man is always "experiencing" the fact, although in ordinary life he knows nothing of it, that he, as an etheric being, inhabits an elemental world. When he becomes conscious of this state of things, the consciousness is quite different from that of ordinary experience. This new consciousness sets in when man becomes clairvoyant. The clairvoyant then knows about that which is always present in life, though hidden from ordinary consciousness."

We learn to experience that we live in two worlds, one about which we know, the other of which today we are usually unaware. Such deeper consciousness may be achieved through meditation, the essential preparation, however, being to strengthen the soul through inner and outer discipline. Meditative practice must rest on clear and active thinking, while warmth of feeling and strength of will are cultivated *in an active and responsible life in the day to day world*. Always, the path involves surrender and devotion to what is outside one's own egoistic self, without losing one's own true ego.

The first realm to be met with, beyond the everyday world of things and visible forms is the one which opens the soul to an awareness of the ether-body in the elemental world. Here, instead of the world of separate existences, we meet with *Beings*—first the elemental beings of earth, water, air and fire—the beings we hear of in the old fairy-tales. It is a realm of sympathies and antipathies, of beauty and ugliness, light and darkness.

At each stage of meditative development the soul learns to meet—even to create—an empty space, giving everything away, except wakefulness. Into such moments of empty, relaxed, waking consciousness (Leerheit des Bewusstseins), a new birth may take place.

Only through sacrifice can new life arise, by experiencing the "NOT I" in oneself.

This is the essence of the new social order, towards which the whole of humanity is struggling with greater or lesser consciousness. Today, as though in one great cauldron, heated by the fires of the nether world, humanity—individuals and nations—meet and learn to know one-another, that new gold may be smelted out, cosmic gold, needed for the future development of creation. In the meeting of human being with human being is expressed the deepest and most spiritual task of our time. To learn not to pass one-another like phantoms—"ships that pass in the night"—even in the bustle and hurry of modern life—is one of the tests at the Threshold of the Mystery Temple, into which we may step more consciously every day. Gradually, the truth dawns; the soul must seek freedom in the spiritual life of thought; all men are equal in the eyes of God; fraternity must be the rule in the economic life. The heart of this Threefold Commonwealth lies between the poles of thinking and doing—in the human hearts of gold.

In the living flow of the elemental world, the soul finds itself obliged to change many of the ideas which it acquired in the physical world. The tendency is to shrink from doing this and to continue thinking along the old and acquired pathways. If, however, the faculty of sound judgement is cultivated, through the exercise of right thinking and honest willing, and there is a readiness to let go of old ideas and to undergo a transformation of self, then we may learn to awaken to the elemental world through the forces of the etheric body. In so doing, we may learn to transform the forces of growth into active thinking, for thinking is an etheric force (*Fundamentals of Therapy*, Ch.I).

Then, just as the eye and the ear become aware of colours and sounds in the physical world, so in the elemental world we learn to perceive in quite a new way, sympathies and antipathies. Then gradually the capacity dawns to feel within oneself the sorrows and joys of another being—the joy and suffering of creation (Figure 47).

Thought-pictures, old and new, inspired by geometry and the new morphology, act as guiding principles both in scientific research and in sociology. Truly, we see what we think we see! In science we see perhaps only particles, points, explosions, catastrophes! In social life today the picture is somewhat similar. It is the world of separation.

But slowly the world is changing. In social life at least, the old picture of cultures dominated by a central figure, whether a king, a pope, or a dictator, is giving way to one of circles of individuals, attempting to work together with equal responsibility. It is not easy, for "old forms die hard", as the saying goes. In the future, we shall learn through mutual endeavour, to create truly such sun-circles—receptive organs in the social organism—for instance, as a "college of teachers" in a school.

In Euclidean geometry, points are *separate* entities; it is an important truth. The new morphology, in which the planes and lines reveal their quality of *togetherness*, by which forms are created in another way, gives a new picture—a new imagination. As we learn to change our ways of thinking so—in the words of the Baptist—we learn to change our ways.

Darkness is powerful in the world today, fear lurks in human coldness, in the hunger and strife, and in the shadow of Chernobyl. But the way leads through the darkness, where clear judgement and discrimination must prevail, when we learn to perceive the *whole*; not only the Cross in its three dimensions—picture of gravity—but also the Sun on the Cross, picture of the forces of Resurrection.

Light, too, is powerful in the world, in the hearts of the young humanity of today and tomorrow; world-wide, there is a changing consciousness. The young today perceive as yet dimly the essential nature of the *meeting* between human being and human being. We may look for this light and warmth, guided by the spirit of positivity, as it was taught by the Risen Christ, walking with His disciples, when he pointed out to them the beautiful teeth in the stinking mass of a rotting carcass, from which they had turned away in disgust. (An old legendary story.) It is a law of life, that the old must pass away, making way for the new, which is already there in seedling forms the world over. Listen to the words of the old Rosecrucian: "In a mustard-seed, if you can understand it, is the image of all higher and lower things." Angelus Silesius.

Sieh, du mein Auge	See thou, mine eye,
Der Sonne reine Strahlen	The Sun's pure rays
Aus der Erde Formenwesen.	In crystal forms of Earth.
Sieh, du mein Herz	See thou, my heart,
Der Sonne Geistgewalten	The Sun's Spirit-power
Aus des Wassers Wellenschlägen.	In Water's surging wave.
Sieh, du meine Seele	See thou, my soul,
Der Sonne Weltenwillen	The Sun's cosmic will
Aus der Lüfte Glanzgeflimmer.	In quivering gleam of Air.
Sieh, du mein Geist	See thou, my Spirit,
Der Sonne Götterwesen	The Sun's indwelling God
Aus des Feuers Liebeströmen.	In Fire's abounding love.
Rudolf Steiner. Autumn 1924 Wahrpruchworte.	Translation in *Verses and Meditations*: George and Mary Adams.

Ethereal Spaces of the Plant World

Two fundamental principles stand before us as guiding themes; they are intimately related. First, that added to the pointwise way of thinking we must cultivate a perception of planar, peripheral qualities in all types of forms, perceived through outer perception and inner experience. Secondly, that this way of perceiving phenomena opens our eyes to the significance of realms *not* filled with substance—receptive, virginal realms of seeming *emptiness, nothingness*.

There is an abyss to cross, which requires the courage to let go of substance, of old ideas, in order to experience them in a new guise.

All seeds contain such a virginal realm, like a seemingly empty space, and they offer up their substance, created in the past, in order to be receptive to the formative forces which pour in from the cosmos into this *empty* space, thus bringing about new, living substance. Nature reveals in her forms and processes and principles of memory and fantasy, or Imagination,—a memory of what *has already been created*; imagination concerning what *may become in the future*.

Goethe rejoiced in the fact that once having conceived the Idea of the "Archetypal Plant" (Urpflanze), he would be capable of calling forth in his mind all possible shapes of plants, which even Mother Nature has not fashioned.

Rudolf Steiner has taken up Geothe's ideas and developed them further. In the book, *The Plant between Sun and Earth*, we have brought to bear the idea of space and counterspace on Goethe's morphology of plants and related both to Rudolf Steiner's spiritual descriptions. A great deal of study material is available, and an enormous amount of work and research is still waiting to be done.

The theme of the interpenetration of centric and peripheral formative principles is, in Rudolf Steiner's own words, quite fundamental. To quote again from the lectures in the Hague in 1922, this time in answer to a question, at the end of a lecture, with the accompanying blackboard sketch (Figure 48):

"When, for example, one contemplates the root of the plant within the Earth, one is looking at a development in the realm of gravity and concerned with the ordinary dimensionality of space. If, however, one wishes to explain the form of the flower, those ordinary ideas of three-dimensional space are inadequate. For then, instead of starting at the mid-point of the three co-ordinate axes, one must begin in infinite space, which is in fact the other form which answers to the central point. Then, instead of going outward centrifugally, one comes inward centripetally. One comes in to this wavy plane (see drawing).[18] Instead of the process bursting outward, there is something pressing inward from without; one finds gliding, shearing movements, which one would understand wrongly, if one tried to explain them on the basis of the co-ordinate axes from the mid-point outward. One must take the infinite sphere as the place to begin and come inward towards the centre with a qualitatively opposite co-ordinate system. As soon as one comes to the etheric realm, one reaches this polar opposite aspect. It is because this is not taken into account, that the theories about the ether are incorrect. That is the difficulty in defining the ether; it is regarded as a fluid realm or a realm of gases, but the mistake is that one still thinks of it in relation to a co-ordinate system from a centre outward. As soon as one comes to the etheric realm, one must imagine the sphere and then describe the whole process not from the centre outward, but in an opposite way."...

As so often, not everything is explicit in the texts which remain to us of Rudolf Steiner's lectures (as distinct from his books). This is particularly important to take into account in the scientific lectures. (The wavy line can be approached through the idea of the "twice-curved surface" (*zweimal gebogene Fläche*) which is the leitmotif in relation to the ethereal quality of the forms of the First Goetheanum.[19])

In the picture of the "gliding, shearing movements pressing inward from without," the peripheral, planar formative process is described, coming from the infinite sphere, pictured here by the *concave* curve above and related to a "qualitatively opposite co-ordinate system" in an etheric realm. Below, in the *convex* realm of earth and root, one is concerned with the ordinary dimensionality of space, in the realm of gravity. In the concave and convex, a lemniscatory quality underlies this picture.

So often, in his lectures, Rudolf Steiner uses the mathematical curve of the lemniscate as illustration of the interplay of the polar opposite forces, though more often than not, he illustrates *both* directions in the usual way, with arrows. His descriptions, however, always lead us to experience the *planar, but upwards "suctional" quality* of the peripheral formative forces. This is all-important and so often misunderstood.

The lemniscate and the accompanying curves of Cassini may as we have seen be brought into being by the interplay of polar opposite families of circles (Figure 35). Flowing together, they form the bipolar organism of curves containing the lemniscate with its concave and convex loops. The two foci, common to all the curves, are polar opposite; the upper focus pictures the innermost point at infinity of a cosmic space; the lower focus the point-centre of an earth-space. *Between the two foci is the realm of balance—-the crossing over between the two worlds.*

Bring the picture into movement in the imagination and experience the polar dynamics of which it is a representation; it can become a guiding imagination towards the understanding of the universal polarities, and of the "twice-curved surface".

Coming inward from cosmic expanses, from the universe of stars, is a field of forces functioning according to the laws of the polar-Euclidean type of space. The cosmic forces, through the medium of the etheric realm, pour into the hollow and seemingly empty spaces and are able so to transform substance, that it behaves in a way not dominated by the laws of gravity. Forms of all kinds come into being and die away in the interplay of cosmic with earthly rhythms, (see, for instance *Fundamentals of Therapy*, quoted on page V. 42).

An example of this interplay between a hollow receptive centre and a realm of created substance is in the photomicrograph of a lengthwise section of a grain of maize (Figure 49), the tiny hollow in the heart of the plumule within the seed is clearly visible. This is an archetypal phenomenon, the significance of which it is necessary to begin to understand, wherever new life of any kind begins, in whatever medium.

This tiny, hollowed-out, concave space is empty of matter, and our mathematical imagination sees in it the "infinitude within" of an ethereal space. A seed bears within it two types of centre. A kind of *void* must be there at the ethereal infinitude, to enable the formative forces to engender form anew. The "innermost point" is *not the source* of the ethereal forces, but rather *the infinitude within* of the ethereal space, the realm infinitely receptive to cosmic forces. *The origin of those forces is the cosmic sphere, their goal is the "intensive" point within.*

Ether-spaces are formed and dissolved again in the life-cycles of organisms. Wherever new life unfolds from a germ-cell—a germinating realm in an already created organism—whether such a germ is immersed in watery, living substance, or, as in the plant shoot, freely poised above the growth cone, and enveloped in the leafy surfaces, we may discern the presence of an "all-relating point", the inward infinitude of an ethereal space. The term "all-relating point" is due to E. Lehrs (See Bibliography).

As a general principle, it is clear that in the region of new growth the matter must in some degree surrender its once-established molecular or pointwise structure and become "chaotic", like an unwritten slate—a receptive matrix, a *materia* in the original sense of the Greek word χάος. We may use this word, rather in the ancient sense, in contrast to "cosmos," which means manifest and ordered form. Matter that holds fast to its given structure, will be unable to surrender itself to the formative forces of living growth, maintaining its form, it remains a "cosmos." It is all-important to understand Rudolf Steiner's meaning rightly in the use of the words "chaos" and "cosmos."

Water in the form of ice is such a cosmos, static and cold. As soon as light and warmth begin to play upon the waters, movement begins. Warmth and light are the origin of rhythmic movements in the water, which can become tremendous and stormy, when the wind rises. In the turbulence, drops and vortices come into being; spaces hollowed out by the spiralling surfaces and the spherical droplets, spaces wherein water becomes alive and fresh. These are χάος-spaces, receptive to the universal forces.

In the plant world, and the other living kingdoms, the young forms spring, one from within the other, each holding for the next one to come, the hollow, virginal space in which the formative forces work (Plate IV & Figure 50). The upward, unfolding growth-cone of a plant is closely akin to a water-vortex, the cosmic forces, received into the spiraling hollow of surfaces in the plant, calling forth substance and drawing it upwards, away from the influence of gravity, ever and again creating new organs.

Place the seed—the little point-like entity, seemingly composed only of material substance—into the moist earth; give it over to the powers of the water, light and warmth, and presently the living forms will reveal, in the quality of their gestures, the interweaving polarity of ethereal formative principles and physical substance. Moisture must always be present, a certain range of temperature, varying with the different plants, and free oxygen for breathing. The physical form must be given over to the other three elements, water, air and fire, before any living form can be conjured from it. Water is the essential element. After the seed has been well soaked for a time, the radicle will appear first and grow downward, later to become a fully developed root, with side-roots shooting from it. Secondly, the plumule will grow upward to form the first green shoot.

A detailed study reveals the fascinating development of the bipolar form of the plant-embryo, in which the consolidated form of the root, and also the little plumule, formed of planar organs, are already present and often visible even to the naked eye, before any form appears outside the seed coat (Figure 49).

In the tiny seed is a space hungry for form, and as the forces of the universe relate to it, so form upon form appears, growing (always at first) *vertically* upward. The substances of which plants are formed, are taken up into a sphere of forces, freeing them from the downward pull of gravity.

Think, for instance, of the Lombardy Poplar, towering high with a great girth of trunk below, the bole extending up and up, becoming more slender, surrounded with leafy branches and shoots, each shoot with its growing-point; a myraid seedlike spaces, capable of further growth.

In earth-space, the plant grows upward; its *process of growth*, however, brings about a *consolidation downward*, from the young, growing tips.

Mineral substances are sucked in by the root-tips and drawn upward, while through the mysterious process of photo-synthesis in the green shoots, new substances are materialized and gradually become densified into more woody forms. In truth, the plant grows upward and downward at the same time; upward, through the upward streaming of the sap, enabling the young organs to be formed at the growing-points, downward in the consolidating and densifying process which overtakes the young forms. In the rising of the sap, we see once more the cosmic aspect of water, which attends all new birth.

Each time a seed is planted into the earth, the hollowed-out, inward emptiness is placed there, into which the planar forces will pour, to fill it with nutritional substance. It is a spring or source of ever-renewed life. We touch here on the realm of divine *magic*, and may understand that in less materialistic times than ours, springs were holy places and the deeds of sowing and reaping were accompanied by acts of worship and prayer. There was the recognition that here is a realm of human activity, which reaches beyond the human being into the spiritual depths of all earthly existence. In the picture of the well, dated 1625, an inner, hidden world is pictured. The secrets of water are symbolically expressed and at the four corners are to be seen the four elements, Fire, Air, Water and Earth (Figure 51).

The Plant and the Human Form

To stand erect is enjoyed alike by plant and human being, while the animals are variously related to the horizontal dimension. The animals' bodies enfold the earth, being mostly parallel to its surface, while man and plant (at least the higher plants) live with their lower parts orientated towards the centre of the earth, their heads towards the sky.

The plant has three main parts: root, leaves and flower; the human being also: head, rhythmic system and metabolic-limb system. Rudolf Steiner has developed his conception of threefold man in great detail.[13] Very often, he compares the threefold human being with the plant, comparing the human head with the root and relating it to the earth, the rhythmic system with the leaves and branches, and the metabolic-reproductive limb-system to the flower and fruiting process. Equally often, however, he relates the limbs to the earth and the head to the cosmos. This is a very bald statement about a most illuminating and entirely new field of human science, requiring detailed study. "Threefold Man" underlies and permeates the whole of Anthroposophy.

Our task here is to draw attention to some morphological comparisons, with a view to encouraging further study in line with the theme of Sun and Earth. The whole field is full of polarities, both in terms of form and of process; we can but touch the fringe of it here, pointing to the need for more research of an inter-disciplinary nature.

As the plant develops, the sheathing bract- and leaf-forms, surrounding the sun-space at the growing-point, open out; node upon node, branch upon branch appear, growing out into earth-space, surface upon surface. At last, the individual shape of the plant is fully there, as in the beautiful form of the tree in Figure 52.

If I look at a tree, as a child might, I feel the comparison of its strong trunk with my strong limbs, holding me up from the ground. Above, on the other hand, the plastic shape, moulded as though from without in a form characteristic of that particular species of tree, is like my head, with sense-organs open to the formative light. How come, that all those twigs and later on the leafy surfaces, associatively, create such a shape, unfolding to such a plastic outline?

So it is with the human form. I can stand, feet together, and stretch my arms out sideways into the horizontal plane around my shoulders (Figure 53), with the palms of my hands facing upward or downward. These palms—little planar surfaces—are my eyes for the planar space of my ether-body. They tell me about my living body, just as when, standing still, I know intuitively that my whole form is well orientated into the space of the earth. If, standing there, palms upward, I raise my arms sideways into the vertical, it is quite natural to feel compelled to allow the whole body to be *drawn up* on to the toes. My palms are now facing inward, as though looking *planewise* into the inner, vertical line of light, *which also holds my form erect*. It is not that I am simply pushing up from below, though my legs are doing this; I am being *drawn upward* and can, in time, come to *know*, in the unity of willing, feeling and thinking, that I am a microcosm in the macrocosm.

Turning the palms outward and lowering the arms downward again, I can return to the normal standing position, aware, through what I have experienced through my hands and thus through the whole body, that I can live consciously in *both* spaces at once, while awake and alive on the earth. I experience intuitively, but can also think clearly, the polar-reciprocal process.

These are intuitive experiences, into which every healthy child grows, and which the new art of education is at pains to keep alive in modern children.[20] One only has to watch the human being moving—a living morphology—and add the other pole to the one-sided imagery, which the cartesian space- and force-concept supplies, and then one can move on from the one-fold, earthly concept to the *threefold*, poised as it is between Sun and Earth. The art of the marionette has an essential part to play in reminding the human being of his true origin, that he is born of the Father-God, whose hands have held him upright, since the days of creation, thus distinguishing him from the animals.

Goethe's eyes saw in the plant, not only a physical staff, manifest in the strong, woody growth, but also what he called a "spiritual staff" (ein geistiger Stab).[21] Contrary to what takes place in the root, the developing organs of the shoot arise from the peripheral layer of cells (cambium) and the centre of the stem may even be hollow. Goethe attached great importance to this innermost realm of the plant shoot, the vertical axis of the plant, which he regarded as formatively powerful, in respect to the spiralling process of the leaves around it (phyllotaxis). We see in it the *line at infinity within*, the innermost line, receptive to the ethereal formative forces, in relation to which, leaf upon leaf, new organs are born. In their vertically, plant and man share an infinitely distant, cosmic horizon, while each has an individual inner vertical line. The plant lives in relation to the ether-body of the earth, while each human being has an individual ether-body. The plant remains tied to one spot, while the human being enjoys the freedom of moving over the earth, for besides an etheric body, he has soul and spirit.

The plant is poised, for the human being to see and perceive, between a vertical axis and a line at infinity; the human being, too, as he walks out on the plane of earth, is poised between his innermost line of light and the horizon about him,—the "encircling round." The plants, which bedeck the earth, the buds on every tree, breathe the rhythms of life between their horizon and the innermost infinitude of their "spiritual staff."

The question must arise: what about the animals? Even in the circus, no animal can perform in a way which compares with human movements, yet each, according to its speciality, far outstrips the human achievement. The birds can fly; the cat jumps superbly onto a fence many times its own height; the cows lie patiently chewing their cud, while their male counterparts may perhaps exhibit a fire of will, hidden in that massive body.

The story of the animals is one of sacrifice towards human evolution; it is concerned with the soul and not only the life-forces and this whole field is therefore more complicated.

In our present study, it will be helpful to think in terms of the three great differences among the higher animals, characterised by the three: Eagle, Lion and Bull. The bird like the head, has a peripheral, bony skeleton, quite opposite to the solid, squarely shaped vertebrate, the bull. The lion, which lives more in its rhythmic system, expresses a balance between the other two.

We meet here with the imagery of the old alchemists, and are reminded of the task of the Rosecrucians, to prepare the way towards modern science. Though still in the soul-mood, which related them intuitively to nature and to the whole universe, those early scientists sought to know the hitherto hidden realm of the human body. They were inspired by the direction in which their time was leading, foreshadowed by the mood of analytical mathematics and Descartes' abstract idea of space. Medicine led the way into the world—so long forbidden—beneath the human skin.

Powerful, already in the 16th century, was the work of the Belgian physician, Andreas Vesalius, who spread the view that the only reliable way to understand the human body was by the practice of autopsy. He was the first to make a whole sequence of drawings of the disected corpse. First, he takes away the skin, then layer upon layer of the muscle fibres, revealing at last the skeleton. Two of these very early drawings are included here in Figures 54 and 55.[22]

Rudolf Steiner sees in the skin and the muscles, organs of the etheric body. The layers of muscles are like congealed streamings of the blood. Vesalius has taken away one etheric surface after another in his drawings, to reveal at last the bony form. In his wisdom, Vesalius stands the skeleton upright, in a thoughtful, meditative gesture; but he sets it squarely in the world of three dimensions—in the vertical dimension, surrounded by the world of the senses. It may perhaps not be surprising that Rudolf Steiner describes the skeleton as the organ for living thinking; the brain, rather than being the producer, is the *vehicle* for abstract thoughts. We think with our bones! (Do we not say in English: "I know it in my bones.")[23]

Look at the long bones, their parallel and right-angled qualities, so different from the spherical form of the skull. In between is the spinal column with the thorax, which has also a spherical tendency; then there is another hollow form, the pelvis. Three hollow forms!

Vesalius makes it seem as though the inner light of thought were still holding the skeleton up. The mineralized form of the skeleton, so clearly set in the space of earth, is, in fact an organ for a most spiritual principle of the human being—the ego. Thanks to these trusty servants, our skeletons, we walk the earth; but we walk it as spiritual beings, who have descended through three spiritual stages of the earth's evolution, before it reached this physical stage, in which, for the first time we can speak of measure, number and weight and the three dimensions.[24]

The long bones—at least the legs—reach down to the three-dimensional earth, which we pace out in equal steps on our two feet. The gesture of form of each of the three hollow spaces speaks a different language. Are they not memories of the cosmic past of humanity, before the descent into the world of three dimensions?

As well as being an earthly sphere of bone, the head is a cosmic space, in which the brain is buoyed up by the cerebro-spinal fluid. The pelvis, too, is an earthly bowl, through which, however, cosmic processes can work in the giving and receiving of new life. In this realm, too, living waters function. These are all cosmic spaces—*Gegenräume*, Saturn, Sun or Moon spaces—receptive to the forces of planets and constellations.

Between the poles of head and metabolic-limb system, is the spine with the thorax, the rhythmic system of heart and lung. This is the realm of the soul of man—the true Sun realm, and it compares with the leafy part of the plant—the true plant, between the poles of root and flower (or flower and root). See, how the heart lives between the lobes of the lung, just as the growing-point of the plant lives in the Sun-space provided for it by the leaves! (Figure 56, in which an anatomical diagram is simply inverted.)

The old alchemists experienced this realm in terms of the ancient symbol of healing—the Caduceus, or Staff of Mercury. They saw the world of substances in terms of salt, mercury and sulphur (Sel, Merkur, Sulphur). The rhythmic system is the true realm of balance, between 'sel' above and 'sulphur' below; Mercury holds the balance.

The Greeks revealed so completely the balance expressed by the human body. In the grandeur of their sculpture, they expressed what they still knew intuitively as a bodily experience. True art can always call to mind the feeling of balance, which we bear within us (Figure 57). Today it is science's turn to learn to know the laws of this world of balance. Forms speak, according to the *laws* of form, which may live in the mind of the beholder.

See how beautifully the bones of the human hand reveal the quality of a growth-measure! (Figure 58a). Then look at the form of the human spine, as Vesalius drew it in those early days of medical research (Figure 58b). Between the radial bones, built to stride the Earth in equal steps, and the head—this kingly sphere, meant to be quietly carried along, surveying the world with its circling movements—is spanned this astonishing column of bones!

The spine pictures the kind of measure, based on the relationship of proportions, which we learned to know in Figure 20. This is not step-measure; it runs between *two* infinities. But now we must recognise it in its projective form. I have drawn it beside Vesalius's picture, in a projective transformation. The gesture of such a *projective growth-measure* has a character of its own, which is clearly recognizable, though living Nature, creating in substance as an artist does, will not necessarily achieve exact measurements. The two infinite points of the logarithmic measure now *both* appear as functional infinities in ordinary space both are like the innermost realm of the "spiral of life". In the spinal column of man and also of the animals, the *quality* of the growth-measure sequence is clearly evident (as it also is in the plant stem).

What is this gesture of form saying? It is telling us that the rhythmic system is poised between poles, *both of which can be regarded as cosmic as well as earthly*. It is the realm of balance *par excellance*, where roles can be interchanged and the cosmic and earthly unite.

Look also at the forms of the single vertebrae (Figure 59); each has a solid, bony part and a part where the bone surrounds a hollow space, through which, in life, the spinal cord runs, serving the nerve-senses aspect of the organism. These bones have the character of a figure-of-eight or lemniscate, in which one part is filled with substance and the other part is hollowed round the organ which serves sense-perception; the bony processes here are also planar. A transition takes place from the more substantial and grown-together forms of the sacral region to the wide open, hollowed out forms of the neck, where then the metamorphosis takes place into the plate-bones of the skull. The transformation runs from the balanced forms of the thoracic and lumbar regions, upward and downward, as though in the growth-measure sequence from infinite to infinite. Atlas, at the top, is almost more hollow than bone! Animal spines reveal the growth measure still more dramatically, but are horizontal—parallel to the earth's surface.

It is of the greatest importance today that the cosmic and peripheral aspects of *form* and *force* should be understood and become a directive in scientific research. In the course of lectures entitled *Boundaries of Natural Science*, given in 1920, Rudolf Steiner deals exhaustively with the question of mathematics in science, and the urgent need to go beyond its abstract aspect, and to cultivate the inner activity of the soul, which we need ''in the wonderful architecture of mathematics.'' He speaks of the ''latent mathematics'' (geometry) in the body of the young child and the inner faculty for the perception of balance. ''Consider how the child gradually gains control of itself, how it learns first to crawl on all fours, how it gradually achieves through its sense of balance the ability to stand and walk, how it finally is able to maintain its own balance... And if one can attain a certain insight into what is happening there, one sees that there is at work in the sense of balance and the sense of movement nothing other than a living ''mathematicizing'' (ein lebendiges Mathematisieren)... We thus see a kind of latent realm of mathematics active within man.''

Compare Figure 47 with Figure 60. Watch the children teaching themselves to walk; learn to see them sensing the play of the peripheral forces of the light, in their efforts to overcome gravity! (Figure 60). Look not only with thoughts concerning the mechanics and physics of the earth, but with the universal forces in mind—the truly celestial forces in mechanics.[6, 14] This is urgently important in education today, where all too often the opposite tendency is revealed in the deportment of young people, whose zest for life has been driven out of them by what they meet in education, for instance, in biological theories based on the materialistic concepts of physics.

Deep is the intuition that man is born in the Image of God, that the human form is of divine origin. To watch the child, intuitively attaining an erect posture and taking the first steps into life on the earth, is one of the greatest wonders. So too is the knowledge that hidden away in a densest bone of the human head—as though in a hollow of the hardest rock of earth-—is the tiny organ of balance, three semi-circular canals, formed in the three right-angled dimensions of earth space, and together with it the spiralling form of the cochlea, a *growth-measure* spiral—the cosmic vortex, receptive organ for speech and tone; the two are joined by a hollow vestibule. The tiny, threefold organ, in the dark cave of rock, contains vital fluid, on the rhythmic wave-motions of which, the sounds of the world are metamorphosed into the inner perceptions of the human soul. The eye, too, on the periphery of the head, lives within a hollow of the rock, an organ receptive of the light and forms of the world, capable of metamorphosing them into inner human experience.

It is urgently necessary that science today should begin to recognise the cosmic as well as the earthly script of the forms and the functions of the human body. The head is like a Sun! (So, too, is the heart, and when it is pregnant, the womb also.)

> In Rudolf Steiner's words: "...because science—the general world conception of our time—does not recognise the meaning of what is "emptier than empty", it is locked in materialism. There is in the human being, if I may express it so, a place which is emptier than empty—not in its whole, but included in its parts. The whole human being—and I mean the physical human being—is a being, which fills out a material space; but a particular member of this human nature...has actually an aspect which is sunlike—is emptier than empty. This is—you may take it or leave it—the human head. And just because the human being is so organised that his head can always empty itself and in certain of its parts become emptier than empty, through this the head has the possibility of allowing the spirit to enter into it." (26.VIII.18).

The head is a replica of the whole human form; the dome, a temple for the reception of the light of thought, of colours and tones; the jaws, like limbs, are active in the reception of physical food, but also in relation to the creativity of speech, and in between is the realm of the breath, the rhythm, which lasts from birth to death. The very science which today has wrested itself free and turned first towards matter, will one day come to recognize the laws of metamorphosis, and, learning to understand the head as the metamorphosis of the whole threefold form of the body, will also be in a position to recognise a still deeper law, that of the metamorphosis through which we pass from one incarnation to the next.

Du selbst, erkennender, fühlender, wollender Mensch,	You, Self, knowing, feeling, willing Man,
Du bist das Rätsel der Welt.	You are the riddle of the world.
Was sie verbirgt,	What it hides
In dir wird es offenbar, es wird	Is revealed in you; it becomes
In deinem Geiste Licht,	In your Spirit, Light,
In deiner Seele Wärme,	In your Soul, Warmth,
Und deines Atems Kraft,	And the power of your Breathing
Sie bindet dir die Leibeswesenheit	Binds for you your bodily Being
An Seelenwelten,	To worlds of Soul
An Geistesreiche.	To realms of Spirit.
Sie führt dich in den Stoff,	It leads you into Matter,
Daß du dich menschlich findest;	That you may find your humanity;
Sie führt dich in den Geist,	It leads you into the Spirit,
Daß du dich geistig nicht verlierest.	That you, as Spirit, do not lose yourself.
Rudolf Steiner, Wahrspruchworte.	Translation by Olive Whicher

Metamorphosis.

Goethe's great contribution to science is his development of the idea of metamorphosis, particularly in relation to the plant.

> "Goethe," says Rudolf Steiner, "demands...in a truly mathematical spirit, that one inwardly permeate phenomena with mathematics. He writes that we must see the archetypal phenomena in such a way that we are able at all times to justify our procedures according to the rigorous requirements of the mathematician. Thus, what Goethe seeks is a modified, transformed mathematics, one that suffuses phenomena. He demands this as a scientific activity. Goethe was able, therefore, to suffuse with light the one pole that otherwise remains so dark, if we postulate only the concept of matter... We moderns must, however, approach the other, the pole of consciousness. We must investigate in the same way how soul faculties manifest their activity in the human being, how they proceed from man's inner nature to manifest their activity externally. We shall have to investigate this. It shall become clear that we must complement the method of investigating the external world offered by Goethean phenomenology with a method of comprehending the realm of human consciousness. It must be a mode of comprehension justifiable in the sense in which Goethe's can be justified to the mathematician...
>
> At the pole of matter we thus encounter the results yielded by Goethean phenomenology and at the pole of consciousness those attained by pursuing the method that I sought to establish in a modest way in my *Philosophy of* Spiritual Activity." (29 IX.20. The Boundaries of Natural Science, Lecture IV).

One of the ways of transforming mathematics is along the path, the very first steps of which we have been following. There can enter into mathematics, which otherwise remains purely intellectual, and appears to interest only the head, something that engages the entire man. Its creative world of pictures can lead into realms of Imagination, Inspiration, Intuition.

As we know, mathematics can lead mankind into the darkness as well as towards the light. There live in and through us the two cosmic beings of light and darkness, known from times past as Lucifer and Ahriman,[25] to whom also we should be thankful for our existence. But the human being must find the pathway of balance between these two great Beings, and this has always required the development of higher soul forces, such, for instance, as control of thinking and of willing, perseverance, positivity, open mindedness, equanimity.

What is *balance*? Is it merely expressed by setting two pounds of flour on either pan of the scales? (Here the physicist may pause for a moment, to ask the question: By what force is the "upthrust" maintained in the column, which supports the two pans?[14])

More pictorially, we may ask: What happens, when Light and Darkness are in interplay with one another? Goethe says: That is when the colours arise; they die, when either the one or the other of the two poles dominates.

Lucifer is the name given to the Light-bearer. Satan pulls in one direction and can lead to an extreme. The other antagonist is Ahriman, or Beelzebub, the Lord of Darkness. Thus we must learn to see that the devil has two faces, one alluring and light-filled, the other cold, hard and materialistic.

The task of today is to recognize these two faces of evil and to strive to hold the balance between them. Facing them both, we learn to realize that they are good powers, when in their right places in the world of nature, and that we are free to recognise them in ourselves. Clearly the world today is out of balance; to find inner and outer equilibrium is an individual and all-human task; each one stands before this task in full inner freedom.

What science says today has an enormous influence, not only on the physical well-being of humanity, but also on the spiritual life. Change lies within the reach of each one, to develop enhanced powers of observation and thinking through exercise. At the pole of matter, the exercise of Goethean phenomology develops a method of deeply involved observation; at the pole of consciousness, Rudolf Steiner adds the method of training towards the enhancement of thinking. Love of the phenomena and warmth in thinking create a synthesis, through which materialistic, intellectual thought will be stirred to life and transformed.

Here is where the threshold is encountered—the meeting of two worlds—that of observation and the world of thinking; which is why it is so immensely important to understand the Idea of Metamorphosis.

A classic example, by means of which the opportunity is given to practise observation and thinking and to begin to understand the laws of metamorphosis, is the organic change, which takes place in the development of the higher insect, as it transforms from egg to butterfly. It goes hand in hand with the picture of the transformation of the leaves of plants and their metamorphosis into the organs of the flower.

As children, we watched the tiny green caterpillar, for example, of *Vanessa*, creeping from an egg on a Stinging Nettle plant and beginning to eat away great quantities of green leaves, growing bigger and bigger, until one day it would hang itself up, head downward, with a silken thread, spun from within its body. (Another method used by some caterpillars is to tie themselves head upwards, with the silken thread attached to the plant stem and passing around the body.

After some time, the skin would split at the back of the head and out would wriggle a new, bigger and greener caterpillar, still with black hairs, which would immediately begin ravaging the leaves again. This would happen about four times, the little animal then becoming so restless, that it would walk and walk, before hanging itself up for the last time. Then, after a time of waiting—oh wonder!—the last skin would split open one day and out would wriggle, not another caterpillar, but a much younger-looking, delicate green form, with no legs and no hairs—a chrysalis or pupa—which after a short time would be covered with sparkles of pure gold! It was an astonishing sight, one not to be missed.

After a time, the gold and green faded, leaving a light-brown, closed-up form—no legs, no mouth—but with an abdomen that wriggled when touched, its segmented shape reminiscent of the caterpillar, which had disappeared. On this form were clearly to be seen the impressions of the forms, which *would be there* in the future! As yet, there were no forms inside, but they were—like a prophesy—all moulded on the outside of this young form, at first shining with gold, while inside there was only a formless, milky-white substance. (See the writings of E.L. Grant Watson.)

Very much patience was then required, perhaps through weeks, or a whole winter, and then, presence of mind, not to miss the next incredible event. One day, there would again be a split at the back of the head and out would come the butterfly, drawing its head, antennae, proboscis and crumpled wings, with an extraordinary gesture, up and out of the *ventral* part of the pupal form. Wings, proboscis and antennae—all sensory organs in the insect—had been laid down along the region previously occupied by a string of nerve-sense ganglia in the caterpillar! (Figure 61). Out of the closed, hollow space, empty of form, there appeared a quite unexpected creature. It would sit there, a perfect, intricately formed insect, while the crumpled organs would gradually spread out into the beautifully marked wings of a Red Admiral, or Tortoishell butterfly. Some more time would elapse, while the butterfly moved its wings in the way typical of butterflies, before fluttering away into the sunshine.

The biologist knows that the butterfly's sense-organs are scattered over its wings and the surface of its body, as well as in its multiple eyes. It is an embodiment of a *planar* kind of consciousness—the kind we are learning to achieve—not so self-centred; this is embodied in insects and birds alike. How else can the peculiar "space-wisdom" of the bee, or of migrating birds be accounted for? It is surely not with a centric space-consciousness like ours that these physically tiny beings know how to map their route from point to point, and fly from south to north pole, or forage for pollen and honey from a particularly placed hive! Every bee-keeper knows that if the hive is moved, even a very small distance, the foraging bees will return to where it was before. It is as though centre and environment were together part of their organism.

These winged beings are not living in the Cartesian space-consciousnes in which *we* are imprisoned! The bee is one with the hive, the migrating bird with Mother Earth; these are not in the full sense earth-beings, they live in the universe of Saturn, Sun, Moon, as well as Earth. The scientist must admit that we do not fully understand the phenomenon we call "instinct."

Rudolf Steiner describes the butterfly as *just wings*; the body is like an appendage. "Just as the butterfly lays its egg, so the flower develops its seed for the future. Looking at the butterfly as it flutters in the air, we see it as a plant raised into the air. What the butterfly becomes above—from egg to perfect insect—under the influence of the sun and higher planets, the plant becomes here below, under the influence of the earth (and the lower planets)" (Man as Symphony of the Creative Word 26.X.23). The plant, he says, lays its seed in the earth, while the butterfly *will only* lay its egg in the realm of the sun. This means, in other words, in the *sun-spaces* of the vegetative plant.

In great detail, Rudolf Steiner describes the symbiotic panorama involved in the relationships between planets, insects, plants, elemental beings and the earth; the butterfly's egg is like a seed laid in the realm of the sun, the caterpillar is like a leaf, the chrysalis is like a bud or calyx and the butterfly like the flower.

We can follow this Imagination of the developing forms, which tell of the secrets of Resurrection. Compare in detail the transformation and metamorphosis of leaves into calyx and corolla. (See Figure 61 and also *The Plant between Sun and Earth*, Chapter VIII.)

The leaves open out and away from the innermost vertical axis of the plant; the nodes progress usually in growth-measure up the stem, and then in the calyx the leaves grow together to form a bud, from which, in time, the quite new form of the flower will appear.

This is a typical plant process, leading, however, to a formation from the leaves to the flower, which heralds quite a new stage of development, involving a curtailment of the purely vegetative growth. When the beauty of the corolla is revealed, it is still an etheric, plant process, but it tells of other worlds. Goethe calls it an enhancement, and describes in detail the transformation from the leaves to the flowers, which he calls a metamorphosis.

The caterpillar, however, is a little animal, with sense-organs for the light enclosed within its body, as well as on the surface. There is a nerve-sensory system, a string of ganglia, running from the brain, down its ventral part; and down its back runs a dorsal vessel, a circulatory, but also nutritive system. This vessel can be compared to the midrib of the plant-leaf, but whereas the vegetative leaf opens its leaf-edges out and away towards the light, the little animal is rolled up around the gut (which extends from mouth to anus) like a rolled up leaf grown together at the leaf-edges (as is actually the case in a calyx formation or bud.) The caterpillar encloses physically in its body, what for the plant is its inner axis of light.

When, then, time after time the caterpillar sheds its skin, revealing the new form within, we may be reminded of the unfolding of the leaves at the growing-point, repeated again and again up the stem. At last the closed form appears—the calyx or flower bud in the plant and the chrysalis in the insect.

Here the hollow form is created, quiet and more long-lasting. In both plant and insect, something comes into being of a much higher order than what went before, revealing forms which have changed beyond all recognition!

Figure 61 shows the bodies of caterpillar, chrysalis and imago in section. Comparing the dorsal vessel with a leaf-midrib, imagine the leaf grown together at its edges (as in the pod of a pea) and compare it with the forms of the insect's body, closed around the ventral ganglia of the nerve-sense system. In the case of the caterpillar, the gut is a tube, through which passes the substance of the green leaves, to be transformed into caterpillar. Like a rolled up leaf, the caterpillar absorbs leafy substance, just as the green leaves assimilate sunlight.

The refinement of the forms in the regions of inflorescence, is to be seen also in the insect transformation. The insect body becomes progressively more aerated and the nerve-sense system more dominant and peripheral. In terms of chemistry, also, there would be much to be said, concerning these processes of enhancement and metamorphosis.

Goethe recognized the idea of metamorphosis, when he saw *abnormal forms* in the plant—half-leaf, half-floral organ—betraying the secret, the plant having failed fully to achieve it. Steiner sees the whole symbiotic process involving plant and insect as a cosmic drama taking place in a world of Elemental Beings, alive in the realms of the ethers and elements; they relate the planetary spheres from Saturn to Moon with Mother Earth. Servants of the Hierarchies, these beings have always been known to human beings in the past. They wait, longing for us to find new ways of perceiving them again today.

Wherever metamorphosis takes place, in whatever realm, there will be an ''empty'' space, through which the change is made possible. There must be a space, an enclave, which is fully given over to forces, not of the world of *created forms*, but of the world of *creative processes*. Rudolf Steiner used the word "ausgespart", which translated literally, would mean "spared out", emptied out. He often described the sun as such a space, in which the scientists would be surprised to find "less than nothing", a spared-out space, where no substance would be found, but a vacuum—"more than a vacuum!" It is a space completely polar opposite to our conception of earth-space.[26]

Such matriarchal spaces are realms of χάος (not cosmos), where the egoism of substance has receded and where the force of gravity has no power. In botanical terms, we speak of heliotropism, in contrast to the geotropism of the root. Not only in the plant, but wherever living processes unfold, such anti-gravitational realms give the opportunity for something new to come about.

These are the silent, hidden, inner spaces, which, in the world of life, or of soul or spirit, need to come about, if metamorphosis is to take place. Here is a turning inside-out; substance no longer goes on and on accumulating extensively, but withdraws, leaving a hollowed out "intensive" space. This is a cosmic space, a Saturn, Sun, Moon, or other such heavenly space. In such a space, quite new forms arise, which are in no way direct physical continuations of what went before.

Human actions based on egoism will destroy. The human being who knows how to create contemplative spaces, empty of noise, and given over to the spirit, can cultivate an inner quiet of forethought, until it becomes a part of action. Thoughtful awareness of the result of an action will, in due course, be transformed into an understanding of karma and reincarnation, the knowledge that every action has as its counterpart, or polar transformation, a resulting action.

In a future, more advanced state, we shall learn to perceive, with each action, a picture of its karmic result—its future, metamorphosed form. The Beings in Nature know the secret of metamorphosis in plant and insect, and they know the sacrifice involved in going through the void, to attain a new form of life—a life resurrected from a tomb. So, too, the Spirit lives as a seed in human thought and must be brought to flower and fruit in Science, gradually to recognize the laws of reincarnation.

But metamorphosis takes time. When, for example, in a lower realm of plant-life, the mushroom hurries over-night to ripen and drop its spores, there is no metamorphosis, as there is, for instance, in the field poppy, which has taken time to mature, hanging its head for a long time, before opening to reveal its uncrumpled petals and the glory of its colour. What the flower reveals in the realms of the earth's ethereal body, the insect shows forth in an astral realm; both are dramatic, metamorphic phenomena.

One is reminded of the cromlech and dolmen (Figure 78), stone altars left standing in the countryside of northern Europe by a far-off culture, like reminders—markings in the book of history. Rudolf Steiner saw in detail and described how the Druid priest was able, in the *shadow* of the stones (in the hollow, one might say, where the stone *is not*), to read and experience the secrets of the Spiritual Sunlight.[27] No longer able to experience the spiritual world as such, he was able to use the arrangement of the cromlech to perceive the invisible powers of the Sun, and to translate this wisdom into the knowledge needed to guide the affairs of human beings on earth.

These were times before the dawn of our own era. A Turning-point of Time was marked by the Mystery of Golgotha. The Druids could still learn of the secrets of the Sun, before the time, when the Sun-Being would walk the Earth. Today, near to the change of a millenium, it is the task of science to rediscover ancient truths—*but* in a modern way.

Listen to some words of the physicist Max Planck (1858-1947) delivered to a scientific audience:

> "Gentlemen! As a physicist—that is someone, who has his lifelong served a sober and objective science—I may surely not be suspected of mere flighty enthusiasm. And so, out of my researches into the atom, I will say the following: There is no such thing as matter on its own. All matter comes about and persists only through a force, which brings the particles into vibration and holds them together in the tiny sun-system of the atom. But as in the whole universe there is neither an intelligent nor eternal (abstract) force—humanity has never been able to achieve the much desired "perpetuum mobile"—so we must assume that behind this force there is a conscious, intelligent Spirit. This Spirit is the basis of all matter. It is not the visible, though perishable matter, which is the reality, the truth, (for matter, as we have seen, would not exist without this Spirit!), but it is the invisible and immortal Spirit, which is the Truth. But as Spirit cannot exist for itself alone, and to every Spirit there belongs a Being, so we are forced to assume Spirit-Being. But as Spirit-Being also cannot exist out of itself alone, and must have been created, so I am not shy in naming this mysterious creator, as have all peoples of all the ancient cultures,—God! (Translated from the journal, *Lebendige Erde*, No 3/84, page 133.)

Du selbst, erkennender, fühlender, wollender Mensch,
Du bist das Rätsel der Welt.
Was sie verbirgt,
In dir wird es offenbar, es wird
In deinem Geiste Licht,
In deiner Seele Wärme,
Und deines Atems Kraft,
Sie bindet dir die Leibeswesenheit
An Seelenwelten,
An Geistesreiche.
Sie führt dich in den Stoff,
Daß du dich menschlich findest;
Sie führt dich in den Geist,
Daß du dich geistig nicht verlierest.

Rudolf Steiner. (Found in a notebook.)

You, Self, knowing, feeling, willing Man
You are the riddle of the world.
What it hides
Is revealed in you; it becomes
In your Spirit, Light,
In your Soul, Warmth,
And the power of your Breathing
Binds for you your bodily Being
To worlds of Soul
To realms of Spirit.
It leads you into Matter,
That you may find your humanity;
It leads you into the Spirit,
That you, as Spirit, do not lose yourself.

Translation; Olive Whicher.

Chapter VII

SCIENCE AND SPIRITUAL UNDERSTANDING

> A theory is the more impressive the greater the simplicity of its premises is, the more different kinds of things it relates, and the more extended is its area of applicability.
> Albert Einstein in *"Autobiographical Notes."*

In his home town of Vienna in September 1923 (26.IX.23), Rudolf Steiner said the following:—

"We can observe the magnificent contribution which scientific research has brought us even up to the most recent time... For instance, we may call ettention to the fact that, through the conscientious, earnest observation of the laws and facts of the external world of the senses, as ia supplied by natural science, very special human capacities have been developed, and that just such observation and experimentation have thrown a light also upon human capacities themselves...

If we only give a little thought to what this light has illuminated, we see that human thinking, through the very fact that it has been able to investigate both narrow and vast relationships—the microscope and the telescope—has gained immeasurably in itself: has gained in the capacity of discrimination, has gained in powers of penetration, to associate the things in the world, so that their secrets are unveiled, and to determine the laws underlying cosmic relationships, and so forth.

We see, as this thinking develops, that a standard is set for this thinking, and it is set precisely for the most earnest of those who take up this research: the demand that this thinking must develop as selflessly as possible in the observation of external nature and in experimentation in the laboratory, in the clinic, etc.

The human being has achieved tremendous power in this respect. He has succeeded in setting up more and more rules, whose character prevents anything of the inner wishes of the heart, of opinions, perhaps even of fantasies regarding one's own being, such as arise in the course of thinking, from being carried over into what he is to establish by means of the microscope, the measuring rule and the scales, regarding the relationships of life and existence."

But, in the very achievement of this objective way of thinking, it has at first become very abstract. A fear of becoming lost in fantastical vagueness causes the scientist still to study the living world only in accordance with the inorganic laws.

Research into Streaming Media.

In the latter years of Rudolf Steiner's life and slowly in the years following his death in 1925, there developed practices in several scientific fields, based on his indications and initiatives. The widening of conventional medical practice grew, under the direction of Dr. med. Ita Wegman (1876—1943); the department of general science and the development of biodynamic agriculture was in the hands of Dr. Günther Wachmuth (1893—1963); and the mathematical-astronomical research was led by Dr. Elisabeth Vreede (1879—1943). Dr. Vreede in particular was very aware and supportive of the scientific impulse of George Adams, and gave him the opportunity to write and publish *Strahlende Weltgestaltung.*

In the forties, the field of specialization into cancer research grew out of the work in the Ita Wegman Klinik in Arlesheim, Switzerland, especially through the initiative of Dr. med Alexandre Leroi (1906—1968), who, together with his wife Rita and others, developed Rudolf Steiner's suggestions towards the remedy for cancer—Iscador—and later founded the Lukas Klinik in Arlesheim, centre for the treatment of cancer patients. Since his tragically early death, his wife, Dr. med. Rita Leroi has continued indefatigably to carry this work further, to its present advanced state (see bibliography).

In 1959, Alexandre Leroi, together with George Adams, Theodor Schwenk (1911--1986) and Georg Unger (see Introduction), generously financed by the anthroposophist and industrialist, Dr. Hanns Voith (1885—1971) founded the water research centre in Herrischried in the Black Forest, the *Institut für Strömungswissenschaften im Verein für Bewegungsforschung.* (*Institute for Research into Streaming Media in the Society for Research into Movement.*)

Concerned as he was with the development of the cancer remedy, Leroi wanted research into various aspects of movement—human, biological, the movements of water and also movement from the aspect of theories in physics.

Already the question of the influence of *movement* in the method of homoeopathic dilution needed research; furthermore, in regard to the remedy for cancer, Rudolf Steiner had indicated that this preparation should take place outside of a gravitational field. Adams had already worked with the advisory team concerned with this research in the lifetime of Ita Wegman and Elisabeth Vreede, both of whom had died during the war.

It was their common interest in the phenomenon of homoeopathic potentisation, and in the problem set by Rudolf Steiner in regard to the method of preparation of the cancer remedy, which brought the small group of scientists, Leroi, Adams, Schwenk and Unger, together in the Institute in Herrischried.

George Adams, convinced of the relation of the concept of polar spaces and forces to the etheric world, continued his researches during and after Rudolf Steiner's lifetime, and especially in the years from 1947 until his death in 1963. In those years he was able to work intensively with Michael Wilson and others, in the setting provided by the Goethean Science Foundation, which they founded in Clent, near Stourbridge, Worcestershire. Michael Wilson became known internationally for his work in Goethe's Theory of Colour and Optics. He was elected Chairman of the Colour Group of Great Britain, affiliated to the London Physical Society, and contributed to various scientific journals. Wilson pioneered the whole field of Art Therapy, particularly in music and colour; he had almost finished a book entitled "Living with Light and Colour," when he died in 1985 (see Bibliography).

Adams had discovered in the works of Sophus Lie (1842—1899), and Felix Klein (1849—1925), a long-forgotten realm of mathematics, concerning surfaces of a higher order than spheres, hyperboloids etc., or even lemniscatory surfaces. They are much more intimately touched by their tangent planes and were therefore, in his view, *qualitatively*, that much closer to an etheric force-field.

It was to this field of forms that he turned, setting to work to develop the necessary mathematical techniques, in order to create such form-types in a variety of shapes. Adapting the name given to such curves in two dimensions by Lie and Klein, who called them W-Kurven, Adams called them *Weg-Kurven*, or *Path-Curves* and *Path-Curve Surfaces* (Figure 63 and Plate III).

The task was to create surfaces, which would in their very nature have a quality akin to the forms which flowing water assumes naturally. It is better known today, than it was in those years, largely through Theodor Schwenk's publications, that by straightening the water-courses and by subjecting water to the force of gravity in long, straight pipes down the mountain-sides, it is rendered inert and without vitality. Adams thought that by creating channels with surfaces of an intensely ethereal quality, through which the devitalised water might be caused to flow, a compensating process might be included in the practical techniques employed for the purpose of drawing power from water.

It has long been a habitual method to purify water through movement in gravel-beds, where vortical flow and the creation of turbulence aerate the water. In recent times this is no longer sufficient and it has been necessary to resort to chemicals.

Why not intensify the ancient, organic method of purifying water, just as in modern bio-dynamic agriculture, the natural, organic methods of growing plants are intensified?

To the farmers, Rudolf Steiner had given directions towards the making of biological preparations for the purpose of intensifying the organic life of soil and compost. To the scientists he had made suggestions as to how to set up laboratory experiments in order to show the existence and the efficacy of the etheric forces, about which he was speaking.

Basic to all these indications, is the plastic, planar quality of the etheric world, which functions according to the laws of *negative* space. In the three test-methods so far devised, it is a question of bringing about *pictures on surfaces*; watching the flow of the liquid substances and then assessing the final forms they achieve.

Lili Kolisko received instructions from Rudolf Steiner to create conditions in which various salt-solutions, followed by biological liquids, would flow together in a surface of filter-paper (Capillary Dynamolysis). To Ehrenfried Pfeiffer, Steiner suggested a method of crystallisation in thin surfaces, to discover in what way the crystal-formation would be altered by the inclusion of a biological juice (Kapillary Dynamolysis). Years later, Theodor Schwenk adapted this picture-making method in his *Tropfen-Bild Methode*

(*Drop-picture method*). In all these types of experiment, the experimentor must learn through long experience to interpret the different forms and also the manner in which they arise *in a surface*. An experienced experimentor acquires the facility of recognising what processes or substances underlie the various forms, which make up the whole picture. Responsible assessment relies on individual human judgement.

Again, in the making of the bio-dynamic preparations, it is a question of surfaces, *organic sheathes* in which substances are laid or wrapped and given time to undergo change in what might be called an inner, vital space.[28] The picture is similar to those we have been considering in the living realms of water-drops, plant-seeds, growing-points and animal or human organisms. They are "negative", receptive spaces, created by the farmer, using organs and substances, as directed; they are then placed somewhere in ordinary space to mature. Such preparations, in their sheathes, are perhaps buried for a period in the earth, perhaps left to the influence of water, perhaps to the air and light; they are subjected to seasonal rhythms for some specified period of time.

What happens in such a space, in respect to the transformation of substance, cannot be compared with ordinary chemistry, for *these are not ordinary spaces; they are focal realms, receptive to cosmic forces*. There are, in our universe, hidden processes, which, given the right conditions, take place between stars, planets and the earth. Moreover, the well-known quantitative laws do not hold here; only small amounts are needed of the matured preparation to spray large areas of land.

Practical experience of the efficacy of these methods is growing, and the result of decades of experimentation is becoming impressive. But, as things are, in the present stage of human understanding, the modern scientist has a right to be sceptical.

Fortunately, the methods do work, even if those who carry them out, cannot fully explain why. It is true, Anthroposophy meets with difficulties, when it comes to science, for it requires more than only to take into account what can be seen, measured and weighed, in the world of the senses. This, however, is for the most part, the present requirement of science, and it was for this reason that Rudolf Steiner looked towards the further development of mathematics, which would give a scientific basis towards the understanding of the etheric laws. (Here again we should be reminded that mathematics does not necessarily mean calculations, but geometry—morphology).

We can, indeed, be thankful that Rudolf Steiner had the courage and forsight to propose practical methods for medicine and agriculture, which appear ridiculous, according to the rules of mechanistic science, without waiting for scientific theory to come abreast with his thought. Homoeopathy, too, faces such criticism.

It was out of such considerations, that Adams had seen the importance of the long forgotten work by the German and Scandinavian mathematicians, concerning the forms of a highly planar order, which he called in English Path-curve Surfaces. He set to work to research such surfaces and to teach us their laws, and particularly Lawrence Edwards[29] became proficient in drawing them. The time came, when it was decided to work experimentally with laboratory models of such forms in the Institut für Strömungswissenschaften.

It must be realized that models can only show a small part of these *ideal* surfaces, which in their reality extend out to the infinite! In Adams' mind, it was the *quality of the surface*, over which the water would be invited to flow, which was all-important.

John Wilkes,[30] the sculptor, was brought in, actually to build and cast these minutely calculated forms, of which two are shown in Figure 64. These and other models were finished and photographed by him after the death of George Adams. It was an exacting and very skilled task, to follow in detail Adams's calculated figures and reproduce them in physical shapes, when he was no longer there to see them.

The death of Adams, and of Dr. Alexander Leroi a few years later, meant that this specific aspect of the work at Herrischried could no longer find direct continuation. Dr. George Unger, working in Dornach, and Lawrence Edwards, were the only two left, who at that time had a competent mathematical understanding of the path-curve surfaces. To John Wilkes, Adams had imparted a great love and recognition of the task in hand, and he has been able to continue experimenting with water, based on his qualitative understanding of the new surfaces and his skill as an artist. He looked further into the intimate relationships, which flowing water can have with empirical and also mathematical surfaces.

As a result of his many years of continued perseverance, combined with his creation of the Sculpture department at Emerson College, his Flowform method made it possible for Wilkes to generate rhythmical, lemniscatory oscillations in water flowing through a channel. He and his colleagues have continued investigating what effects such surfaces and rhythms have upon the quality of water. The work is meeting with wide interest among people deeply concerned about the condition of water in many countries of the world.

In the years, since George Adams died, a great amount of quiet and intensive work has been going on, in direct connection with his scientific impulse. Supported by Dr. Georg Unger's genius for illuminating the content of modern scientific research from the anthroposophical point of view, the Mathematical-Astronomical Section at the Goetheanum has through the years provided a forum for the interchange of individual fields of research and a ground for the development of educational methods in mathematics and physics.

In particular, two recent publications, one by Dr. Renatus Ziegler on the history of geometrical mechanics in the nineteenth century, and the other by Dr. Peter Gschwind on the problem of space, time and velocity, make significant strides forward. Ziegler describes in detail the historical development of thought in mathematical physics, which led Adams to the conception and formulation of the idea of "*Universal Forces in Mechanics*",[14] Gschwind shows that one meets with the mathematics of the path-curves, when one attempts to develop a concept of velocity, which does not take its start from the usual idea of space and time. This presupposes the possibility of new experiments in physics, based on the theory put forward by George Adams concerning the universal forces also at work in mechanics.

Path-curve Surfaces—Fact or Fancy?

So far, the relating of Rudolf Steiner's idea of negative space to science has been in the realm of thoughts and inner experiences, theories and hypotheses, based on mathematics and on a certain degree of understanding of anthroposophy. At the end of a lifetime of research, Adams had been very relieved and full of gratitude for the opportunity at last to put theory into practice, and he worked beyond the powers of his physical body to leave behind sufficient mathematical detail for the furtherance of the project begun at Herrischried.

Lawrence Edwards, is one of those who has assimilated the mathematical aspect of George Adams's scientific work most competently. His book, *Projective Geometry* brings together in textbook form a large part of what Adams was researching and teaching, but unfortunately it does not allude to the conception of Space and Counterspace.

Edwards was able to continue working at the path-curve surfaces, on the basis of what he had been given. He, too, was convinced of the validity of the idea of cosmic forces functioning in the "negative spaces" of plant growth, and he shared the view that to picture the flowering and fruiting processes in the plant on the basis of lemniscatory forms was only a first step, and not a fully adequate or elegant mathematical description (see *The Plant between Sun and Earth*).

It was for this reason that Adam's researches had led him to seek for forms of a higher mathematical order than the logarithmic spiral or the lemniscate. His research into the path-curve surfaces had shown him that they appear most naturally in two types, egg-shapes and vortical forms. At first, he had been interested in the egg-shaped form. So obviously, a cosmic form, related to life, it underlies, for instance, such forms as the human head, the heart, buds, and other natural shapes.[31] In connection with the flow-form work in Herrischried, Adams concentrated on developing vortical shapes. In achieving the desired model-forms, he was helped on the pictorial side by Lawrence Edward's skill in imagining and drawing the beautiful forms, given the required parameters, and by Georg Unger's skill in mathematical physics.

To give a very simple analogy: just as we have seen that families of circle-curves can be drawn projectively, between a fixed (invariant) line of four harmonic points and a fixed point of four harmonic lines (Figure 25), so now we are led to picture a projective transformation of higher order curves in relation to an *invariant triangle* (Figure 63) and of surfaces in relation to an *invariant tetrahedron* (Plate III and Figure 65).

The whole plane, in the one case, and the whole of space in the other, is streamed through and through by the path-curves and their surfaces, as they transform into one another. Space itself is transformed by them. Finally, it must be said, that the invariant triangle—or tetrahedron—may have many different aspects; for example, it may have some of its parts at infinity, or they may be *imaginary* (in the mathematical sense).[4]

We reach the limit of what may be brought here by way of elementary description of the path-curve surfaces. Suffice it to say that, just as we have learned to conceive of a sphere in its *full sense*, so here we are contemplating forms *in which this completeness is fully manifest in the visible form itself. As visible form, each surface reveals both its pointwise and its planewise aspect: it is a complete synthesis of physical and ethereal form.*

Looking at the single path-curve surface, we must see it as just one moment in a whole sea of moving forms, flowing between a line at infinity within (vertical in the picture), and a line at infinity in the (horizontal) infinite (Plate III).

A number of years after George Adams' death, Lawrence Edwards took this field of research a significant step forward. He began to realise that *certain forms in nature are actually path-curve surfaces, while others are not*, and he developed a method for making minute and detailed measurements by which to demonstrate this fact. A first step revealed that the forms of pine cones, flower buds and vegetative growing-points are in fact path-curve surfaces,—that is to say, shapes, which, *in their outer form*, show that they are of the nature of a negative or sun space (Figure 65).

Further remarkable discoveries followed, notably in relation to the fertilization of the flower, to forms and processes of the human heart and of the uterus. In the latter case, for example, investigation revealed that the uterus, when actively engaged in the first stages of pregnancy, takes on the shape of a path-curve surface, evidence of which disappears later on (see Edwards: *The Field of Form*).

Edwards most recent experiments demonstrate clearly the fact of cosmic influences on vegetative processes. Distinct changes in the shapes of vegetative buds on, say, an oak tree, can be measured and shown to be related to the movement of (in this case) the planet Mars in relation to the Moon. A parameter in the calculation of the path-curve surface, to which Adams assigned the Greek letter lambda λ, can be clearly monitored and set down in a graph. A very evident change in the value of λ shows up at times of conjunction or opposition between Mars and the Moon.

The λ value is a most important and also a very sensitive parameter, appearing as a *projective growth measure*, along the central axis of the bud, from base to tip;[32] in other words, it is a function of the line at infinity within—the functional infinitude—of the bud. From our previous considerations it is not difficult to imagine that this sensitivity (which involves a minute, but measurable, rhythmic movement of the shape of the bud) might well be due to a relationship in ethereal space between an aspect of the form closely related both to its own innermost ethereal axis, and to a process taking place in the outer cosmic spheres between Moon and Mars.

At all events, the fact is that it has been possible to register this relationship in terms of measurement, thus bringing the idea of a negative space, or sun-space, in which the cosmic, universal forces function, into the realm of measurable fact. It is surely an epoch-making discovery!

Of course, these and similar experiments now being carried out also by others in the field, must be regarded as pilot experiments, which will have to be checked over and over again, before scientific scepticism is appeased. Furthermore, in the excitement of having translated a cosmic process into a measurable value, *it is very easy to forget that it is indeed a parameter belonging to a process in negative space* and not only to the three-dimensional aspect of the bud. There is a real danger of losing sight of the very raison d'être of the whole procedure, so great is the bias towards thinking materialistically and in terms of quantitative measurement in earth space.

Just think what it means! Even thinking only of buds on trees, we begin to catch sight of the living realm of the formative forces body—the ethereal body—of the earth, related and in tune with the whole cosmos. Ideas to be met with in Paracelsus or Novelis or Culpepper (or, for that matter, Rudolf Steiner) of the relationships of the planets to specific plants, metals or other substances,[33] find confirmation in these experiments, in a form, which a scientist asking for objective proof in terms of measurement cannot justifiably ignore.

Towards Global Thinking

Looking back to what the world was like in those last years of Rudolf Steiner's lifetime, one can hardly believe that such a change has come about in so short a time.

It is, however, true to say that Rudolf Steiner was already describing much of what we now learn about phenomena made available to research through recent technical achievements.

Ecology, which did not exist as a science at that time, and sociology, which only recently ranks as a science, contain ideas and even practices suggested by him. Involved, is a thinking in terms of *association*, rather than spatial and psychological *separation*. Ideas about living relationships, such as plant associations, environmental inter-relationships, even parents-teachers associations and workers' unions, were not as commonplace then as they are now.

The World Power Conference (now known as the World Energy Conference) which was first founded by the British anthroposophist, D.N. Dunlop (1868—1935)[34] in 1924, was originally intended as a first step towards the forming of an international body of experts—producers *and* consumers—in technical enterprises, industry and agriculture, in order to safeguard the interests of *all* nations, concerning the commodities upon which life on the earth depends. The intention was, and ideally it still is, that internationalism and not nationalism should prevail. Humanity is struggling, but it is moving on. That 5,000 members from all countries of the world could meet together (in October 1986 in Cannes) to concentrate on one of the world's greatest problems today, is a fact not to be under-estimated, however controversial opinions may be, concerning the very difficult issues.

The successes of science in technology have led in the first place to the state of imbalance of today, but through this very fact, humanity is faced with the necessity to think in terms of the whole Earth, including its environment. With a growing understanding of social and ecological principles, the "laws of science" are changing.

Molecular Biology—The Living Environment of Organisms

That entrenched opinions do eventually give way to change, is instanced by the remarkable case in microbiology involving Barbara McClintock,[35] the pioneer geneticist, who, as a young woman at Cornell University in the early twenties, achieved a high level of recognition in the field of cytology and genetics, which she helped to create. When, however, in the fifties she upset the dogma of the fixed, linear sequence of genes, which were thought to hold the key to the unfolding of the organism, by introducing the view that *movement* occurs in the genetic elements of the cell ("transportation" in the chromosomes), she had to suffer three decades of entrangement and isolation from the mainstream of biology. Now, the scientists have come to regard her view as an indisputable phenomenon, and in 1982 she received a Nobel prize for her work, which some regard as the beginning of a new revolution in biology. Dr. McClintock combined the techniques of observation of the whole plant and even of its environment with the study of the configurations of the chromosomes as they appeared under the microscope. Rather than seeking a molecular mechanism, with a stable structure, she looked for a more functional structure, and saw that the "activator" genes did not correspond to fixed places on the chromosome, but that they *moved*.

With the discovery of genetic mobility, the idea of a static, linear message inscribed in the sequence of DNA is superceded by the thought of a dynamic structure, in which *the movement of the genes is itself* part of the "programme" of instructions to the cell.

It all becomes more complicated—but life *is* complicated; and when the question is asked: Where do the instructions come from? McClintock's answer is that they come from the *entire cell, the organism as a whole, perhaps even the environment.*

What seemed like a wild idea to many biologists in the fifties and sixties, may well still seem uncomfortable to some, but the fact is that biologists have begun to move on beyond a picture of the organism—and even the universe—based on the Newtonian idea in physics of the interaction of point masses, which for biologists is translated into the idea of a smallest and simplest living organism.

Perhaps Barbara McClintock set more in motion in science than the theories concerning chromosomes and genes. Her vitality, extreme self-determination and unlimited love for what she had chosen to do, made her such a good scientist. Her biographer writes that what was truly exceptional was the extent to which she maintained her childlike capacity for absorption throughout her adult life. A crucial component of this capacity was her wish "to be free of the body". She'd had a taste of this freedom—first as a young child "flying" along the beach, and later, at moments of special concentration in her studies. As a child, Barbara had loved to go out to the beach and run in a special style that she had discovered herself. "You stood quite straight, with your back just completely straight, and you practically floated. Each step was rhythmically floating, without any sense of fatigue, and with a great sense of euphoria." Years later, she read of the Buddhist monks in Tibet, "Running Lamas", who cultivated the same technique. She loved skating and physical activities and at the same time, she loved to sit alone, intensely absorbed, just "thinking about things."

It is surely significant that the pioneer scientists in the twentieth century, in search of the causes and processes of development in seed and germ, took the pathway of observation into the infinitessimal worlds within substance, patterning their thoughts upon physical chemistry and the achievements of physics and the inorganic sciences. This has resulted in the practice of genetic engineering, with its immense potential for life and also for death.

A deep inner conviction, however, led at least this scientist to look for causative factors outside the tiny, observable genes themselves. Following the scientific method conscientiously in all detail, she is nevertheless convinced that "Things are much more marvellous than the scientific method allows us to conceive."[35]

It is surely also significant, that when research into molecular biology was beginning, in the early twenties of this century, Rudolf Steiner was drawing the attention of doctors and scientists in detail to certain developments in human embryology, which now, sixty years later, are being studied through microscopic and clinical observation.[36] He was then also calling attention to the fact, as we have already quoted, that:

"Through the conscientious, earnest observations of the laws and facts of the external world of the senses, as is supplied by natural science, very special human capacities have been developed: just such observation and experimentation have thrown a light also upon human capacities themselves"...(Vienna 27.IX.23).

"Thinking",...he continues, "is capable of energizing itself inwardly to activity. It may energize itself in such a way that, although not exact in the sense in which we apply this term to measure and weight in external research, it is exact in relationship to its own development in the sense in which the external scientist, the mathematician, for example is accustomed to follow with full consciousness every step in his research. But this occurs when that mode of supersensible cognition of which I am here speaking replaces the ancient, vague meditation, the ancient indistinct immersion of oneself in thinking, with a truly exact development of this thinking."

The belief that experimental science and intellect, given time, will in the end be able to explain the universe on the basis of molecular physics, is indeed being widely questioned by science itself today. Evidence of this is the number of rival theories of the origin of the universe, eg., big bang, steady state, anti-matter, varying gravity constant... Quite a galaxy in fact; the picture is capable of multiplication, representing the offspring of serious and for the most part devoted minds.

These theories are food for thought for millions of ordinary people today, including growing children, who look to science for answers to their inner questions. But why is it, one might ask, that the picture—one might even call it, the imagination—of a Big Bang, an explosion, plays such a prominent part in our world today? It lurks in many things, from a conception of the origin of the universe to celebrating with fireworks and crackers. We have in our time forgotten the power of pictures on the imagination, and few ask where the origin of such pictures lies and what causes their perpetuation.

In spite of—or is it because of—the dark thunder-clouds, there is indeed a strong wind of change blowing today; but the way of picturing the human being and the universe in terms of tiny particles or units of material substance in physical space strongly resists change.

New ideas, such as "morphogenetic fields" and "explicate and implicate orders" (Bohm) are progressive, but mostly illustrated by examples taken from technical fields, such as the telephone, television, telecommunication, even though the underlying mathematics has long gone beyond ordinary space-concepts.[37] It all makes fascinating reading, and with due discretion, one's imagination is fired by the scientists and other writers, who brave untrodden routes. But the ideas are disappointing. They evoke, at least in my imagination (I use the rather fascinating idiom of one recent publication) the picture of point-like entities, busily moving and searching through a spatial world, finally bumping into the plane at infinity—the looking-glass!—through which, unlike Alice, they do not penetrate! While the cage of ordinary spatial conceptions is still well locked and bolted, the way is barred to an understanding of the creative environment of organisms.

The idea of Wholeness (Holism), towards which scientists are aspiring today, lives indeed in the idea of Physical and Ethereal Spaces and Forces, but this involves transcending in thought the plane at infinity and metamorphosing one-sidedly physical-spatial forms of thought, in order to reach a synthesis, which accords with the *whole* truth.

John Davy, for many years science correspondent of the London newspaper, *The Observer* and decorated for his services with the Order of the British Empire, was a deeply versed anthroposophist. In his capacity as correspondent, he gained an intimate knowledge of the world-wide scientific scene, in conversations with eminent scientists holding both orthodox and "new age" views. In an article on evolution—he was himself a biologist—-he made an interesting comment:

"It is curious that while science postulates all kind of unobservable entities to explain, in particular, atomic and sub-atomic phenomena, it shies away in alarm if asked to postulate supersensible spiritual entities to explain other phenomena. Yet Rudolf Steiner asks, to begin with, little more than science asks of itself— namely that his descriptions of events and beings in a spiritual world, not immediately accessible to the senses, should at first be neither accepted nor rejected, but *tried out*, by considering them side by side with natural phenomena to see if they are mutually illuminating..."

It is valuable here to draw attention to the selection of essays by John Davy, published after his premature death in 1984 under the title: *Hope, Evolution and Change*.

It is given to science today, in an entirely new way, to uncover the great wisdom, which the thousands of centuries of evolution have laid into the physical world of nature and into our own bodies. Scientists are free to discover the wonderful laws, hidden in the world of phenomena, without being influenced by myth and saga or religion, just as ordinary people are free to find their own individual guide-lines through life. Yet the binding effects of old cults and cultures is only too evident today, when nations and individuals cannot break from old traditions and beliefs. The resulting fanaticism indicates all too clearly that the spiritual values have been lost; rigidity then sets in.

Freedom is like a two-edged sword, and the task is to learn how to use it, for the idea of freedom is so new! The book *The Philosophy of Freedom* contains a sentence, which serves as a simple reminder:

"To live in love of the action and to *let live*, having understanding for the other person's will, is the fundamental principle of *free human beings*."

It lies within the scope of free and objective scientific thinking to overcome its present one-sided forms of thought, and to encompass areas of knowledge, which have until now remained inaccessible to it.

We have here followed the development of mathematical thinking through the centuries, seen it move from the fixity of finished form to movement and transformation in the light of perspective. But, although mobile, thinking in a perspective transformation is still spatial and still accords with familiar experiences on the earth. When, however, thinking and imagination are activated through the exercise of polar reciprocation, we begin to unlock the cage of cartesian space (Chapter IV). This third step, which gives access to the idea of polar spaces, requires a thinking capable of "energising itself inwardly". It is an essential step, requiring flexibility; it involves a turning inside-out of one's habitual way of thinking and leads to the consciousness of another kind of space, interweaving the first.

In coming to terms with the modern conception of "lemniscatory space" (physical and ethereal spaces interwoven), the facility is acquired in pure thinking, to create imaginations which supercede the old forms without losing or negating them. It is rather like climbing a mountain, learning to find the new footholds, without being afraid to lose hold of the old ones. Every mountaineer knows how fatal it is to cling to the mountain; one summons one's sense of balance, using that force about which the running lamas knew. It is the force of the etheric body, warmed through by the love of the pursuit and the determination of the ego to reach the summit. Every human being knows this intuitively; it is an open secret, and modern science can and surely must compass it.

The Lord of Darkness would perpetuate the lie that the universe and all its forms are merely matter; the Lord of Light would have us close our eyes to the cares of the earth. In truth, just as the plants are ether-forms, made visible by the substances that fill them, so the human being indwells a cosmic, Divine Form, made visible in flesh and blood. Living in it, we may learn to know the Being who helps us to hold the Balance,—and who is also the Lord of Karma.

Plate Tectonics and the Shape of the Earth

Already in 1924, Steiner made pronouncements concerning the earth, which at that time seemed very far-fetched, but have since become recognised earth science. It concerns the form of the tetrahedron (see chapter IV). Regarded in the light of polar reciprocation, this is the simplest possible regular form, and it is *self-polar*, with respect to a sphere (Figure 41).

In September, 1924, in a lecture to the workmen, who were engaged in building the second Goetheanum (Dornach, 18. IX. 24), Rudolf Steiner described in a detailed and most graphic way, that the earth is not a globe, but has a tetrahedral shape.

> "Yes, but actually it is not true that the earth is a globe!... It is only a fantasy that the earth is a globe." Picture the form of a tetrahedron, but now "the sides of the triangles, which were straight before, are rounded. Can you picture that? There arises now a body, which is actually a tetrahedron become round! And you see, our earth is actually such a rounded tetrahedron. This can even be established to the extent of finding the edges, the sides, of the earth-tetrahedron."

Rudolf Steiner then continued to describe the tetrahedron, with its four points, one in central America, at the volcano Coseguina, one at the south pole, one in the volcanic mountains of the Caucasus and one in Japan. Then, in detail, he described how the lines of the tetrahedron are traced out by the lines on which the most important volcanos are found on the earth.

Continuing, in the very direct and descriptive manner in which it was always his wont to speak to the workmen, from whom he met with immediate and confident understanding, Rudolf Steiner described the earth as being formed of four plates or surfaces, stuck together, as in a tetrahedron. The plates, he describes as being flung in from the periphery and then not securely stuck together (like a model made by a child!). Where the plates, are not securely cemented together, but leave weak edges, so that the material from within the earth can be squeezed out, this is where the volcanic eruptions occur.

Rough and ready though the description is (and it is woven through with other considerations), it nevertheless accords with most recent discoveries in geology, as a result of the possibilities of observation and measurement provided by advanced techniques of today. It is now known that, far from being a rigid structure, the earth is a far more fluid mass than it was thought to be. The science of Plate Tectonics, arising from the study of "continental drift," describes the continents as plates or surfaces, which move.[38] On the surface they push together, while on the ocean-bed they open up, with the result that two kinds of volcano appear, spread over the earth and roughly marking out two interlacing tetrahedra, the one with a point at the north pole, while the other, described by Rudolf Steiner, has a point at the south pole.

These two tetrahedra are of contrasting types, in that the volcanos of one are alkaline and of the other acid! The whole field is full of surprises and is crying out to be approached, using the thought-forms of space and counterspace—which is as far as we can take it here. The Swiss geologist, Hans Ulrich Schmutz, in his recent book, points toward such further research; Figure 66, taken from the coloured design on the cover of the book, indicates a way in which to seek relationships between the physical structure of the earth and her cosmic environment.

If the science of geology has taken the enormous stride it has taken in recent decades, based on the mathematics in general use today, may it not be time to approach these phenomena also in the light of a development of mathematics leading further, thus bringing two fields together, to see, (in the words of John Davy) "if they are mutually illuminating."

Not only had Rudolf Steiner developed his powers of spiritual investigation to an unusually high degree, and as a scientist, was also deeply versed in the classics and the arts; he also kept fully abreast of the times. George Adams would describe how, while waiting for him in his study, he would see all the most recent publications on his desk and in his book-shelves (brought there by Dr. Wachsmuth). It should therefore not surprise us to meet with statements by Rudolf Steiner, which will perhaps only find confirmation in the far future.

Der Wahrheit Same liegt in der Liebe;	In Love lives the seed of Truth,
Der Liebe Wurzel suche in der Wahrheit	In truth seek the root of Love:
So spricht dein höheres Selbst.	Thus speaks thy higher Self.
Des Feuers Glut wandelt	The fire's glow transmutes
Holz in wärmenden Strahl,	Wood into warming rays.
Des Wissens lösender Wille	Wisdom's resolving Will
Das Werk in die Kraft.	Changes the outer work
	Into abiding strength.
Dein Werk sei der Schatten,	
Den dein Ich wirft,	So let thy work be the shadow
Wenn es beschienen wird	Cast by thine I
Durch die Flamme	When it is lit by the flame—
Deines höheren Selbst.	Flame of thy higher Self.

Rudolf Steiner (1902)
Wahrspruchworte

Verses and Meditations.

Chapter VIII

CHRISTIANITY AND SUN SPACE

> Das Gewahr werden der Idee in der Wirklichkeit ist die wahre
> Kommunion der Menschheit.
> Rudolf Steiner
>
> Becoming aware of the Idea in Reality is the true Communion
> of Mankind.
> (Goethean Science, G.A.1)

The Being of the Sun

Among the surprising statements made by Rudolf Steiner are those concerning the Sun as a heavenly body in the solar system and those concerning the Incarnation of Christ. In the lecture course entitled *Man and the World of Stars—The Spiritual Communion of Mankind* (Dornach 1.XII.22), Rudolf Steiner describes the human being's relation to the Sun as follows:-

"Now when we look into the countenance of a man and his glance falls on us, when we see his expression, maybe the flushing of the face, then indeed the eyes of our soul are looking right through the physical to the soul and spirit. Indeed, it cannot be otherwise in our life among our fellowmen. In like manner we must accustom ourselves also to see spirit-and-soul in the physiognomy—if I may call it so—and changing coloring of the plant-world on our Earth.

If we are only willing to recognize the physical, we say that the Sun's warmth and light work upon the plants, forming in them the saps, the chlorophyll and so forth. But if we contemplate all this with spiritual insight, if we take the same attitude to this plant-physiognomy of the Earth as we are accustomed to take to the human physiognomy, then something unveils itself to us that I should like to express with a particular word, because this word actually conveys the reality.

The Sun, of which we say, outwardly speaking, that it sends its light to the Earth, is not merely a radiant globe of gas but infinitely more than that. It sends its rays down to the Earth, but whenever we look at the Sun it is the outer side of the rays that we see. The rays have, however, an inner side.

If someone were able to look through the Sun's light, to regard the light only as an outer husk and look through to the soul of it, he would behold the Soul-Power, the Soul-Being of the Sun. With ordinary human consciousness we see the Sun as we should see a man who was made of papier-maché. An effigy in which there is nothing but the form; the lifeless form, is of course something different from the human being we actually see before us. In the case of the living human being, we see through this outer form and perceive soul-and-spirit. For ordinary consciousness the Sun is changed as it were into a papier-maché cast. We do not see through its outer husk that is woven of Light.

But if we were able to see through this, we should see the soul-and-spirit essence of the Sun. We can be conscious of its activity just as we are conscious of the physical papier-maché husk of the Sun. From the standpoint of physical knowledge we say: 'The Sun shines upon the Earth; it sparkles upon the stones, upon the soil. The light is thrown back and thereby we see everything that is mineral. The rays of the Sun penetrate into the plants, making them green, making them bud.' —All that is external. If we see the soul-and-spirit essence of the Sun, we cannot merely say: 'The sunlight sparkles on the minerals, is reflected, enabling us to see the minerals,' or, 'The light and heat of the Sun penetrate into the plants, making them verdant'—but we shall have to say, meaning now the countless spiritual Beings who people the Sun and who constitute its soul and spirit: 'The Sun dreams and its dreams envelop the Earth and fashion the plants.''

Very often, Rudolf Steiner describes the sun as a negative space, in contrast to the earth[39]. There is an example in the lecture on the tetrahedral structure of the earth, to which we referred in Chapter VII: ''The sun is very different from what the physicists of today imagine. They would be much astonished, if they were to approach it: they would find no fiery gas, but would find something that causes any earthly substance to be sucked in and to disappear. The sun is an empty space that exerts suction. It is not a globe of gas, but resembles a pearl in the universe, a suction globe with nothing within it...''(18.IX.24).

Or again, in a lecture, describing an experience, which the human being may have in the spiritual existence between death and a new birth (Oxford, 22.VIII.22), he says:

"What do you imagine the interior of the Sun to be? If you could enter there, you would find it altogether different from what our physicists naively and unwittingly suppose. The interior of the Sun is no mere ball of gas; it is in fact something less than space—a realm where space itself has been taken away. If you begin by imagining an extended space in which some pressure is prevailing, you must conceive the interior of the Sun rather as a realm of suction. It is a *negative space*— space that is emptier than empty. Few people have an adequate idea of what this means."

It is beyond the present endeavour of this book to enter the field of solar physics, but for those equipped to do so, it becomes clear that the gap between Steiner's picture and present-day views is not as wide as it was, at least in as much as that many of the phenomena described by the scientists appear to be opposite to what is familiar on the earth.[40]

We touch here on a theme, fundamental to Steiner's thought, which is difficult and only too often ignored. It is, however, of deep significance. Very often he tries to awaken the picture by describing a familiar experience; one can have a pocket full of money, then an empty purse and then reach the state of being in debt! It is clear that here he has other aspects in mind,—those of economics. The progression is from fulness to emptiness and then to the complete polar opposite of fulness—a state, which is *more than just empty*. It has an intensely receptive potential!

It is here that the idea of a *polar* Euclidean space—an etheric space—provides us with another kind of mathematical imagination, with which to approach such descriptions, provided this idea has become part of an intuitive way of thinking and is no longer merely an intellectual concept (which at first it must needs be, of course). This concept must have been raised, through constant practice in observation and thinking, first into an Imagination; then gradually it grows and blossoms into the realms of Inspiration and Intuition. Without constant work and attention, of course nothing will grow.

What is an "empty" bowl, with *more than nothing* in it ? It is surely a space of the kind one can learn to conceive of in mathematical thought. I can go round with an empty pocket and disturb no-one, but to be in debt involves other factors—this hollow must be filled, for it brings with it social obligations. Looked at from another angle, a similar picture is given by the widow's mite, shining in the bottom of the bowl, towards which other mites can find their way. The problems and perplexities of modern economics are met with here, and an invitation to learn how to see the Christ walking in the market-place. This touches the all-human social question.

It is only in recent times that the Sun is thought to be a mere ball of hot gases in the sky. It was always known in ancient times and cultures, that the Sun is the expression of a great omnipresent Being, and it was known that this Being would one day descend to the Earth. We read about it still in the ancient teachings of India, Persia, the Greeks and the Hebrews, which have become popular again today. Perhaps the imagination of a child in the Ecole Perceval (Chatou, Paris), pictured in Plate V, comes nearer to the truth.

Rudolf Steiner did not simply repeat the old teachings, which have come down to us in various forms and have sometimes become changed and mistranslated through the ages. He described the results of his own individual spiritual investigations, which were not mediumistic, but carried out in full consciousness.

Describing the descent of the Christ Being to the Earth, through the ancient cultural epochs of India, Persia, Egypt and Chaldea, Greece and Babylon to Roman times, Rudolf Steiner shows that it was the *same Being*, who was referred to with different names, as the One who once dwelt in the Sun and gradually came nearer and nearer to the Earth (London 24th April, 1922).

In Ancient Persian times, Zarathustra, the great teacher sometimes called Zoroaster, could still see the Being in the Sun—the all-embracing Spirit, who enkindled the higher man of soul and spirit, to which the ordinary man aspires. He taught of the spiritual forces, which come to the earth with the rays of the Sun—for which reason he was himself called Zoroaster or Radiant Star.

Then came a time, when man no longer saw the Sun as *radiant*, but only *shining*. They spoke in those times of Ra, whose representative on the Earth was Osiris. Ra signified for them the Sun, which moved round the Earth, giving light. The initiates of Egypt and Chaldea saw the forces of light and movement—the *deeds* of the Being, but not the Being Himself; for them, there was One, who represents on Earth the forces of the Sun that man carries within him, and they called him Osiris. He was cut into pieces and strewn over the Earth, for Isis to find again.

By the time of Greece, in the eighth to the fifth centuries before the Mystery of Golgotha, human beings had lost all power of looking into the Mysteries of the Sun, and could only see the effect of the Sun's influence in the environment of the Earth. They beheld the working of the Sun in the ether that fills all the space around the Earth and permeates the human being himself also. The Greek initiates called this ether Zeus.

These were the three aspects of the Sun, of which Julian the Apostate knew, as a tradition; firstly, the aspect of the earthly ether; secondly, the aspect of the light of heaven that is behind the earthly ether—the cosmic life-forces in the activities of water, light and fire ; and lastly the aspect of pure spiritual Being. This is the teaching of the Threefold Sun.

Then came the prosaic and external civilisation of Rome. The only remnant of this knowledge, left for later generations, is the symbol of it in the triple crown worn by the Popes of Rome (London 24.IV.22).

Wisdom and Love

As in the parts of this book related to natural science, the intention is simply to bring examples, in order to encourage further research in the light of the idea of physical and ethereal spaces. With few examples, we shall attempt to understand that in the centuries just before and during the lifetimes of the great mathematicians, who were opening up new ways of thinking, the artists, in their realms of imagination, were also revealing the same secrets!

At a time when the mathematicians began to release their thinking from the prison of rigid Euclidean space-conceptions, the great renaissance painters began to show the way in pictorial imaginations, towards the understanding of perspective, and, furthermore, towards the deeper underlying idea of the hidden, other-worldly spaces from which life proceeds. Though still pictured in the garb of earthly, spatial forms, these other spaces of angelic worlds are brought together with the scenes in earth-space, revealing the *wholeness* of the visible and the invisible worlds in union.

If, through the activity of thinking, the soul has begun to be imbued and enlightened towards the understanding of a "lemniscatory" type of space, in which *physical and ethereal flow together and interweave to form a whole*, it will in time reach to a fuller comprehension of the great cosmic picture—the Coming of the divine Being of the Sun into Earth evolution.

In the years 1909 to 1913, Steiner gave the lectures on the Gospels and the as yet hidden aspects of the Gospel narratives. He explained in great detail the paradoxes concerning the differing descriptions in the Gospels of St. Luke and St. Matthew of the genealogy, birth and childhood of the boy Jesus.[41] The stories in those two Gospels are so very different.

It is not surprising that this aspect of the Christian teaching is very slowly assimilated today; it requires long and open-minded study, through which, however, so very much is explained, which seemed puzzling. Rudolf Steiner showed that there are in fact two different children, who figure in these two narratives; the one described by St. Luke comes from the Nathan line of the House of David, while St. Matthew describes the coming of a child into the Solomon line of the House of David.

The picture of Mother and Child as a religious imagination, existed in antiquity long before the advent of Christianity, and in their way the early Church Fathers knew that the Being had come—as had been foretold, for instance by Zarathustra—Who would bring a quite new element into the whole of human evolution.

The evolution of humanity has two great aspects, which when taken together form a whole—Wisdom and Love.

In very ancient times, consciousness was different from what we experience today, for humanity had not developed the intellect as we now know it in the so-called civilized parts of the world. Just as each individual goes through a path of development, leaving behind the garden of childhood and gradually developing the faculties necessary to deal with the world and with fellow human beings, so it was and is with humanity as a whole. We learn to know the world and ourselves, and in time will come to understand that knowledge and love represent, so to speak, two sides of the same coin. *True knowledge is born of love and love finds its way to knowledge.*

Through the light of the different aspects of thought, the scientist discovers so much wisdom in the created world and becomes himself creative. But without the warmth of enthusiasm for knowledge and the creative process, there would be no science. Only the full human being, using and enhancing all capacities that become possible on the Earth and in the realm of substance, may become free to learn—or not to learn—what love really is, in the same degree that we already know so much of the wisdom hidden in the created world.

The Christian Churches, through the centuries, have proclaimed the truth of Mother and Child, while at the same time they have withheld the ancient truth of reincarnation. In the present century, however, new ways of understanding are beginning to dawn, in the intermingling of cultures and the emancipation of individuality. The cold intellect, without becoming vague and mystical, must be infused with the quality which lives, for instance, in the gaze of a very small child. True art lives in this element, and the artists often portray truths, which ask for the right thoughts with which to perceive and understand them.

In the time of the development of the "consciousness soul", better described as the spiritual, or thinking soul, religion based only on faith does not satisfy large numbers of people, who nevertheless continue in the search for truth, aided often by the most sophisticated achievements of modern materialistic science.

The archaeological discovery of the Qumran texts in 1947 and subsequent research, described in the book about *The Two Jesus Children* by Hella Krause-Zimmer[42] has confirmed that there were, indeed, two families, and that the two boys (as well as the boy John the Baptist) figure in paintings and frescoes, depicting their lives up to the time, when the twelve-year-old Child was found by his amazed parents teaching the Elders in the synagogue.

In S. Ambrogio's picture (Figure 67) one Child is turning quietly away towards his anxious Mother, while the gaze of the other Child is firmly upon him, as he continues to speak.

Rudolf Steiner was able to explain this scene, of which there are a surprising number of pictures still to be found. He was aware of the connection of the two boys, one embodying the Love of Buddha and the other the Wisdom of Zarathustra. He tells of the departure of the ego of Zarathustra, embodied in the slightly older Child, into the other Child, who was then found preaching to the Elders, whose soul was one with the soul of Buddha. The older Child then faded away and later died, to make way for the other, whose soul from then on bore both Wisdom and Love in the highest possible degree.

Much has been lost or expunged of the historical facts, since the beginning of the dark ages in Europe, following the first three or four centuries A.D., but in folklore, in art and in the hidden streams of Christianity, the truths remain. "Today the time has come, when it is urgent that humanity should look back and remember the spiritual way in which Christianity was understood in the first Christian centuries" (London, 24.IV.22).

In the Burg Valeria in Sion, high up in the Swiss Alps, is a painted fresco—very faded—in which the two Families are clearly to be seen, and behind them both stories are depicted (Plate VI). The Jesus Child described by St. Luke is in a winter landscape, with angels on the snowy roof, shepherds and sheep on the slopes behind, and the Father God looking down from the heights. The "Matthew Child" is in a sunlit, Eastern landscape; streams of people, some with black faces, many crowned heads, are pouring down on horseback, with banners unfurled, to where the Three Kings are paying homage to the Child. This Child is standing up and responding actively, while the other little Child is lying down and is surrounded by the golden rays of his aura. A surprising feature of this picture is the house. The two parts, belonging to the two Families, are joined by a central part, which is shared between them and in which the animals are housed. It would seem to be a threefold house!

It is by no means rare to find the two families both depicted, either in one picture or in two separate paintings mounted together. They are clearly to be seen, for instance, in the painting by Hans Memling (c.1480) in Munich, "The Seven Joys of the Virgin". Another beautiful example is an oil painting on two panels in the Fitzwilliam Museum in Cambridge; it comes from the Flemish School in the early sixteenth century (Plate VII). The picture by Maitre Franke (Figure 72) is itself part of a whole, in which both the Adoration of the Shepherds and the Adoration of the Kings are pictured.

In such pictures, Mary and Joseph may seem to be the same people; they are often even dressed alike, while in the great multitude of single paintings, there is little doubt as to which Child is pictured. The one will be upright, standing or sitting, often very active, perhaps holding a ball or an apple, or looking with great interest at some natural object (Plate VIII). The other will be quite or, even in His Mother's arms, almost horizontal, very often on the ground and sometimes on a little square cloth, surrounded by his widely spreading, golden aura (Plates IX and XI).

Why two Jesus Children? The reader must turn to the great wealth of detail in Steiner's lectures, explaining the scriptural texts and telling of all that had to come about in order that the Jewish people might bring into being a Body, with its pure etheric and astral sheathes, worthy to become the habitation of the God, Who had been descending and was now to become Man on Earth. It does not seem difficult to understand that such a human being, into whom the Divine Being could descend, might be one in whom Wisdom and Love would be balanced and fused into one great Whole.

Perhaps surprisingly enough, a helpful thought is at hand, following our attempts to understand anew the human being in his relation to space and time and to the other realms of creation. The conception of the "Verticon", described in Chapter VI, once it has taken root in the imagination, lights up and becomes a guide. Goethe's idea of the "Spiritual Staff" has been clothed in a clear, mathematical thought-form in this concept of the "Verticon." Horizon and verticon belong together; this mathematical concept underlies Steiner's spiritual picture of the "Umkreis" ("Encircling Round") in its relation with the innermost vertical line—the spiritual realm of light—in the upright, human ego-being in physical and ethereal space.

In the practice of Eurythmy and Bothmer Gymnastics, this inner axis or column of light can be experienced. A true experience in Eurythmy of the spiritual nature of the vowel sounds, reaching deeper than a merely intellectual concept, gives access to the certain knowledge of the secret of life in the plant and also in one's own upright, human form. A consciousness begins to dawn of the all-pervading, all-relating quality of Light (Wisdom), and of the all-embracing, creative being of Warmth (Love) in the "Encircling Round". In the new arts of speech and singing and in Eurythmy, we experience the inner column of sound and of light in our upright stature, together with the great horizon's round. Only the Human Form, especially in movement, experienced here on Earth, can hold together and harmonize these two cosmic aspects of human life.

The opportunity is given in the free individual's struggle for balance in life, to grasp the hand of super-human Powers, awaiting the moment in which to help the human being to see anew the Colours of the Rainbow and to hear again the Harmony of the Spheres.

It is of the utmost importance to understand the fact, made clear by Rudolf Steiner, that it is from the time of the scene in the Temple (Figure 67), that one can think of the single person, Jesus of Nazareth, and follow his life from his twelfth, until his thirtieth year (Oslo, 5 and 6.X.13). Then, at the Baptism by John in the Jordan, the Christ Being enters the Man, Jesus of Nazareth. Only after this event, can one speak of Christ Jesus. The Being of the Sun entered into a prepared Human Being, permeating Him more and more during the three years, until the Crucifixion.

In the three years, not only did the Divine Being live among men, teaching and bringing about miracles, healing and the raising of the dead, He experienced bitter loneliness, suffering and the loss of his God-like powers.

"Stage by stage the God became a Man...until the similarity was so complete that he could feel anguish like a man;...on the Mount of Olives...the Christ Being had upon His brow the sweat of anguish... In the same measure in which this etheric Christ Being grew to greater identity with the body of Jesus of Nazareth, in the same measure did the Christ become Man... And forthwith the multitude, who had once gazed in amazement at the manifestations of the super-earthly, wonder-working powers of the Christ Being, no longer stood in astonishment around Him, but stood before the Cross, mocking the powerlessness of the God, Who had become man... From the fulness of divine power, to the complete loss of it—this was the Way of the Passion, a way of infinite suffering, to which was added the sorrowing for a humanity that had come to be as it was at the time of the Mystery of Golgotha. But this suffering gave birth to the Spirit, which was poured upon the Apostles on the Day of Pentecost. Out of this suffering was born the all-prevailing Cosmic Love.

"These are things of which we must be mindful, if we would understand the full significance of the Christ Impulse, as it must be understood in times to come. Men of the future will need to understand it in this way, if they are to make progress along their path of culture and evolution." (Oslo.3.X.13).

Rudolf Steiner's pictures are dramatic, human, and for the most part very understandable, for they dispel many misunderstandings. In the gradual descent into the Earth, the Being of the Sun was first *conceived* at the Baptism by John, in the waters of the Jordan. On the Cross, Jesus of Nazareth felt alone and forsaken, and when the agony was over, the Being was *born*. Through the infinite suffering, the "all-prevailing Cosmic Love" was born out of the cosmos into the world, the divine Love, that had previously been everywhere, around and outside of the Earth, now entered into it.

"When Jesus of Nazareth died on the Cross, at that moment there was born for the Earth, something previously to be found only in the Cosmos" (2.X.13).

This is the archetypal picture of the entry of Life into any earthly realm. In order for life to be born, there must be a complete void, an emptiness, such as is described by the Greek word χάος,—a matriarchal realm, into which new life and ordered form can grow. It is necessary rightly to understand Steiner's use of the words "chaos and cosmos."

Life is not identical with substance, not even with minute particles, such as atoms or cells and their derivatives. The Cross of substance must be there, at this stage of earth evolution; it is necessary that life be born into the three-dimensional world, but it is important to realize that *life is the primary factor and that matter is secondary*. Living substance, in answer to the formative forces of the universe, is born into a realm which, qua substance, is at first "emptier than empty—less than a vacuum."[39].

An ethereal space must be present, if anything new is to be born, whether in plant or animal, or in the spiritual life of human beings. Rudolf Steiner also describes how, when Jesus of Nazareth was finding His way to John in the Jordan, after the departure from Him of the Ego of Zarathustra to make way for the Christ, that with only the three sheathes—physical, ethereal, astral and no ego— He was as though in a condition of "nothingness" (Oslo, 6.X.13). It is this same secret, concerning a condition of "nothingness", through which deep trials of life bring the human soul, that Shakespeare deals in his tragedies. (See L.F. Edmunds).

As modern science develops, the understanding becomes clearer that, rather than to look for the origin of life as part of the substance, it is possible to conceive of non-local origins of a force bringing about development. The conception that all living forms are held and sustained by a formative principle, which remains invisible, unless we acquire "eyes" to see it, becomes quite tenable.

In the living gestures of a human form, it is indeed true to say that one sees, "a spiritual form, filled out with earthly substance". The Risen Body (the Phantom) was not clothed in substance, and therefore not visible to all who were looking.

The Christ Himself suffered solitariness and went into the dark depths of the Earth, in order to redeem the body of the Earth, and the bodies of all human beings. With the Blood that flowed, even the Body was actually received by the Earth. With this, the cosmic forces of Light, Love and Life entered into it, and the Earth became a Seed in the cosmos. (1.II.25, Letter XIX.)

Rudolf Steiner describes how, at the Crucifixion, not only was there darkness over the land, but there was also an earthquake.

> "That earthquake followed upon the darkening of the Sun. It shook the grave in which the Body of Jesus had been laid and the stone covering it was wrenched away; a fissure was rent in the Earth and the corpse was received into it. Another tremor caused the fissure to close again over the corpse and when the people came in the morning, the grave was empty, for the dead Body of Jesus had been received into the Earth," (Oslo, 2.X.13).

This Body was actually received into the Earth, but the Body bore within it the Being of the Sun, and this invisible Etheric Being rose again. For the Earth, this was a macrocosmic event, which took place once and for all time, but it is mirrored in all microcosmic life and repeated in rhythms and cycles of life, ever again, in living things. We have learned to see the plant as an ethereal form, revealed before our very eyes by the substances which fill it out, given to us as nourishment. Every time we plant a seed in the moist, warm and sunlit soil, a similar event takes place, for the seed is not just a little piece of substance only, like a stone, it contains its living germ and will grow. The Christ grew down into the Earth and gave it the forces, whereby the plants continue to grow.

The Christ will not come again in a physical body, for that has already been accomplished. The Second Coming, which is in this century, is into the etheric realm, the world bordering on the physical; it is the realm of the Elemental Beings, and the Angels. The Christ comes today into the realm of those Beings who take care of the life on the Earth.

Our own etheric bodies give us the power of thought and since the fifteenth century, thinking becomes more and more a capacity we can take hold of individually and activate. Therefore the time has come, to grow towards the Mystery of Golgotha, not only through devotion and feeling, but also in the clear light of thinking.

The Mystery of the Sun-Being revealed by the Artists

Once more, let it be said that the intention here is not to attempt an exhaustive study of such a deep and important field, but simply to point to a fundamental, underlying truth. Love will join with the Wisdom of the East, which flows to us from the past, whether we can believe it yet or not; the two belong together and make up the whole. Wisdom and Love together hold the balance in life. The great artists, who painted their Imaginations, to help guide humanity at the dawn of the modern age, clearly knew the hidden Christian Mystery, which we have lost today. It is revealed by the love and tenderness and at the same time, the wisdom, in the faces of the Children as they look at one another, as, for example, in Leonardo da Vinci's, *The Virgin and the Child* (Figure 68), and the similar picture, painted by Bernadino Luini, which is in Milan. The second Child is usually referred to as St. John the Baptist (although he does not carry the little cross, with which he is often distinguishable). In Raphaël's Madone del Duca di Terranova (in Berlin) the *three* Children are clearly portrayed (Figure 69).

So many pictures of the Descent of the Being of the Sun into the darkness of Earth have been created by so many human beings in the various Arts since this great moment in Time. The Love, which poured into the world has been recognized and striven for by countless human beings. The artist knows the meaning of the struggle for creative expression, which can only happen by grace through love of the deed. Now the time has come for *scientists* today to recognize this same principle.

Included here are a very few illustrations of the way artists have portrayed the cosmic and earthly spaces together, from about the 12th century on. Figure 70 dates from the 11th century. Especially at the dawn of the Spiritual Soul, around the 15th century, this polar spatial aspect of the Christian Mystery was pictured by great artists. It is a Mystery, which has only just begun to unfold, for it is hardly two thousand years old!

Over and over again, the great masters, but also the lesser painters, show, on the one hand, the three dimensions of earth space, in stone or wood: cubical shapes of buildings, cradles or tombs, with the step-measure patterns of squares or hexagons side-by-side, in varying degrees of perspective. On the other hand, different ways are employed to evoke the picture of the opposite kind of space, which also features in these surprising events. The hollowed out spaces—concave, and not convex—are clearly evident, and the events are taking place *between the two spaces*.

One only has to *look with thoughts capable of seeing* the ethereal spaces, as well as the three-dimensional one, and one sees a clear message.

We are left free to see this message or not, for pictures always leave us free.

The Annunciation scenes, in which Gabriel appears with the Lily, invariably reveal a winged presence, appearing to a maiden, sitting in an earthly house; three-dimensional, often with the pattern of squares on floor or wall. The Angel has come in, perhaps, through a hollow space in the roof, from a world, where other winged beings are at home. (Wings, we must remember, and also haloes, are pictures of the ethereal, planar world.) In Figure 71, the quaint little angel is tightly holding on to Gabriel's ribbon and gazing longingly back into the world to which he belongs! Often, in the old paintings, the Gospel Word is written on a furling and unfurling surface—a twice-curved surface![19]

And the Child, once arrived, is pictured as, for example, in Plate VIII by Lucas Cranach the Elder. This is the Child described by St. Matthew, very active and alert, studying the objects being shown to him for all the world as though he were a little scientist. Cranach pictures this scene within the darkness of earth, and the little angels looking in from the outside are in a perspective measure! This Child is virtually always vertical, looking wise and awake.

Or else, we may see the Child as in Plate IX, lying horizontally in a cradle (or is it a tomb?). This Child, who was greeted by the Shepherds, while the Angels sang, is often pictured as though hovering, surrounded by His golden aura.

In Figure 72 the Father God, looks out of a hollowed-out space, which is surrounded with red stars in step-measure; in the original, the angels' wings are red too! In this picture, there is a strange inter-relationship between the two spaces. The Mother also, and the Child, with their raying, golden auras, seem not yet to be on the ground, while the animals and their three-dimensional manger, are just on the inside edge of the dark cave of Earth.

The Baptism, less often pictured, is here shown in Figure 73. The Father God looks down from a heavenly space, similar to the one in which the Dove is descending. There are horizontal rings on the surface of the water, in which Jesus is standing. There is a mixture of realism and symbolism in all these pictures, which are, of course, really Imaginations.

Strange, yet with a clear message, is the scene in Figure 74. Crowds of people stand in the aisle—on the earth, while hierarchical beings (are they angels or priests?) are sitting in a perspective, which moves towards and around quite a different space. We are in the nave of a Gothic cathedral, at the far end of which one would expect, either to see the altar, or a screen closing off this further space. In this picture we are confronted with the hidden world in terms of a powerful three-dimensional scene. Can this be an ethereal space? There is much food for thought in this picture.

In Plate X, God looks down from His Heavenly Space upon a circle of people surrounding the altar and the Child, Whose presence transforms this into a Sun-circle—a Seed-space of Future Mysteries. A serious, almost sad mood prevails; this Child looks towards a figure standing there. Is this not Judas?

Rembrandt, nearly two hundred years later, deals very differently with this space. In his *Adoration of the Shepherds* (Plate XI), Rembrandt reveals so wonderfully the secret of the social aspect of this Mystery, (as did likewise Georges de la Tour and others). It is the human beings themselves, who, all together, create the warm, cosmic light-filled space, into which the Child of Love has descended. One person holds the lantern of earthly light in one hand, while with the other he reveals his wonder, looking into the other space of light in the surrounding darkness. Rembrandt's genius shows in a similar way, the Risen Christ, together with the pilgrims at Emmaus; the light, shown also by the white surface of the table-cloth, shines in the darkness (Plate XII).

The Mystery of Golgotha is revealed through history in two ways, by those who were there on the spot, and witnessed the amazing things that happened, and also by others, who were not there physically, but who nevertheless also experienced the event of Golgotha, which happened for the whole Earth. After visiting Tintagel in Cornwall, Steiner described how the Druid priests saw in the elements of water, air, and light, what was happening in space in Palestine.

One Christian revelation is the historical one, represented by the Churches, and celebrated by spacial monuments, while the other is more hidden and is related to the legend of the Holy Grail, on the one hand, and to the legendary Knights of the Round Table of King Arthur and the Celtic Mysteries, on the other.

The two invisible streams of Christianity came together in the ninth century, the

Grail stream, which spread through the blood and hearts of men, moving from East to West, and the pre-Christian, cosmic stream of the Christ of the Sun-Mysteries, which was spread by the Knights of Arthur, from West to East (London, 27. VIII, 24).

Among those who were not direct witnesses in Palestine, belongs St Paul. who, as Saul, even persecuted the Christians, until, in a blinding flash on the road to Damascus, he *saw* and recognized what had happened.

Rembrandt's pictures speak intimately of the Child of Love, this warm, inner light born to human beings in the darkness. His pictures, with their unique handling of the light within the darkness, tell of events between human beings, revealing dramatically the active social lives of men and women in earthly circumstances.

Turner, too, is aware of the secret and is equally a master of the play of light and darkness, but in a very different way. He paints the drama, as it happens out there in Nature, among the elements. He reveals the colours as the "deeds and sufferings of the light" in the darkness, to use Goethe's words.

Where Rembrandt reveals the light in the hidden world of a human heart, or in a circle of human beings, surrounded by darkness (Plate XI) Turner looks for the spiritual aspect of the sunlight—the cosmic, ethereal world of light in Nature. This he seeks to conjure forth in his paintings, to reveal the laws of the elements in living nature (Plate XV). Like Goethe, whom he greatly admired, Turner shows the natural-scientific way to the Sun Mystery.

Many artists, working with Rudolf Steiner in the first Goetheanum, developing a new art of painting—one of the first was the Russian artist, Margarita Sabaschnikowa-Woloschina—have pictured the timeless Christian themes in such a way that the Sun Space, the space of the "Umkreis", is eloquently revealed.

The charmingly physical scenes of the Last Supper, by the painter Grigor, for example, by Giotto in the fourteenth century and by the Meister des Hausbuches (Figure 75), have been raised into pure colour by Woloschina in her imagination of the Last Supper, which shows an unbroken circle of figures.

The pictures of the Resurrection show the ethereal space and its forces very clearly. Mathias Grünewald, for example, in his famous altar pictures in Colmar, paints the great granite blocks of the tomb hurled aside and the Christ rising with tremendous vigour, drawn upward by quite other forces. Chagall painted an almost whimsical scene, in deep blues and a touch of red and yellow, the Crucifiction with also a Resurrection taking place. His stained glass window, in a village church in Kent, also shows the Crucifixion with the quality of the Resurrection already in it.

Fra Angelico (Figure 76), in his gentle and pure way, pictures the empty, three-dimensional space, into which the women are looking, while the Angel, all the time, is sitting right down on the tomb and pointing down and also upward to the Figure rising in the space of light and bouyancy, which the others do not see. Even the water, as it is pictured also in scenes of the Baptism, is rising with the Risen Christ. These early pictures, showing the two spaces, do nevertheless still speak strongly in terms of cartesian space, while Rembrandt leads beyond it.

Liane Collot d'Herbois paints the archetypal scenes in great, transparent, interweaving surfaces and planes of colour. The forms arise out of light-woven colour. Her painting entitled "Nole me tangere" is an imagination of the Sun-Being, still standing on the

Earth and visible to some, *before* his Ascension.(Plate XIII). Beppe Assensa, in his "Easter", has raised the three-dimensional Cross of Earth-substance up into the Resurrection Space—the Space of the Sun. Both spaces are thus united in one, as in a seed (Plate XIV). It is indeed the same space as that painted by Turner, to which he gave so many titles depicting new birth and relating to Goethe's theory of the colours arising between darkness and light (Plate XV). In every seed and wherever life comes into being, the two worlds are joined.

The work of the painter Gerard Wagner creates a bridge between the inner Imaginations to which Christianity has given rise, and the way of Goethe and Turner, in the contemplation of worlds of light and colour in the outer manifestations of earthly scenes. Turner and Goethe and also Wagner show a scientific pathway through art, leading to an understanding of the Mystery of the Sun. The painting in Plate XVI is called by the artist "Plant Growth"; to the scientist it may speak also of the secret of the "Verticon"—of the "Spiritual Staff" of the plant.

Moving through the centuries, we may see a remarkable progression from Imaginations clothed in more physical terms to those which approach more closely to the purely spiritual conception of the modern mathematician, who seeks to understand and describe in scientific terms the eternal truths of the polar worlds of substance and of life.

Suche im eignen Wesen	Seek in your own being
Und du findest die Welt,	And you will find the World
Suche im Weltenwalten	Seek in the rulings of the World
Und du findest dich selbst,	And you will find yourself.
Merke den Pendelschlag	Mark the pendulum-beat
Zwischen Selbst und Welt:	Between Self and World:
Und dir offenbart sich	And it will be revealed to you
Menschen-Welten-Wesen,	Human—World—Being,
Welten-Menschen-Wesen.	World—Human—Being
Rudolf Steiner	Translation: Olive Whicher
Wahrspruchworte, 1935	

The World-embracing Problem of Economics

The Imagination of the Last Super—a historical *and* cosmic event at the heart of Christianity—lives deeply in the heart of humanity, though still largely unrecognized. It has been stated recently that statistics show that one third of the world's population is Christian. More widely spread, however, and by no means restricted to orthodox Christianity, is the simple urge to find ways of living together as individuals and nations, so that none dominates, but all find their place at the Earth's Table.

The task has become an all-human one, as never before; through the modern communication systems, the whole world has, as it were, become our village—our living space; its survival depends on every human being, who strives towards maturity, and this, in our time means finding a balance between thinking, feeling and willing.

Today it is the thinker, who must decide for himself, whether or not the world contains more than the materialistic eye can see.

It is no longer a question of different religions or faiths, but the guidance of their archetypal pictures is accessible also to the thinking of our time, in relation to the tasks facing the modern human family and each single individual today.

We have mentioned the two great spiritual Beings fundamental to existence on the Earth; Lucifer is the Being of Light and Heat, while Ahriman rules amid Darkness and Cold. When they are not held in balance, they are both hostile to life. Steiner makes clear the difference between Lucifer and Beelzebub and he describes in detail the Three Temptations of Christ, one by Lucifer, one by Lucifer and Ahriman together, and one by Ahriman alone. He shows that it is in the nature of the case, in the present stage of evolution, that Ahriman could not be entirely repulsed in the Third Temptation.

Ahriman came to Christ alone and said, "Turn these stones into Bread, in order to show thy power." Rudolf Steiner continues: "Ahriman cannot be driven entirely from the field. Ahriman, Mephistopheles, Mammon (these concepts are synonymous) are hidden in gold (money): in everything however, that brings egoism into play in the material world. Inasmuch as some element of materialism must inevitably be part and parcel of human life, Ahriman must be reckoned with.

"If Christ was truly to help man on Earth, he was compelled to allow Ahriman to work. For Ahriman must work; the material element *must* persist, until the end of Earth evolution. The activity of Ahriman had to remain unvanquished by Christ; Ahriman was not fully conquered. Christ must lend Himself to the struggle with Ahriman, until the end of Earth-evolution, for Ahriman had to remain." (18.XII.13).

The picture of a circle has its earthly and also its cosmic aspect, expressing separateness on the one hand and togetherness on the other. In Figure 75, the Circle around the square, white tablecloth has a break in it, where the one without a halo is busy with earthly matters. Yet the Circle is held together by the Being who reaches into its centre, as into an inner infinitude, where the Lamb is, while St John, "the disciple whom Jesus loved," is pictured in such great contrast to the one, whose attention is turned to his money-bag. All are nevertheless seated round the Table.

It is within the power of every human being to face and overcome the first two of the Three Temptations, but the third is connected with the deepest mystery of all, that of the transmutation of substance. The world in our time is face to face with difficult and *seemingly* insoluble problems in the economic realm, in which not only governments, but every individual is involved.

The picture of turning stones into bread has very many aspects. One is doubtless the task of transforming our one-sidedly quantitative, intellectual thinking, so as to reach the deeper understanding of life, for instance, in the realms of medicine and agriculture. Another is the overcoming of egoism, both collective and individual.

Today it is the turn of the scientists to recognise that there is more to the world than meets the eye, unless it has opened itself to see. In the new developments of Antroposophical Medicine and Agriculture, we have seeds for the future in our hands, which are now beginning to be used in many parts of the world. To forge the bridge of understanding between industrialised science and these new developments is more and more urgent.

The time will come, when it will be generally understood that since the "Turning-point of Time," the seed of Love *is* within the Earth; for ever since that time, there have been human souls, who have known it; and there will be more and more. Many today are being drawn back by Lucifer, following cults, which have their roots in the past. But many know that Ahriman must be faced by a power of intellect equal to his own, yet raised, clarified and warmed through by the quality of the love which will grow from the Seed, which has been sown for the future.

The path inevitably leads through pain and suffering. It is the picture of the Cross of the Three Earth Dimensions, which dominates in the world today. (The cross was actually only introduced as a symbol in the third or fourth century after the Mystery of Golgotha.) Millions are starving in a world of seeming plenty, there is so much suffering, the forests are dying, in an otherwise all too light-hearted world. Humanity, too hangs on the Cross.

Today, it is not only the One Being, the Three-in-One and One-in-Three, Who makes the supreme sacrifice, but men, women and children the world over. Human violence is echoed in our day by the very violence of the Earth herself, as the wrath of the Elemental Beings is expressed in civil and natural catastrophe.

We are called to awaken to what is really happening, and to begin to recognize in truly modern scientific terms the laws and truths, which have always been and always will be those of the ethereal worlds of Spiritual Being.

Rätsel an Rätsel stellt sich im Raum,
Rätsel an Rätsel läuft in der Zeit;
Lösung bringt der Geist nur,
Der sich ergreift
Jenseits von Raumesgrenzen und
Jenseits vom Zeitenlauf.

Rudolf Steiner
Wahrspruchworte

Riddle untold in the widths of Space,
Riddles untold in the rounds of Time!
Only the wakened Spirit can solve them,
holding its own
Beyond the confines of Space,
beyond the flow of Time.

Verses and Meditations

Chapter IX

PAST AND FUTURE

> Assuming heat and similar subjects to be matter, we shall then have a very marked division of all the varieties of substance into two classes: one of these will contain ponderable and the other imponderable matter. The great source of imponderable matter, and that which supplies all the varieties, is the sun, whose office it appears to be to shed these subtle principles over our system.
>
> Michael Faraday*

Cromlech, Dolmen, Tumulus of the Past.

The Celtic Crosses and Standing Stones, left behind by Celtic Christianity, serve also as powerful Imaginations preserved in stone, memories of a past at which we gaze today. The symbolism of plants and intertwining branches speaks of the fact that the Druid priests were still able to work with the healing forces of the world of life, although they could no longer see clearly into the spiritual world. There are patterns in step-measure on the stones and the spirals are also of that kind—Archemedian. But the circle is also to be seen on the cross of three dimensions (Figure 77).

Rudolf Steiner describes the ancient Mysteries of Hybernia as foreshadowing the Mysteries of the Future.[43] The Sun Being was on the way down to Earth and the Druids practiced healing rites. They knew when the starry constellations decreed that the time was ripe to cut mistletoe with a golden knife—as the legends tell—and use it for healing purposes (foreshadowing, too, the modern Weleda medicament *Iscador*, which is made from mistletoe).

We now know the difference between the Archemedian spiral and the logarithmic one, the spiral of life, and we also have learned that there is another aspect to the circle than the one Euclid taught. To bring these modern aspects of mathematics to bear on pictures and symbols left by an earlier humanity, heading downward to take hold of the measure and the substance of Earth, is very instructive. In the pre-Christian pictures, step-measure prevailed, in the Temples and in the Stone Alignments of the megalithic cult-centres, such, for instance, as at Carnac in Brittany.

On his return to the continent from England in the autumn of 1923, Rudolf Steiner described to the friends in Stuttgart something of what he had experienced, while visiting the Druid circles near Penmaenmawr in Wales (14.IX.23):

"You come to realise how these old Druids chose for their most important cult-centres, just such places in which the spiritual, as it approaches mankind, expresses itself to some extent in the quality of the place. Those Druid circles we

---

* The Life and Letters of Michael Faraday (1791-1867) by Bence Jones, Vol 1, p. 215.

visited—well, if we had gone up in a balloon and looked down from above on the larger and the smaller circles, for though they are some distance apart you would not notice that, when you are a certain height above them, the circles would have appeared like the ground-plan of the Goetheanum which has been destroyed by fire. It is a wonderfully situated spot! As you climb the heights, you have wide views over land and sea. Then you reach the top and the Druid circles lie before you—there where the hill is hollowed out, so that you find yourself in a ring of hills, and within this ring of hills are the Druid circles. It was there that the Druid sought his science, his knowledge, his wisdom; there that he sought his Sun-wisdom but also his Nature-wisdom.

As the Druid penetrated into the relationship between what he saw on Earth and what streamed down from the heavens, he saw the whole processes of plant-growth and vegetation quite differently from the way in which they appear to our abstract thought of later days. If we can properly grasp the true quality of the sun, on the one hand the physical rays which enter our eyes, on the other the shadow with its various gradations, we come to realise that the *spiritual* essence of the sun lives on in the various grades of shadow. The shadow prevents only the physical rays of the sun from reaching other bodies, whereas the spiritual penetrates further. In the cromlechs which I have described to you, a small dark place is separated off. But it is only the physical sunlight which cannot penetrate there; its *activity* penetrates, and the Druid, as gradually through this activity he came to be permeated by the secret forces of cosmic existence, entered into the secrets of the world.''

In the dolmen, such, for instance, as in Figure 78: a small, dark space is separated off, through the physical arrangement of the stones; a space into which the physical sunlight does not penetrate, but only its activity. The *spiritual* essence of the sun lives on in such a space.

Do we not recognize once more the archetypal picture, which we have been learning to perceive, when our mathematical thinking reaches the realm of Imagination? It is not in the physical, molecular substance of the stones that the secret lies, but in the way their arrangement on the Earth leaves a small, dark place, separated off—a space in which the *cosmic* sun is active.

Wherever we look for the activity of life, especially where it germinates, whether in plant seeds and buds, in animal realms of fertilization, or in human activities of soul and spirit, this quiet inner space, separated off on the one hand, yet ethereally wide open on the other, is essential for any living development to take place. It is the emptied out space (ausgesparter Raum) and it is indispensible, if, in *any* realm of life, cosmic forces are to work into earthly conditions.

It is a wonderful experience to enter a tumulus in Ireland, for instance, at Knowth, not far from the well-known New Grange tumulus. One finds oneself inside a *hollow cross*, which lies under the mound of earth, in contrast to those standing above ground, where the many crosses are to be seen, standing side by side, or alone. One enters in at the foot of the cross and makes one's way along a dark passage lined with stone slabs, to the actual cross and circle at the end. The construction is such that the reflected rays of the rising sun at the winter solstice shine in at the foot of the cross and up the passage, shedding a glow of light on one of the upright granite slabs, which line the circle from within. As a result of the precession of the equinoxes, the glow does not appear on the stone upon which it would have been seen in Druid times, but it has moved round the circle a small distance. It is still moving round! On the ground within the circle of stones, there lies a stone slab, with a shallow hollow, a saucer-like form.

Archaeologists are beginning to recognise today, that besides being used for burials, these cairns were used by the Druids to enable them to perceive the mysteries of stars and planets, of sun and moon, in relation to the tasks of agriculture, healing and medicine.

Steiner described how the Druid priest, in his Sun-Initiation, lived within the activity of nature and saw the unity of cosmos and earth, not in the form of abstract laws, as we do today, but still experiencing the elemental beings in nature, who sustain life on the earth. Today this experience has completely left us, and the time has come to find a new and modern way of understanding and experiencing these same laws, essential as they are to life on this planet. The elemental beings are still there, whether we experience them or not.[27]

The hidden secrets concerning life were given to humanity in the past by means of the ancient mystery cults and more recently in religious ceremonies. Today and on into the future, as the Spiritual Soul develops in mankind, a true understanding of the forces of life must be rediscovered. The manner in which this will come about must not, and cannot be of a mediumistic kind, but in the clear and conscious thought proper to the free individual and to science, in which mathematics must play a part.

Science must recognize a fresh possibility for itself. Rather than looking to the past for answers, it begins to see that it stands at the threshold of quite new possibilities. Many scientists today do recognize that the future of modern science already lies hidden within its own basic tenets, namely in the observation of *all* phenomena, objectively and without preconceived ideas, irrespective of whether the phenomena belong to material or more psychological or spiritual facts of human experience.

It lies within the reach of science, in a manner properly consistent with its own laws, to penetrate into the spiritual aspects of phenomena, so as to complement the purely atomistic comprehension of the laws of the material realm. The future of science is to learn to know the *whole* nature of a seed and not only its chemical constituents, thus ultimately incorporating the spiritual fact, that since the "Turning-point of Time"— the Mystery of Golgotha— the Earth has become a Seed in the Universe.

The nature of this threshold in science becomes clear as soon as the idea of an ethereal, or polar-Euclidean space becomes clear in thought and complements the cartesian conception of earth-space. Both spaces interpenetrate one another and form a Whole. In the Path-curve Surfaces the pointwise aspect of the form is in a most intimate way integrated into the planewise aspect. The Path-curve Surface (see p. 77) is an ethereal space of a higher mathematical order than the upper loop of the lemniscate. Working in this field, which was rediscovered and further developed by George Adams, Lawrence Edwards has achieved a method of proving that a Path-curve Surface—that is to say, an ethereal space—is actually manifested in the bud of a living plant. Moreover, he can demonstrate that delicate rhythmical movements may be measured along the axis of the bud in the very early stages of its development, and that these rhythmical movements are indeed related to planetary movements, in respect to which the moon acts as mediator. (See Bibliography.)

In principle, there is little difference between what the Druid priest was still able to understand, with the aid of his cromlech, and what the modern mathematician is beginning to understand by means of his path-curve surface and his tree-bud. The difference lies in a different state of consciousness. The modern research is based on the clarity and objectivity of mathematical thinking, albeit in a field of mathematica, which is not yet widely accessible. As, in an age of fading spiritual consciousness, the physical arrangement of stones enabled the Druid to receive information from spiritual worlds, so in our time, we have the opportunity to achieve a growing clarity concerning the spiritual principles involved, for instance in homœopathy, Anthroposophical medicine and in methods of agriculture, which take the modern movement of organic farming and gardening a stage further, through the use of specially made preparations.

For example, the process by means of which, for many years now, the production of the cancer remedy, Iscador, has been carried out in the Hiscia Laboratory of the Lucas Clinic in Arlesheim, Switzerland, requires a similar mode of approach, in order to describe what is there involved. The Misteltoe, from which the medicament is made, grows parasitically on trees and, unlike plants with normal roots, can be considered to have little connection with the earth as such. This principle is retained in the method of preparation of the plant juices, which sees to it that they are mixed under conditions whereby they are removed from the influence of the force of gravity. By means of a high-powered centrifuge, the mixing process takes place, in effect, in a space, which is separated off from the gravitational field of the earth. Such a space, though mechanically contrived, can be compared with the anti-gravitational spaces of plant growth, which, as we have seen, give the opportunity for cosmic forces to work in living substances.

Cancer is a disease of the present time, during which humanity faces a predominantly quantitative world. The disease shows itself in the abnormal proliferation of cells, which would under normal circumstances be controlled through the formative forces of the etheric body, forces which are under attack by the stress under which life finds itself today.

We have here been describing scientific experiments and processes, leading towards a fuller means of dealing with the life-processes which sustain our earth and its inhabitants. It is, however, equally important to realize that the laws of ethereal space and ethereal forces apply also to the social experiment of today. Social forms are being saught today, which would do away with autocracy, and its mode of control by means of a rigid, central authority.

The ideal form of a modern parliament lies in the association of all its single members, gifted individuals, who *together* may find the answers to the social problems and run the country so as to be at peace with all the other countries of the world. In the Steiner Schools, the ideal is to run the school, not with a headmaster or mistress, but with a circle of committed people, all of whom give of their services and take full responsibility together. This ideal, which is at the heart of the Waldorf School movement, is difficult to follow, for it asks for the inner and outer participation of every single individual in the circle. It is essential to strive towards this ideal— "The work of each for the weal of all"—for the future of institutions and nations, and the well-being of humanity depends on it. Wherever this ideal is striven for, in the freedom of the human spirit, there, the guiding Spirit of the Time can give a helping hand.

Modern consciousness—so different from that of the ancient Druids, or event of St Augustine and the other early Christian Fathers—had begun to dawn in the time of Descartes and Desargues and the other originators of modern mathematics and of modern science. We have, in the cause of freedom, lost access to an earlier form of consciousness, in order to achieve, in the fullness of Ideas, a truly human consciousness. Mankind faces adulthood in the loneliness and cold of a civilization face to face with Ahriman, the Spirit of Materialism.

In England, Shakespeare (circa 1564—1616) and Bacon (1561—1626) played great and opposing parts in this drama of a changing consciousness. Shakespeare's great heart always shows the path for today, if we can but understand what he is saying. But while we are living in a "muddy vesture of decay" we cannot hear the angel voices "quiring to the young-eyed cherubins." Only the experience of the "nothingness" will open the way again. It is in the spirit of freedom that we must seek the spirit today, by facing the emptiness within and the emptiness without. The words of the Mysteries, which are the Mysteries of the Future, sound forth, if we would hear them: "Know Thyself! Know the World!"

Rudolf Steiner wrote, in the last of his written letters, published in the News Sheet of the Goetheanum—messages from his sick-bed to those, who had put their hands with his to the plough:

> "In the age, when there was not yet a technical industry independent of true Nature, the human being found the Spirit *within* his view of Nature. But the technical processes, emancipating themselves from the Spirit caused him to stare more and more fixedly at the mechanical-material, which now became for him the really scientific realm. In this mechanical-material domain, all the Divine-Spiritual Being connected with the origin of human evolution, is completely absent. The purely Ahrimanic dominates this sphere.
>
> In the Science of the Spirit, we now create another sphere, in which there is no Ahrimanic element. It is just by receiving in Knowledge this spirituality to which the Ahrimanic powers have no access, that man is strengthened to confront Ahriman *within the world*." (Anthroposophical Leading Thoughts. March 1925).

The Science of the Spirit is the modern science which begins to assimilate into itself an understanding of the Christ, with the help of the Spirit of the Time. With this science of the spirit we learn the true nature of Balance.

Since Rudolf Steiner wrote that message, so shortly before his death, the world has become infinitely more aware of what the confrontation with Ahriman means. We are no longer staring quite so fixedly at the mechanical-material realm, completely *empty* of spiritual values; it begins to hit so hard now, that perhaps the world is waking up.

It is the artist in us, the heart, which begins the waking-up process, but today it must be the thinker, who stands at the threshold of Good and Evil. William Blake, one of the sons of our island—"this jewel, set in the silver sea"—spent the forces of his life at that threshold, shedding light towards the understanding that without ceasing to use the Sword of Mental Fight, we must seek the path of "those feet in ancient time." Blake proclaimed the divinity of the Human Form and saw, with Shakespeare, that "man is the measure of all things."

Each grain of Sand,
Every Stone on the Land,
Each rock and each hill,
Each fountain and rill,
Each herb and each tree,
Mountain, hill, earth and sea,
Cloud, Meteor and Star,
Are Men seen Afar.
William Blake (1757—1827)

The Goetheanum Forms of the Future

During the greater part of the time in which Rudolf Steiner was engaged in the formulating and teaching of Anthroposophy, he was renewing the arts and designing and building the First Goetheanum in Switzerland, with its quite new approach to Form (Figure 79).

While the Goetheanum was being built, during the 1914 war by many members of the different nations engaged in that war, Rudolf Steiner attempted to open people's minds and hearts to this new kind of architecture. It is a style of building which intends to surround human beings with the kind of forms, which will sustain, rather than suck away the Spiritual life-forces. The lectures on this theme are full of descriptions concerning the peripheral, ethereal forces and the way they may be expressed in *surface-like forms*. In lectures to teachers, given in the later years, also in lectures about the teaching of science in schools, Steiner spoke very often in specifically mathematical terms about the theme of the formative principles in such forms.

In her foreward to the 1926 edition of the lectures entitled "*Ways to a New Style in Architecture,*" Marie Steiner quotes a well-known American architect, whose appreciation of the first Goetheanum building knew no bounds:

"The man, who has solved this problem is a mathematical genius of the highest order. He is a master of mathematics, a master of our science: from him we architects have to learn. The man who built this has conquered the heights, because he is master of the depths."

It is well to remember that although Steiner's capacities reached far beyond those of his contemporaries, his way of working was essentially to work with others, inspiring them also to use all their skills—architects, mathematicians, sculptors, painters, masons. He spoke always of "our building."

The development of Temple Architecture, from Greek and Roman times, through the age of the great Gothic Cathedrals to the First Goetheanum, mirrors the picture of the development of geometrical thinking. We have followed it here, from Euclidean geometry, through perspective transformation to the idea of polar-reciprocal forms and eventually to the mathematical formulation of the idea of Ethereal Space.

In the Greek and Roman Temple buildings, it is gravity which prevails. At that time, the human soul was beginning to come to grips with the Earth. In facing gravity, man learns to overcome it. The intuitive experience of learning to stand upright in Euclidean space is such an example.

Through the skill and artistry of the men of the medieval guilds, who built the cathedrals, forms were created, which, though still dominated by the gravitational mode of perception, could draw the soul upward to the heights of the vaulted nave and onward, towards the altar. The soul feels the onward movement, forward towards the altar and the spiritual world beyond it; it is drawn towards the space of the "beyond"—the invisible space, which even architecturally is often hidden by the reredos. (This is the space, pictured in Figure 74 which is made to look so extremely physical, almost to the extent of stating an untruth!)

A predominant experience conveyed by the Gothic cathedral is that of movement in perspective towards a "vanishing point", beyond which it is not yet given one to see. The mathematical laws of a perspective transformation make it clear that this vanishing point, or indeed any points on the vanishing line, do *not form a fixed boundary, but a threshold, beyond which modern mathematical thinking can see.* This threshold is crossed, as soon as the restricting conception of a centric and finite spatial world is overcome. In other words, the "space" beyond the altar is attainable spiritually, but not physically. To the sense of touch is added the sense of sight—of insight—and *the two together create a whole.* The world of substance must become enlightened.

In the Cathedral of Chartres, the late morning summer sun still shines down through the high, coloured windows, and bathes the old stone pillars and floor with breathtakingly ethereal colours; as the sun moves, so the colours move round, as though in a great spatial, colour-filled sundial. It reminds one of the cromlech and at the same time of the colour-flooded space of the first Goetheanum.

Those who described to us the experience of being in the colour-flooded inner space of this building, also called the "Johannesbau" (St John's Building), saw Goethe's theory of colour in action, as the surfaces of colour interpenetrated and created the complementary colours—the *ethereal* colours—which every human eye sees, though for the most part unconsciously. When painting the inner surface of the smaller cupola and in showing others how to help him and to do the same for the larger cupola, Rudolf Steiner developed a new art of painting in thin layers of colour. This is taught in the schools of painting of Gerard Wagner, Liane Collot d'Herbois, Beppe Assensa, Anne Stockton and by many individual artists in the world today.

In designing and building the first Goetheanum, Rudolf Steiner helped the artists to imagine and create a space, in which the working together of planes and surfaces was primary. This is the creative principle in the Goetheanum forms and colours, into which the peripheral forces of the light can flow, engendering new forms and colours. The spaces below the two different-sized cupolas came into being by virtue of the fact that the walls functioned like the inner surface of a mould, so that something living (he compared it to the cake!) might be received into the spaces. Two receptive spaces were open to one another, and the whole was ethereally open to the universe—this was the picture embodied in the St John's Building (Figure 79).

The walls were formed in the art of relief; the artists were taught to chisel in such a way that surfaces arose and not rounded-off forms.

"We learn to love the surface we are creating,—the surface that is coming into being under the mallet. I, for my part, must admit that I always feel as if I could in some way caress such a surface. We must learn to love it, so that we live in it with inner feeling and do not think of it as something that is merely there for the eye to look at" (7.VI.14).

In the earlier temple buildings, the walls were intended to shut off the outer world. "Our building must not shut off anything in the universe: its walls must live, but in accordance with the truth itself. Truth flows into the beauty of the relief" (17.VI.14). The windows were not for the purpose of looking out, but to allow the spiritual beings and the spirit of the world to look in. Light flooded into this space through the different coloured windows, interpenetrating, to create secondary and complementary colours, filling the space with ethereal colours.

In the setting of the columns, which were compared to the human legs, step-measure appeared naturally. Between the columns and the cupola forms, compared to the human skull, lived the forms of the architraves, in which, in perpetual breathing interplay, convex flows over into concave. "The one influences the other—is the complementary of the other."

The architecture of the first Goetheanum deals with the question of the threshold between the two spaces embodied by the two cupolas.

The rostrum is set at the place of transition between the two cupolas, as though at the point of transition of a lemniscatory space. This is the place, in this "House of the Word" or "House of Speech," at which the cosmic Word might speak through the human word to the human beings, who were there to hear it.

We may compare this picture of a building to the picture of a blossom, seen as a lemniscatory form, raised aloft by the plant and revealed through the metamorphosis of the green leaves. In a Rose, for instance, the pollen is received, having been ripened in the Sun-filled air; it then makes its way to the ovules, waiting to receive it in the more earthly of the two parts of the flower; from this there results the fruit. The fruit comes about as a result of the plant having raised its substance into the form of the flower, which can receive sun-like forces of fertilisation into a moon-like receptacle, thus to create new life. (*The Plant between Sun and Earth.*)

The Goetheanum forms speak of the laws of polarity and metamorphosis; they raise these mathematical laws into forms of art, which express the truth of the etheric world. They express not only the truth about the gravitational space, as in the Greek Temple, and of the perspectives of Earth-space, as in the Gothic Cathedral, but they also express the Sun-like Space—the space which before was invisible. The Goetheanum forms express the whole truth, as the plant does, when it blossoms and receives fruit and seed, and as the Human Form does, in its threefold nature.

Science must aspire towards understanding the whole truth. Contemplation, for instance, of the threefold plant, in the light of polarity and metamorphosis, opens the human heart to its task of holding a living balance between the poles of thinking and willing. Words of Rudolf Steiner concerning the effect on human souls of the architecture and works of art, which speak out the truth belonging to the spirit of a particular time, are appropriate also to the contemplation and understanding of the forms in nature, including the form of the human being himself.

"However much study may be given to the elimination of crime and wrong-doing from the world, true redemption, the turning of evil into good, will in future depend upon whether true art is able to pour a spiritual fluid into the hearts and souls of men. When men's hearts and souls are surrounded by the achievements of true architecture, sculpture and the like, they will cease to lie, if it happens they are untruthfully inclined; they will cease to disturb the peace of their fellow men, if this is their tendency. Edifices and buildings will begin to *speak*, and in a language of which people to-day have no sort of inkling" (17.VI.14).

Reduced to a symbol, polarity and metamorphosis are expressed in the form of the lemniscate, *but only when the qualitative difference between the two loops is rightly understood*. One loop may express an earthly process and then the other will express the cosmic pole. Steiner uses this picture constantly, in describing the relations between cosmos and earth, or spirit and body in his threefold conception of the universe and man. But if the reciprocal nature, for instance, of the polarity between head and limbs, is not absolutely clear, confusion arises. The head, for instance, may well be described in one context as the earthly pole and in another as a cosmic space. From the aspect of *substance*—salt, mercury, sulphur—the human being is like an inverted plant; from the more dynamic aspect of *processes*, the comparison is the other way round (See Chapter VI). The head, with its dome is an image of the cosmos.

In conformity with the fundamental principle, that *in living processes, movement originating from the light-filled cosmic peripheries of the universe precedes the fixity of created form*, Rudolf Steiner showed the teachers who were instrumental in founding with him the new art of education, how first to involve small children in an intuitive experience of the form-creating laws of peripheral, universal forces.

At first, through the will, by running forms, and through the movements of Eurythmy, the child begins to become master of otherwise chaotic processes. Then in free symmetry drawing, at first about a vertical line and then about a central form, the child learns to draw an answering *peripheral* form (Ilkley 14.VIII.23 and Torquay 15.VIII.24). It can easily be missed (and often is by those who are not familiar with the true laws of polarity) that here is an occasion for the child to be given the chance to experience intuitively and artistically (without any intellectual explanations) what such a form is saying. It will speak of centric and peripheral—physical and ethereal—processes, in the same way as Eurythmy does, for example, provided the teacher does not stand in the way.

In the first days at a Waldorf School, the child is not introduced to the fixity of the alphabetical symbols; these gradually crystallize out for him, by means of imaginative drawings, coloured and mobile. Later on, in the symmetry exercises, around a central point or a vertical axis (which is not actually drawn in), the teacher will be all the wiser, if he or she has mastered the law of polarity as pictured in the "verticon," and if the laws of polar reciprocation have become a living imagination in the soul. Figure 80 shows examples of the drawings suggested by Steiner to teachers in Ilkley and Torquay.

Surely, this theme reveals a principle, which, raised into pure art, underlies Rudolf Steiner's "seal forms" and forms of the First Goetheanum. To those who have lived with the mathematical law of polar reciprocation and worked with it (not necessarily with the knowledge of *imaginary* points and lines and the *imaginary circle*), it is abundantly clear that Steiner was showing the way to the experience of formative processes, which would speak to human beings once more of the *wholeness* of creation. Compare, for example, the polar forms drawn with respect to an *imaginary* circle[4] in Figure 81 with the art form, Rudolf Steiner's "Sun Seal," in Figure 82.

The step-measure forms of the Celtic and Greek frieze had their task in mankind's development; so too the form of the Standing Stones and the Cromlech. It is interesting that in the Middle Ages the "Ars Lineandi" of the prehistoric stone carvings reappeared in the plaited braids of the art of the Lombards, before the break-through by the mathematicians from Euclidean to projective and then polar forms. In the forms of the Goetheanum, Rudolf Steiner has metamorphosed the ancient forms into those through which the Divine Word may speak to us today.

The spiritual Word speaks differently today, for we must learn to raise the old order into a new and freer mode, without loosing it. The peripheral symmetry speaks very differently to the child's soul, complementing and sublimating the repetitive step-measures of the earth. (There is some sign today that teenage music is breaking through to a form less dominated and deadened by *beat*, as though a human cry is beginning to find answers.)

Having built the Goetheanum—a "Sun-space" on the Earth (Figure 79), Rudolf Steiner saw it vanish into flames, before it was even quite finished; it disappeared on New Year's Eve, 1922, leaving only the foundations.

Shortly before this happened, in a course of lectures entitled: *Man and the World of Stars*, he gave again a graphic description of the descent of humanity from a far-distant past, when there was no experience at all of space, but simply the feeling of living together with all other beings in Time, to our present state, in which, especially in western civilization, the experience and conception of earth-space has become deeply ingrained and dominant, with the resulting feeling of "aloneness" (17.XII.22). From a time when the predominating experience was one of "togetherness", with no spatial experience, mankind has reached an age, in which there is a feeling of solitariness in an overwhelmingly spatial culture.

Of all the Spiritual Beings, apart from the Christ, Who has certainly undergone the purely human experience of Earth-Space, the Archangel Michaël,* who is the guiding spirit of our time, comes nearest to understanding the human predicament. "Michaël is the active Being, the Being, who, as it were, pulses through our breath, our veins,

---

* In pronouncing this Archangel's name in English, it is important to separate the vowels a and é, as is normal in German.

our nerves, to the end that we may actively develop all that belongs to our full humanity in connection with the Cosmos. What stands before us as a challenge of Michaël is that we become active in our very thoughts, working out our own view of the world through our own inner activity'' (17.XII.22).

In a Michaël Age, the age in which humanity attains freedom and independence of thought, and struggles to bring about a consciousness of human rights and brotherly behaviour, we do not sit down and wait to be told what to do or to think; we go ahead and do what we think is right. It is, indeed, a dangerous situation, but a necessary one; between the dark clouds, there are powerful forces of good today, facing so much evil.

It is not that the divine world is no longer there, but that mankind, in a scientific age, with its roots in materialism, has perforce to find a new approach to it.

"But when, through the spiritualizing of purely spatial knowledge, bridges to the divine world have been found again, then what man has gained from the science of Space—in the very period when he has emancipated his thought most drastically from the divine world, ie., since the fifteenth century—all the spatial knowledge he has gained will become important for the divine spiritual world as well. And man can conquer a new portion of the universe for the Gods, if he will but bring the spirit again into the conception of Space." . . . "The science, which, as anthroposophical Spiritual Science, spiritualizes spatial thinking, lifts it again into the supersensible. This Spiritual Science works from below upwards to grasp the hands of Michael stretching down from above. It is then that the bridge can be created between humanity and the Gods." (17.XII.22).

These words were spoken in the Goetheanum, which, a fortnight later, on New Year's Day, 1923, was reduced to ashes and disappeared from Earth-space. It was an experience of bitter pain—a going through the *nothingness*. Rudolf Steiner never paused; lectures continued next morning and work began on the second Goetheanum straight away.

Es wollte im Sinnenstoffe	Made out of Nature's materials,
Das Goetheanum vom Ewigen	The Goetheanum wanted to speak
In Formen zum Auge sprechen:	through its forms
Die Flammen konnten den Stoff verzehren.	Of the Eternal to the eyes of men.
Es soll die Anthroposophie	The flames were able to consume
Aus Geistigem ihren Bau	the matter.
Zur Seele sprechen lassen:	Henceforward Anthroposophia—
Die Flammen des Geistes,	Her edifice formed of the Spirit—
Sie werden sie erhärten.	Shall speak to the inner soul of man
	In words of fire, tempered by the
Rudolf Steiner, April 1923	flames—
(From a note-book)	The flames of the Spirit.
	Verses and Meditations

In the passage quoted on page 100 (14.IX.23), towards the Michaelmas of that year, Rudolf Steiner compared the ground-plan of the Goetheanum to the Druid circles. The Goetheanum, built all of wood, had indeed been consumed by fire, but not the ground-plan, and the second Goetheanum (one of the very first examples of a building in pre-stressed concrete) was already arising on those foundations.

The *living impulse* of the Goetheanum, far from being destroyed, had been strengthened, and at the end of 1923, when the Twelve Holy nights came round again, Rudolf Steiner laid the Foundation Stone of the Goetheanum Impulse anew—this time into human hearts. The small band of human beings, who had shared with Rudolf Steiner the night of the Fire, among them George Adams, were there again, and they experienced—to put it pictorially—how he raised this ground-plan into the hearts of human beings. He founded then, in what he called the "Christmas Foundation Meeting," a World Movement. The meeting lasted from Christmas morning, 1923 to the evening of the first of January, 1924, during which time he gave, and described how to use, a meditation, which he called the "Foundation Stone Meditation." It is printed at the end of this book.[44]

All spiritual movements have their Foundation Stone; St Peter founded his Church upon a Rock (a cube). The Stone of this Foundation is a Pentagon Dodecahedron, the form to which Plato gave the name "Quinta Essentia."

In verses which voice the Speech of the threefold Hierarchies to the threefold Being of Man, Rudolf Steiner laid the seed of spiritual renewal into the hearts of all mankind. From that time on, it is possible for the seed of this Impulse to be freely and consciously received by any human being, who so wills it, recognising that the task of humanity today is to redress the imbalance of materialism in science and art and even in the way it has crept into religion.

This seed is laid into the invisible realm of the human Spirit, through the deed of the Sun-being, where Ahriman cannot reach it and where human beings of any colour, race or creed, who have Goodwill for the Spirit, can find it. In the Holy Nights of 1923/24, the Sun-Mysteries came close to Humanity.

To approach the reality of the Trinity and the threefold nature of the human being in the light of a true understanding of polarities and their inter-relationships is to tread a modern pathway. It guides us in finding new ways of living together, and for governments, it means continuing the struggle towards freedom of thought, human rights and brotherliness in the realm of economics. Slowly, although painfully, the world is finding its way towards a balanced Threefold Social Order; it means work—good work of all kinds. Rudolf Steiner had great confidence in human beings and a very deep experience and understanding of the pathway mankind is treading.

Already in 1910, he had said:
We are... approaching an age in which man will feel himself surrounded not only by a physical, sensible world but also, according to the measure of his knowledge, by a spiritual kingdom. The leader in this new kingdom of the spirit will be the Etheric Christ. No matter what religious community or faith to which people belong, once they have experienced these facts in themselves they will acknowledge and accept the Christ event. Those Christians who actually have the experience of the Etheric Christ are perhaps in a more difficult situation than adherents to

other religions, yet they should endeavor to accept this Christ event in just as neutral a way as the others. It will, in fact, be man's task to develop, especially through Christianity, an understanding for the possibility of entering the spiritual world independently of any religious denomination but simply through the power of good will (15.III.10).

Here, we come full circle, returning—we hope, on a higher curve of the spiral—to the thoughts with which we opened the fields of research in Chapter II. Through the untiring, sacrificial efforts of untold numbers of individual human beings, modern science, the social life and the deeds of world economy will become Christened.

Des Geistes Sphäre ist der Seele Heimat;	The sphere of the Spirit is the soul's true home,
Und der Mensch gelangt dahin,	And Man will surely reach it.
Geht er den Weg des wahren Denkens,	By walking in the path of honest Thought;
Wählt er des Herzens Liebekraft	By choosing as his guide the fount of Love
Zum starken Führer sich,	Implanted in his heart;
Und öffnet er den inneren Seelensinn	By opening the eye of his soul.
Der Schrift, die überall	To Nature's script
Im Weltensein sich offenbaret,	Spread out before him through all the Universe,
Die er stets finden kann	Telling the story of the Spirit
Als Geistverkündigung	In all that lives and thrives,
In allem, was da lebt und lebend wirkt,	And in the silent spaciousness of lifeless things,
In allen Dingen auch,	And in the stream of Time—the process of becoming.
Die leblos sich im Raume breiten,	
In allem, was geschieht	
Im Werdestrom der Zeit.	
Rudolf Steiner [Meditation given to an individual in 1922]. Wahrspruchworte;	*Verses and Meditations.*

EPILOGUE

It has been my intention throughout this book to let Rudolf Steiner speak in his own words as much as possible, in order to show with what earnestness he awaited from the scientists to whom he was speaking, that they should undertake the further development of modern mathematics, in pictorial as well as in algebraic form, so as to create a new way of approach to natural scientific phenomena.

I have attempted, in a pictorial and non-academic way, to make a realm of higher mathematics more generally accessible and to show how widely and deeply the concept of Counterspace—Ethereal Sun-space—sheds light on as yet unsolved questions in science and in life altogether. This Thought-picture sheds light as a lamp does; but the lamp must be trimmed and lit!

There is no question here of a systematic development of any of the many realms open to further research. Rather is the emphasis laid on *exercise*, and on stimulating the hard work necessary in order to develop thoughts with which to continue building the bridge, which exists between modern Natural Science and Rudolf Steiner's Science of the Spirit.

Building bridges is a deed possible only to a *whole* human being. Therefore it is appropriate to let Rudolf Steiner speak once more, in words used by him in Vienna in September 1923:

"The natural scientist applies exactness to the external experiment, to the external observation; he wishes to see the objects in such juxtaposition that they reveal their secrets with exactitude in the process of measuring, enumerating, weighing. The spiritual scientist, about whom I am here speaking, employs this exactness to the evolution of the forces of his own soul. That which he uncovers in himself, through which the spiritual world and human immortality step before his soul, is made in a precise manner, to use an expression of Goethe's.

With every step thus taken by the spiritual scientist, in order that the spiritual world may at last lie unfolded before the eyes of the soul, he feels obligated to be as conscientious in regard to his perception as a mathematician must be with every step he takes. For just as the mathematician must see clearly into everything that he writes on the paper, so must the spiritual scientist see with absolute precision into everything that he makes out of his powers of cognition. He then knows that he has formed an "eye of the soul" out of the soul itself through the same inner necessity with which Nature has formed the corporeal eye out of bodily substance. And he knows that he can speak of spiritual worlds with the same justification with which he speaks of a physical-sensible world in relationship to the physical eye.

In this sense the spiritual research with which we are here concerned satisfies the demands of our age imposed upon us by the magnificent achievements of natural science—which spiritual science in no way opposes but, rather, seeks to supplement... Just as the seed of the plant lies out of sight under the earth, when we have laid it in the soil, and yet will become a plant, so do we plant a seed in the soul in the very action of conscientious scientific research.

He who is a serious scientist in this sense has within himself the germ of imaginative, inspired, and intuitive knowledge. He needs only to develop the germ. He will then know that, just as natural science is a demand of the times, so likewise is supersensible research. What I mean to say is that everyone, who speaks in the spirit of natural science, speaks also in the spirit of supersensible research, only without knowing this. And that which constitutes an unconscious longing in the innermost depths of many persons today...is the impulse of supersensible research to unfold out of its germ." (27. IX. 23.)

Der Grundsteinlegungsspuch der Allgemeinen
Anthroposophischen Gesellschaft, Gegeben durch Rudolf
Steiner in Dornach, Schweiz. 25. Dezember 1923 bis
1. Januar 1924

Menschenseele!
Du lebest in den Gliedern,
Die dich durch die Raumeswelt
Im Geistesmeereswesen tragen:
Übe Geist-Erinnern
In Seelentiefen,
Wo in waltendem
Weltenschöpfer-Sein
Das eigne Ich
Im Gottes-Ich
Erweset;
Und du wirst wahrhaft leben
Im Menschen-Welten-Wesen.

Denn es waltet der Vater-Geist der Höhen
In den Weltentiefen Sein-erzeugend:
Seraphim, Cherubim, Throne,
Lasset aus den Höhen erklingen,
Was in den Tiefen das Echo findet;
Dieses spricht:
Ex Deo nascimur—
Aus dem Göttlichen weset die Menschheit.
Das hören die Elementargeister
Im Osten, Westen, Norden, Süden:
Menschen mögen es hören.

Menschenseele!
Du lebest in dem Herzens-Lungen-Schlage,
Der dich durch den Zeitenrhythmus
Ins eigne Seelenwesensfühlen leitet:
Übe *Geist-Besinnen*
Im Seelengleichgewichte,
Wo die wogenden
Welten-Werde-Taten
Das eigne Ich
Dem Welten-Ich
Vereinen;
Und du wirst wahrhaft fühlen
Im Menschen-Seelen-Wirken.

Denn es waltet der Christus-Wille im Umkreis
In den Weltenrhythmen Seelen-begnadend.
Kyriotetes, Dynamis, Exusiai
Lasset vom Osten befeuern,
Was durch den Westen sich formet;
Dieses spricht:
In Christo morimur—
In dem Christus wird Leben der Tod.
Das hören die Elementargeister
Im Osten, Westen, Norden, Süden:
Menschen mögen es hören.

Menschenseele!
Du lebest im ruhenden Haupte,
Das dir aus Ewigkeitsgründen
Die Weltgedanken erschließet:
Übe Geist-Erschauen
In Gedanken-Ruhe,
Wo die ew'gen Götterziele
Welten-Wesens-Licht
Dem eignen Ich
Zu freiem Wollen
Schenken;
Und du wirst wahrhaft denken
In Menschen-Geistes-Gründen.

Denn es walten des Geistes-Weltgedanken
Im Weltenwesen Licht-erflehend.
Archai, Archangeloi, Angeloi,
O lasset aus den Tiefen erbitten,
Was in den Höhen erhöret wird;
Dieses spricht:
In des Geistes Weltgedanken erwachet
  die Seele.
Das hören die Elementargeister
Im Osten, Westen, Norden, Süden:
Menschen mögen es hören.

In der Zeiten Wende
Trat das Welten-Geistes-Licht
In den irdischen Wesenßtrom;
Nacht-Dunkel
Hatte ausgewaltet;
Taghelles Licht
Erstrahlte in Menschenseelen;
Licht,
Das erwärmet
Die armen Hirtenherzen;
Licht,
Das erleuchtet
Die weisen Königshäupter.

Göttliches Licht,
Christus-Sonne
Erwärme
Unsere Herzen;
Erleuchte
Unsere Häupter;
Daß gut werde,
Was wir aus Herzen
Gründen,
Aus Häuptern
Zielvoll führen wollen.

The Foundation Stone Meditation of the General Anthroposophical Society, given by Rudolf Steiner in Dornach, Switzerland (25.XII.23—1.I.24)

Soul of Man!
Thou livest in the Limbs
Which bear thee through the world of Space
Into the ocean-being of the Spirit.
Practise *Spirit-recollection*
In depths of soul,
Where in the wielding
World-Creator-Life
Thine own I comes to being
Within the I of God.
Then in the All-World-Being of Man
Thou wilt truly *live*.

For the Father-Spirit of the Heights
　holds sway
In Depths of worlds begetting Life.
Seraphim, Cherubim, Thrones!
Let this ring out from the Heights
And in the Depths be echoed,
Speaking:
　　Ex Deo nascimur.
　　From God Mankind has Being
The Elemental Spirits hear it
In East and West and North and South:
May human beings hear it!

Soul of Man!
Thou livest in the beat of Heart and Lung
Which leads thee through the rhythmic tides
　of Time
Into the feeling of thine own soul-being.
Practise *Spirit-mindfulness*
In balance of the soul,
Where the surging
Deeds of the World's Becoming
Do thine own I unite
Unto the I of the World.
Then 'mid the weaving of the Soul of Man
Thou wilt truly *feel*.

For the Christ-Will in the encircling
　Round holds sway
In the Rhythms of the Worlds, blessing
　the Soul.
Kyriotetes, Dynamis, Exusiai!
Let this be fired from the East
And through the West be formèd,
Speaking:
　　In Christo morimur.
　　In Christ Death becomes Life
The Elemental Spirits hear it
In East and West and North and South.
May human beings hear it.

Soul of Man!
Thou livest in the resting Head
Which from the ground of the Eternal
Opens to thee the Thoughts of Worlds.
Practise *Spirit-vision*
In quietness of Thought,
Where the eternal aims of Gods
World-Being's Light
On thine own I bestow
For thy free Willing.
Then from the ground of the Spirit in Man
Thou wilt truly *think*.

For the Spirit's Universal Thoughts
   hold sway
In the Being of all Worlds, craving for Light.
Archai, Archangeloi, Angeloi!
Let this be prayed in the Depths
And from the Heights be answered,
Speaking:
   Per Spiritum Sanctum reviviscimus.
   In the cosmic Spirit-Thoughts
   the Soul awakens.
The Elemental Spirits hear it
In East and West and North and South:
May human beings hear it.

At the turning-point of Time
The Spirit-Light of the World
Entered the stream of Earthly Being.
Darkness of Night
Had held its sway;
Day-radiant Light
Poured into the souls of men:
Light that gives warmth
To simple Shepherds' Hearts,
Light that enlightens
The wise Heads of Kings.

O Light Divine,
O Sun of Christ!
Warm Thou our Hearts,
Enlighten Thou our Heads,
That good may become
What from our Hearts we would found
And from our Heads direct
With single purpose.

Translation: George Adams.

NOTES

INTRODUCTION AND CHAPTERS I AND II

1 *Anthroposophy* is the name given by Rudolf Steiner to his teaching; it is a modern spiritual and scientific path of knowledge, leading towards an understanding of the relationship of the human being both to the material and the spiritual aspects of life, Anthroposophy is not a religion, but recognises that the Christian Mystery—past, present and future—lies at the heart of all the religions. The word *Anthropos* refers to the Human Being and *Sophia* to Wisdom.

Information concerning the centres of Anthroposophical work throughout the world will be supplied by the Secretariat, Goetheanum, 4143 Dornach, Switzerland, which can give the required addresses for any country. This includes, for example, Educational, Medical and Agricultural centres, and also the various national Anthroposophical Societies, of which the Goetheanum is the world centre.

CHAPTER III

2 Terminology and Translation. Rudolf Steiner used the German language creatively, in order to find words in which to express the actual language of the Spirit, for which the created languages have become too rigid and formal. He chose the German language as a basis, because it is still maleable, and although he could certainly have lectured in English, had he so wished, he always refused, saying that it was difficult enough to translate the Words of the Spirit into German.

George Adams had a close relationship to Rudolf Steiner in the difficult task of introducing Anthroposophy to the English-speaking world. He interpreted personally over a hundred lectures, was present very often when interviews were arranged, and he had opportunity for consultation with Rudolf Steiner concerning the problems of translation into English.

For instance, Rudolf Steiner asked that *Philosophie der Freiheit* be translated as *Philosophy of Spiritual Activity*, saying that it would be impossible to convey the spirit of the German word *Freiheit*, with its wide open sound, by using a word ending with the suffix *dom*. It is in this sense, too, that George Adams prefers the beautiful English word *ethereal*, to the ugly-sounding word *etheric*. Another suggestion made by Rudolf Steiner was that preferable to the clumsy expression *Consciousness Soul*, would be *Spiritual Soul* for *Bewusstseinseele*.

Furthermore, as well as using the mathematical terminology, which is found in the new, as well as the classical textbooks of Synthetic, or Projective Geometry, Adams used a freer and more pictorial terminology. (See Chapter IV). Moreover, he still used the expression *"synthetic"* and *"projective"* mostly in a synonymous way, whereas in the modern literature a distinction is made between Synthetic and Projective Geometry.

3 A.N. Whitehead, Mathematics in *Alfred North Whitehead, Science and Philosophy*, p. 285 (Philosophical Library, New York, 1974.)

CHAPTER IV

4 René Descartes (Cartesius). See F. Cajori: *A History of Mathematics*, Macmillan, New York, 1901, who quotes from a letter to Mersenne, how he excused himself for not more whole-heartedly following the direction in pure mathematics, which was being pursued by his friends, Girard Desargues and Blaise Pascal. His interest lay in developing a mathematical method more immediately applicable in practice to physics, as it was then beginning to develop.

Concerning the realm of the *Imaginary* in mathematics, which was developed in the nineteenth century, see the Bibliography, for example, under Adams, Locher, Edwards.

CHAPTER V

5 First published by George Adams in Anthroposophical Quarterly, journal of the Anthroposophical Society in Great Britain (now called *Anthroposophy Today*).

6 The new art of Eurythmy, created by Rudolf Steiner, and also the new form of Gymnastics (see Note 20 and Bibliography), which he encouraged and helped Fritz von Bothmer to begin creating for children in schools, are based on the understanding and experience of the ethereal, planar forces of *levity*, in interplay with the downward-pulling forces of gravity. The one-sided conception of human movement, based solely on the physical-mechanical picture of the parts of the body, is thus superceded. Both aspects, of course, belong together, and it is becoming more and more evident that the one-sided picture of human movement, exaggerated as it has become in some sports today, has a degenerative influence on body and mind. Many illnesses, such, for instance, as spinal problems, stem from the domination in the soul of the idea that the body is subject to the gravitational laws alone, like the mechanical movements, which take place in three-dimensional space. Here the true imagination of the levitational forces of the ethereal world is sadly absent. The light-filled imaginations of a planar, ethereal space can have a powerful influence on the physical organism and on the psychological disposition.

7 That the ethereal body or body of formative forces is to be apprehended through the quality of planes and surfaces is demonstrated by the different approach to massage, developed by Rudolf Steiner and Ita Wegman and established further by Margaretta Hauschka.

8 Goethe's introduction of the study of morphology is brought out especially in his essays on *The Metamorphosis of the Plant* and *The Spiral Tendency in Plants*. See *Geothe's Wissenschaftliche Schriften*, edited by Rudolf Steiner in the edition published by Kürchner: Erster Band, Union Deutche Verlagsgesellschaft, 1883. English: *Goethe's Botanical Writings*, Bertha Mueller, University of Hawaii Press, 1952. (See Bibliography.)

9 The Lemniscate of Bernoulli: for every point of this figure-of-eight curve, the multiple of the distances to the two foci is constant. This law makes no distinction in quality between the two loops and foci. Rudolf Steiner uses this curve, or variations of it, again and again, to call forth a picture of *qualitatively opposing forces* and processes. In Plate II and Figure 35, the curves arise in the interplay of centric and peripheral, that is, pointwise and tangentially created circles. The two foci then become pictures of *qualitatively opposite* points, one centric and the other functioning as an *infinitude within*, or *star-point* (a "point of lines"). The colouring emphasizes the qualitative polarity and reveals the convex and concave (centric and peripheral) aspects of the two realms. The Cassini ovals, outside the lemniscate, grow more and more circular, until they become a circle in the infinite (which is a straight line). The egg-shaped curves, moving outward, will merge with the lemniscate, while moving inward, they degenerate into the two focal poles. The law of common multiple shows each opposing pair of egg-curves to be actually *one curve*, only *appearing* in their pictorial manifestation as though divided. (For more detail, see the notes in Chapter VI of *The Plant between Sun and Earth*).

10 Lemniscatory Space-formation. See Rudolf Steiner's lecture course: *Das Verhältnis der verschiedenen naturwissenschaftlichen Gebiete zur Astronomie*, 1.—18. January 1921, Rudolf Steiner Verlag, 1983, GA 323. English translation: in preparation, Mercury Press, Spring Valley, NY.

CHAPTER VI

11 Valborg Werbeck-Svärdström: *Die Schule der Stimmenthüllung*. The first edition of this book appeared in 1938; Frau Werbeck was just beginning to establish her work in voice-training in Rudolf Steiner House in London, when the forces of opposition interposed with the outbreak of war.

12 The picture in Figure 43 is of Isabella de Jaager and Marie Savitch in 1924, two of the early pioneers of Eurythmy in Dornach, during the lifetime of Rudolf Steiner. Eurythmy is the new art of movement created by Steiner, which he called "Visible Speech" and "Visible Song" (See also Note 6).

13 Steiner established his conception of man as being of a threefold nature in relation to the spiritual attributes of thinking, feeling and willing and the three bodily systems of head, heart and limbs, thus enhancing the present idea, that man is a being of soul and body (mind and body) only. It is a very detailed spiritual and physiological description, which underlies his whole teaching and, in his view, represents the one thing in it, which is entirely new.

14 Gravity is a dominant force in the realm of the element of earth. Passing from this element to those of water, air and warmth, or heat, we perceive it manifesting less and less, inasmuch as substance decreases. Steiner describes the four ethers (not to be confused with the idea of the "ether", which flourished in the nineteenth century), and he attributes them to the ethereal world. He calls them: *Life-ether*, *Chemical-ether*, *Light-ether* and *Warmth-ether*. The force which becomes progressively dominant in the movement from water to warmth is the "negative" or anti-gravitational force, to which he applies the word "Leichte", which we translate as "Levity" (see page 41). This is the force, which opposes the law of gravity and rules in the realm of the so-called ethers. In his science courses, Steiner indicates the direction science must take to recognise these forces at work, even in substance. The "universal forces" work even into substance and must even be conceived to be at work in mechanics (see under Adams and Gschwind in the Bibliography).

15 Leonard Nilsson: *Ein Kind entsteht*. Mosaik Verlag with illustrations by Bernt Forshland.

16 Wolfgang Schaumann, who is responsible for the Bio-dynamic Agricultural Movement in Germany, put these microscopic photographs of growing-points at the disposal of this publication.

17 Frits Wilmar: *Vorgeburtliche Menschenwerdung*, Mellinger Verlag, Stuttgart, 1979.

18 The printed reproduction of Rudolf Steiner's sketch, made during a question and answer session, during the lecture course of April 1922 in The Hague, is in outline; I have added the shading.

19 The "zweimal—gebogene Fläche" (twice-curved surface) is a conception of form, which is fundamental to Steiner's artistic conception of the Goetheanum forms, in which "positive" and "negative" surfaces are in continual, living interplay. This is the mode in which he translates the laws and qualities of the ethereal world into art forms, which, like all sculptural and architectural forms, must, of course, appear in physical space. The twice-curved surface is exactly conceived of in the mathematical description of a "projective plane", which does not have an upper and an underside, as does a finite plane. Hence the lemniscatory twist, (the "Mobius strip"), which describes the property of a projective plane. This calls for further study, to which access will be found in the Bibliography.

20 Eurythmy relates and educates in the child the ethereal, anti-gravitational experience of human movement (see also Note 6). Bothmer Gymnastics does this too, provided that Bothmer's descriptions concerning the *space* in which movement takes place are fully understood. See Fritz Graf von Bothmer: *Gymnastische Erziehung*, Stuttgart, 1981, and an earlier English edition, *Gymnastic Education*, Stuttgart and London 1959.

21 Goethe's essay on the *Spiral Tendency in Plants* (see note 8). See also Adams and Whicher : *The Plant between Sun and Earth*.

22 From the book: *The Anatomical Drawings of Andreas Vesalius, with Introduction, Annotations and Translations* by J.B. de C.M. Saunders and Charles D. O'Malley. New York, 1982. The actual woodcuts are of unknown origin, thought to be by an Italian artist of the late renaissance.

23 "We think with our bones", see for example, the lectures of 7th and 8th January 1924. G.A. 319.

24 Rudolf Steiner: *Die Geheimwissenschaft im Umriss*, 29th edition, Dornach 1977, GA 13. *Occult Science—an Outline*, Chapter IV. London, latest reprint 1984.

25 Rudolf Steiner: *Christus in Verhältnis zu Luzifer und Ahriman—Die dreifache Wesensgestaltung*, Linz 18.V.15: In *Das Geheimnis des Todes* GA 159/160, 2nd edition, Dornach 1980. *Christ in Relationship to Lucifer and Ahniman,* Spring Valley, N.Y. 1978.

26 References to a space of this kind, with processes polar to the known forces of the earth, and particularly in relation to the sun, occur frequently in lectures, especially after 1919. For example: *Die Wissenschaft vom Werden des Menschen*, 6th lecture (26.VIII.18) GA 183, 2nd edition, Dornach 1987; *Geisteswissenschaftliche Impulse zur Entwickelung der Physik*, Stuttgart 1st—4th March, 1920, GA 321, 3rd edition, Dornach 1982. English: *Warmth Course*, Spring Valley, New York (Mercury Press) 1980. *Das Verhältnis der Verschiedenen Naturwissenschaftlichen Gebiete zur Astronomie*, Stuttgart 1.—18. I. 1921 (lectures 15 and 16) GA 323, 2nd edition, Dornach 1983; English translation in preparation by Anthroposophic Press, New York and Rudolf Steiner Press, London. *Menschenwerden, Weltenseele, Weltengeist*, Dornach 22. VII.—20. VIII. 1921, GA 206, 1st edition, Dornach 1967 (lecture of 24.VII.21). English: *Man as a Being of Sense and Perception, London 1958.*

27 Rudolf Steiner: *Initianswissenschaft und Sternenerkenntnis*. Dornach, London, Stuttgart, 27. VII.—16. IX. 1923, GA 228, 1st edition, Dornach 1964. *Man in the Past, Present and the Future and the Sun Initiation of the Druid Priest and his Moon Science*, London 1966.

CHAPTER VII

28 Directions for making and using the Bio-dynamic Preparations are available by request (see Note 1).

29 Lawrence Edwards taught as a Class Teacher and teacher of mathematics in the Edinburgh Rudolf Steiner School since 1945. He came regularly every year for twelve years to study with George Adams, until the latter's death in 1963. He is the first to show in practical terms, the validity of the concept of the vital space at the growing-points of plants.

30 John Wilkes is in charge of the Sculpture department of Emerson College, Forest Row, Sussex, England, and founder of the *Wirbela Flow Design Research Institute* of the same address.

31 Fundamental to George Adams' scientific impulse is the morphological, picture-forming aspect of synthetic geometry. He was very appreciative of the works of D'Arcy Wentworth Thompson *On Growth and Form* (Cambridge University Press, 1942) and of Theodore Andrea Cook: *The Curves of Life* (Constable and Co. 1914), but even more of the little known work of J. Bell Pettigrew, the Scottish physician, surgeon and anatomist, who compiled three volumes, very fully illustrated, entitled *Design in Nature* (Longmans, Green and Co. 1908). Adams was particularly interested in Pettigrew's researches into the dynamics of bird flight, and of locomotion in animals and the human being, revealing a lemniscatory form inherent in animal and human movement. His imagination was fired by Pettigrew's discovery in 1858, that the muscle-fibres of the heart are coiled upon each other in seven layers, with the direction of the fibres taking on a form which deeply interested him. Following Edwards' discovery, after the death of George Adams, we now know that the path-curve surfaces Adams was investigating are indeed revealed in the forms of the human heart.

32 Take a Growth Measure (Figure 20 p. IV.21), and transform it by projection, so that the function of the point at infinity is taken by a point in the finite (see Figure 58b). It is the type of measure, the *quality* of which is revealed in the sequence of a vertebral column and—though not always quite so clearly—in the sequence of the leaves of a plant between hypocotyl and calyx. Thus, the vertical axis of both human being and plant is pictured as a line functioning as an infinitude within and existing between two points, both of which may be considered as functional infinitudes. It is interesting that the Fibonacci series, which is a special case of a growth measure, may be found in the sequence of leaves in some plants.

33 See the works of Lili Kolisko, Ehrenfried Pfeiffer, Agnes Fyfe, Rudolf Hauschka, A. and O. Selawry and others, the most recent publications being: A. Selawry: *Metal-funktionstypen in Psychologie und Medizin*, Heidelberg 1985, and *Ehrenfried Pfeiffer*, Dornach 1987. See J Bockemühl (and others), *Towards a Phenomenology of the Etheric World,* Spring Valley, N.Y. 1985.

34 Thomas Meyer, *D.N. Dunlop, Ein Zeit und Lebensbild*, Dornach 1987. English translation in preparation

35 Evelyn Fox Keller: *A Feeling for the Organism. The Life and Work of* Barbara McClintock, New York, 1983.

36 See, for example, Frits Wilmar : *Vorgeburtliche Menschenwerdung*, Stuttgart 1979. See also: *Funktionelle Anatomie des Nervensystems*, by J.W. Rohen, Stuttgart—New York 1985.

37 David Bohm: *Wholeness and the Implicate Order*, London/New York reprinted 1984, and *Causality and Chance in Modern Physics*, London/New York 1984; Rupert Sheldrake: *A New Science of Life*, London/New York, reprinted 1984; Fritjof Capra: *The Turning Point*, New York 1982. Briggs and Peat, *Looking Glass Universe,* New York 1984.

38 *Continental Drift. A Study of the Earth's Moving Surface*, by D. H. and M.P. Tarling. *Die Tetraeder-Struktur der Erde* by Hans-Ulrich Schmutz, Stuttgart, 1986.

CHAPTER VIII

39 See Note 26. In Steiner's conception, the Sun is the Heart of our universe and the heart of Man is a microcosmic Sun. Both have their earthly and their cosmic aspects, which are polar-reciprocal. In contemplating the picture of the Threefold Human Being in the light of the Sun-Earth polarity—the cosmic *and* earthly aspects of both head and limb-system, with the Heart in the balance between them—we are on a path of approach to the Michaël Mystery, in a manner in which this Mystery can speak within us today. In his Letter of 31. VIII.24 (*Anthroposophical Leading Thoughts*), Steiner wrote: "The Knowledge of Nature acquired during the age of materialism can be comprehended in the soul's inner life in a spiritual way. Michaël, who has spoken 'from above', can be heard 'from within', where he will begin to dwell. Speaking imaginatively, this may be expressed as follows: The Sun-nature, which for long periods man received only from the Cosmos, will begin to shine within his soul. He will learn to speak of an 'Inner Sun'. This will not prevent him from knowing himself to be an earthly being during his life between birth and death; but he will recognise that this his earthly being is *led by the Sun*. He will learn to feel as a truth, that a being places him, in his inner nature, into a light, which shines indeed upon earthly existence, but which is not enkindled within it. In the dawn of the Michaël Age it may still seem as if all this were very remote from humanity; but '*in the spirit*' it is near: it only needs to be 'seen'. A very great deal depends upon this fact, that the ideas of man do not merely remain 'thinking', but in thought develop *sight.*''

40 George Blattmann—*Gestirn und Gottheit*, Stuttgart, 1972; *The Sun—The Ancient Mysteries and a New Physics*, Edinburgh and London 1985.

41 See under Rudolf Steiner in the Bibliography; see also works of Emil Bock, Stuttgart and Edinburgh.

42 Hella Krause-Zimmer: *Die Zwei Jesusknaben in der Bildende Kunst*, Stuttgart 1977; *Le Problème des Deux Enfants Jésus et sa Trace dans l'Art*, Paris 1977.

CHAPTER IX

43 The Hybernian Mysteries: In recent decades, popular interest in the Druid rites has awakened, often in an all too trivialized form, revealing the influence of both opposing Powers, Lucifer and Ahriman, and sometimes resulting in the degradation of a most significant truth relating to human evolution. Thoughout his teaching, Rudolf Steiner continually refers to the true Rosecrucians, for Anthroposophy is indeed the modern form of Rosecrucianism. In a course of lectures given in Budapest in June 1909, entitled *Rosecrucian Esotericism*, he describes how the great individuality, who was Christian Rosenkreuz foresaw what great demands of understanding would be made by rationalistic thought, and how he realized that already in those centuries it had become necessary to promulgate all spiritual knowledge in a form demanded by the modern age. "The Rosecrucians were obliged to work for an era, when man's thinking would be guided by mathematical principles. They were obliged to make their preparations with this in view and hence were entirely misunderstood" (3.VI.09).

The relationship of the development of mathematics with the unveiling of Rosecrucian Esotericism in Anthroposophy is also as yet very little understood. In the lecture course given in January, 1924, *Mysterien des Mittelalters*, (*Rosecrucianism and Modern Initiation*), Rudolf Steiner describes the polaric experiences undergone by the pupil in the original Rosecrucian School between 1235 and 1315. This is not Eastern, but Western esotericism. He underlines the fact that there was even at that time no question of mediumistic experiences, but a foreshadowing of the modern, clear and objective thoughts and perceptions, towards which humanity was then developing. "It was a tremendous, original human striving, related to inner revelation and outer enlightenment of Nature" (5.I.24). This modern path reopens the understanding of the soul to the elemental beings alive in Nature.

44 The Foundation Stone is the name of the meditation, which lays the foundations for the transformation of the Ancient Mysteries into those proper and right for present and future time. It was given by Rudolf Steiner at the founding meeting of the General Anthroposophical Society in Dornach, Switzerland, a year after the first Goetheanum was burnt down, and while the present Goetheanum was being built. The meeting took place between 24th December, 1923 and 1st January, 1924.

Two books to be recommended which deal with the Foundation Stone meditation (not yet translated into English) are: Jörgen Smit: *Geistesschulung und Lebenspraxis*, and Athys Floride: *Stufen der Meditation*, both published in 1987 by the Philosophisch-Anthroposophische Verlag am Goetheanum, CH-4143, Dornach.

BIBLIOGRAPHY

Works by Rudolf Steiner referred to in the text.

1883—97		*Goethe's Naturwissenschaftliche Schriften* GA 1, 3rd edition, Dornach 1986. The collected introductions, footnotes and explanations to Goethe's scientific works by Rudolf Steiner, published in Kirschner's "Deutschen National-Literatur."
	Translation	Goethean Science, Spring Valley, N.Y. 1988.
1894		*Die Philosophie der Freiheit*, GA 4, 14th edition, Dornach 1978
	Translation	*Philosophy of Freedom*, London 1979.
	Translation	*Philosophy of Spiritual Activity*, New York 1986
1901		*Die Mystik im Aufgange des neuzeitlichen Geisteslebens und ihr Verhältnis zur Modernen Weltanschauung*, GA 7, 5th edition, Dornach 1960.
	Translation	*Mysticism at the Dawn of the Modern Age*, with a foreword by Paul Marshall Allen, New York 1980.
1902		*Das Christentum als Mystische Tatsache und die Mysterien des Altertums*, GA 8, 8th edition, Dornach 1976.
	Translation	*Christianity as Mystical Fact*, London 1972
1904		*Wie Erlangt man Erkenntnis der Höheren Welten?* GA 10 22nd edition, Dornach 1975.
	Translation	*Knowledge of Higher Worlds and its Attainment*, London 1985.
1910		*Die Geheimwissenschaft im Umriss, GA 13, 26th edition*, Dornach 1977.
	Translation	*Occult Science*, an Outline, London 1984.
1910—13		*Vier Mysteriendramen*, GA 14, 4th edition, Dornach 1981.
	Translation	*The Four Mystery Plays*, London 1983.
1913		*Die Schwelle der Geistigen Welt*, GA 17, 6th edition, Dornach 1972.
	Translation	*The Threshold of the Spiritual World*, London 1956.
1919		*Die Kernpunkte der Sozialen Frage*, GA 23, 6th edition, Dornach 1976.
	Translation	*Towards Social Renewal, The Threefold Commonwealth*, London 1977.
1923—24		*Die Grundsteinlegung der Allgemeinen Anthroposophischen Gesellschaft*, 1923—24. Selection from GA 260, 5th edition, Dornach 1986, comprising the "*Grundsteinmeditation*". and its Rhythms.
	Translation	*The Foundation Stone*, compiled by George Adams, London 1957; second edition, compiled by Michael Wilson, London 1979.
1923—25		*Mein Lebensgang*, GA 28, 8th edition, Dornach 1982.
	Translation	*The Course of my Life*, New York 1988.

1924—25		*Anthroposophische Leitsätze*, GA 26, Dornach 1982.
	Translation	*Anthroposophical Leading Thoughts*, London 1985
		Wahrspruchworte, GA 40, 5th edition, Dornach 1981.
	Translation	*Verses and Meditations* by Rudolf Steiner, compiled and introduced by George Adams, London 1979
1925		Rudolf Steiner and Ita Wegman: *Grundlegendes für eine Erweiterung der Heilkunst nach geisteswissenschaftlichen Erkenntnissen*, GA 27, 5th edition, Dornach 1977.
	Translation	*Fundamentals of Therapy*, London 1983.

Lectures by Rudolf Steiner referred to in the text. The German are identified by GA numbers (Rudolf Steiner-Gesamtausgabe in Dornach).

18.—31.5.08.	Hamburg	*Das Johannes Evangelium*, GA 103, 1981.
	Translation	*The Gospel of St John*, New York, 1973.
3.6.09	Budapest	In: *Das Prinzip der spirituellen Ökonomie im
5.6.09	Budapest	Zusammenhang mit Wiederverkörperungsfragen* GA 109/111, Dornach 1979.
	Translation	*Rosecrucian Esotericism*, New York 1978.
27.2.10	Cologne	In: *Das Ereignis der Christus-Erscheinung in
15.3.10	Munich	der ätherischen Welt*, GA 118, 1977.
	Translation	*The Reappearance of the Christ in the Etheric*, New York 1983.
5.—14.10.11	Karlsruhe	*Von Jesus zu Christus*, GA 131, 1982.
	Translation	*From Jesus to Christ*, London 1973.
2.10.13	Oslo	In: *Aus der Akasha-Forschung, das Fünfte
3.10.13	Oslo	Evangelium*, GA 148, 1980.
5.10.13	Oslo	
	Translation	*The Fifth Gospel*, London 1985.
6.10.13	Oslo	
17.12.13	Cologne	
18.12.13	Cologne	
7.6.14	Dornach	In: *Wege zu einem neuen Baustil*, GA 286, 1982.
17.6.14	Dornach	
	Translation	*Ways to a New Style in Architecture*, London 1927.
21.11.14	Dornach	In: *Die Welt als Ergebnis von Gleichgewichts-wirkungen*, GA 158, 1980.
	Translation	*Balance in the World and Man*, Vancouver, 1977.
26.8.18	Dornach	In: *Die Wissenschaft vom Werden des Menschen*, GA 183, 1967.
30.11.19	Dornach	In: *Die Sendung Michael*, GA 194, 1983.
	Translation	*Mission of the Archangel Michael*, New York 1961.
1.—14.3.20	Stuttgart	*Geisteswissenschaftliche Impulse zur Entwickelung der Physik*. GA 321, 1982.
29.9.20	Dornach	In: *Grenzen der Naturerkenntnis*, GA 322, 1981.
30.9.20	Dornach	
	Translation	*The Boundaries of Natural Science*, with a Foreword by Saul Bellow, New York, 1983.
15.1.21	Stuttgart	In *Das Verhältnis der Verschiedenen Naturwissen-
16.1.21	Stuttgaot	schaftlichen Gebiete zur Astronomie*, GA 323, 1983.
	Translation	English edition in preparation, Spring Valley, New York.
5.4.21	Dornach	In: *Die befruchtende Wirkung der Anthroposo-
6.4.21	Dornach	phie auf die Fachwissenschaften*, GA 76, 1977.

Date	Place	Reference
8.4.22	The Hague	In: *Die Bedeutung der Anthroposophie im*
9.4.22	The Hague	*Geistesleben der Gegenwart*, GA 82, 1989.
10.4.22	The Hague	A translation of the lectures of 8. and 9.
	Translation	April, 1922 appeared in the *Golden Blade*, London 1961.
14.4.22	London	In: *Das Sonnenmysterium und das Mysterium von*
24.4.22	London	*Tod und Auferstehung*, GA 211, 1986.
	Translation	*Planetry Spheres and their Influence on Man's Life on Earth and in the Spiritual Worlds*, London 1982.
28.7.22	Dornach	*Das Geheimnis der Trinitat*, GA 214, 1980.
9.8.22	Dornach	
22.8.22	Oxford	
	Translation	*The Mystery of the Trinity*, London, 1947.
1.12.22	Dornach	In: *Das Verhaltnis der Sternenwelt* zum *Menschen*
17.12.22	Dornach	*und des Menschen zur Sternenwelt—Die geistige* Kommunion der Menschheit, GA 219, 1976.
	Translation	*Man and the World of Stars—The Spiritual Communion of Mankind*, New York 1982.
14.8.23	Ilkley	In: *Gegenwartiges Geistesleben und Erziehung*, GA 307, 1973
	Translation	*A Modern Art of Education*, London 1981.
14.9.23	Stuttgart	*Initionswissenschaft und Sternenerkenntnis*, GA 228, 1964.
	Translation	*Man in the Past, the Present and the Future—The Sun-Initiation of the Druid Priest and his Moon-Science*, London 1982.
27.9.23	Vienna	In: *Was wollte das Goetheanum und was soll die Anthroposophie?* GA 84, 1961.
	Translation	In *Esoteric Development*, (Selected lectures): New York 1982.
26.10.23	Dornach	In: *Der Mensch als Zusammenklang des schaffenden*
2.11.23	Dornach	*bildenden und gestaltenden Weltenwortes*, GA 230, 1978.
3.11.23	Dornach	*Man as Symphony of the Creative Word*,
	Translation	London 1970.
23.11.23	Dornach	In: *Mysteriengestaltungen*, GA 232, 1974.
	Translation	*Mystery Knowledge and Mystery Centres*, London 1972.
4.1.24	Dornach	In: *Meditative Betrachtungen und Anleitungen*
5.1.24	Dornach	*zur Vertiefung der Heilkunst*, GA 316, 1980.
6.1.24	Dornach	
7.1.24	Dornach	
8.1.24	Dornach	
24.1.24	Dornach	
15.8.24	Torquay	In: *Die Kunst des Erziehens aus dem Erfassen*
27.8.24	Torquay	*der Menschenwesenheit*, GA 311, 1979
	Translation	*The Kingdom of Childhood*, London 1988.
18.9.24	Dornach	In: *Die Schöpfung der Welt und des Menschen—Erdenleben und Sternenwirken.* GA 354, 1977.
	Translation	*The Forming of the Earth and the Moon; Causes of Vulcanism.* Typescript copy in the Library of Rudolf Steiner House, London. Z. 257.

Works of other Authors.

Adams, George (Kaufmann)	(1933)	*Von dem Ätherischen Raume*, second impression, Stuttgart 1981
		Physical and Ethereal Spaces, second impression, London, 1978.
	Translation	*Sobre el Espacio, Mexico City*, 1982.
	(1934)	*Strahlende Weltgestaltung*, Dornach 1965.
	(1926—1963)	*Grundfragen der Naturwissenschaft*, essays translated from the English. Stuttgart 1979.
	(1926—1964)	*George Adams, Interpreter of Rudolf Steiner*, collected essays, with a biography by Olive Whicher. East Grinstead, 1977.
	(1936—1948)	*Nature Ever New*, essays, Spring Valley USA, 1980.
	(1955)	*The Mysteries of the Rose Gross.* New Knowledge Books, East Grinstead, Sussex, 1955.
	(1956—1959)	Study material:
		Universalkräfte in der Mechanik, Dornach 1973.
	Translation	*Universal Forces in Mechanics*, London 1977.
		Letter from George Adams, London 1978.
		Lemniskatische Regelflächen in Raum und Gegenraum, Dornach (in preparation).
	Translation	*Lemniscatory Ruled Surface in Space and Counterspace*, London 1979.
Adams, George and Whicher, Olive	(1949)	*The Living Plant*, Clent, Stourbridge, Worcs.
	(1952) (with colour)	*The Plant between Sun and Earth and the Science of Physical and Ethereal Spaces*, second revised and enlarged edition, London 1980.
	(1960) (with colour)	*Die Pflanze in Raum und Gegenraum. Elemente einer neuen Morphologie*, Stuttgart, second edition 1979.
	Translation	*Entre Soleil et Terre, la Plante*, Paris 1982.
	(no colour)	*The Plant between Sun and Earth*, Boston 1982.
Adler, Claire Fischer	(1958)	*Modern Geometry*, New York/London 1967.
Bernhard, Arnold		*Projektive Geometrie*, aus der Raumanschauung zeichnend entwickelt, Stuttgart 1984.
Blattmann, George		*Die Sonne, Gestirn und Gottheit*, Stuttgart 1972.
	Translation	*The Sun—Ancient Mysteries and a New Physics*, Edinburgh and New York, 1985.
Bockemühl, Jochen		*Erscheinungsformen des Ätherischen*, see also the article by Hermann Poppelbaum, Stuttgart 1977.
	Translation	*Towards a Phenomenology of the Etheric World*, Spring Valley, N.Y. 1985.
Bothmer, Graf Fritz v.		*Gymnastische Erziehung*, Stuttgart 1981.
		Gymnastic Education, Stuttgart 1959 (translation of an earlier edition).
Bohm, David	(1980)	*Wholeness and the Implicate Order*, London 1984.
	Translation	*Die Implizite Ordnung,* Munich 1985.
Briggs, John and Peat, David	(1984)	*Looking Glass Universe: The Emerging Science of Wholeness*, New York/London 1985.
Coxeter, H.S.M.		*The Real Projective Plane*, New York/London 1949.
		Projective Geometry, New York/London 1964.
Davy, John.		*Hope, Evolution and Change.* Selected articles, compiled by Gudrun Davy, Stroud 1985.

Edmunds, L.F.E.		*Anthroposophy*, Forest Row, 1982.
Edwards, Lawrence		*The Field of Form*, Edinburgh 1982.
	Translation	*Geometrie des Lebendigen. Vom Erleben Gestaltbildender Naturkräfte*, Revised and enlarged edition, Stuttgart, 1986.
Floride, Athys,		*Stufen der Meditation*, Dornach 1987.
Fritzsch, Charlotte,		*Tropfenbilder*, Stuttgart 1982
Fyfe, Agnes		*Die Signatur des Merkur im Pflanzenreich* (Kapilar-dynamische Untersuchungsergebnisse), Stuttgart 1973.
		Die Signatur des Venus..., 1978.
		Die Signatur des Uranus..., 1984.
Goethe, Wolfgang von,	(1793)	*Die Metamorphose der Pflanze* and *Die Spiral-Tendenz der Pflanze*, Dornach 1975.
	Translation	Bertha Müller: *Goethe's Botanical Writings*, Hawaii 1952.
Grosse, Rudolf		*Die Weihnachtstagung alz Zeitenwende*, Dornach 1981.
	Translation	*The Christmas Foundation*, Vancouver, Canada, 1984.
		Das Wesen Anthroposophie, Dornach 1982.
	Translation	*The Living Being Anthroposophia*, Vancouver, Canada, 1986.
Gschwind, Peter		*Der Lineare Komplex, eine Überimaginäre Zahl*, Dornach 1977.
Hauschka, Rudolf	1946	*Substanzlehre*, 9th edition, Frankfurt 1985.
	Translation	*Nature of Substance*, London 1983.
	(1951)	*Ernährungslehre*, 8th edition, Frankfurt 1982.
Hauschka, Margarethe		*Fundamentals of Therapy* (Translation), London 1985.
Jammer, Max	(1954)	*Concepts of Space*, Cambridge (USA).
	(1957)	*Concepts of Force*, Cambridge (USA).
		Das Problem des Raums, Darmstadt 1980.
Kemper, Carl		*Der Bau*. Compiled and published by Hilde Raske, Stuttgart 1966.
Koepf, Herbert		*Landbau, natur- und menschengemäss*, Stuttgart 1986
Koept, Petersen and Schaumann.		*Biodynamic Agriculture, an Introduction*,
Kranich, Ernst Michael		*Die Formensprache der Pflanze*, Stuttgart 1979.
	Translation	*Planetary Influences upon Plants*, Wyoming (USA) 1984.
Krause-Zimmer, Hella		*Die Zwei Jesusknaben in der bildenden Kunst*, 2nd edition, Stuttgart 1977.
	Translation	*Le Problème des Deux Enfants Jésus et sa Trace dans l'Art*, Paris 1977.
Lehrs, Ernst	(1951)	*Mensch oder Materie*, Frankfurt 1957.
		Man or Matter, 3rd enlarged edition, London 1985.
Leroi, Rita		*Die Misteltherapie, Eine Antwort auf die Herausforderung Krebs*, Stuttgart 1987. (About the pioneer medical work of Rudolf Steiner and Ita Wegmann.)
Locher-Ernst, Louis	(1940)	*Projektive Geometrie*, 2nd edition, Dornach 1980.
		Geometrische Metamorphosen, 2nd edition, Dornach 1970.
		Raum und Gegenraum, 2nd edition, Dornach 1970.
Meyer, Thomas		*D.N. Dunlop, Ein Zeit und Lebensbild*, Dornach 1987.
	Translation	D.N. Dunlop, (in preparation) London.
Schmutz, Hans-Ulrich		*Die Tetraederstruktur der Erde, Eine geologisch-geometrische Untersuchung anhand der Plattentektonik*, Stuttgart, 1986.

Schuberth, Ernst		In: Kranich, Jünemann, Berthold-Andrae, Bühler, Schuberth, *Formenzeichnen, Die Entwickelung des Formensinns in der Erziehung*, Stuttgart 1987.
Schultz, Joachim	1963	*Rhythmen der Sterne*, compiled by Suso Vetter, 3rd edition, Dornach 1985.
	Translation	*Movement and Rhythm of the Stars*, Edinburgh/New York, 1986.
Schwenk, Theodor	1962	*Das Sensible Chaos*, 6th edition, Stuttgart 1984.
	Translation	*Sensitive Chaos*, London 1976
Selawry, A and O		*Die Kupferchlorid Kristallisation*, Stuttgart 1957
Selawry, Alla		*Metallfunktionstypen in Psychologie und Medizin*, Heidelberg 1985.
		Ehrenfried Pfeiffer, Dornach 1987.
Sheldrake, Rupert	1981	*A New Science of Life, The Hypothesis of Formative Causation*, London 1984.
Smit. Jörgen		*Geistesschulung und Lebenspraxis*, Dornach 1987.
Streit, Jacob		*Sonne und Kreuz*, 2nd edition, Stuttgart 1986.
	Translation	*Sun and Cross*, Edinburgh 1984.
Struik, Dirk J		*A Concise History of Mathematics*, London 1965.
Teichman, Frank		*Der Mensch und sein Tempel, Megalith-Kultur in Ireland, England und der Bretagne*, Stuttgart 1983.
Unger, Georg		*Vom Bilden physikalischer Begriffe*
		I. *Die Grundbegriffe von Mechanik und Wärmelehre*, Stuttgart 1959.
		II. *Die Grundbegriffe der Optik und Electrizitatslehre*, Stuttgart 1961
		III. *Grundbegriffe der Modernen Physik—Quanten Teilchen, Relativität.*
		Das Offenbare Geheimnis des Raumes—Meditationen am Pentagondodekaeder nach Carl Kemper Stuttgart 1963.
Vreede, Elisabeth	(1927—1930)	*Astrosophie und Astronomie*, 2nd revised edition, Dornach 1980.
Wegman, Ita		*Im Anbruck des Wirkens für eine Erweiterung der Heilkunst*, Arlesheim 1974.
Wilson, Michael		*Living with Light and Colour,* posthumous publication in preparation.
	1949	*What is Colour*, Clent, Stourbridge 1983.
Whicher, Olive		*Projective Geometry, Creative Polarities in Space and Time*, London 1985. second impression.
		Projektive Geometrie, Schöpferische Polaritäten in Raum und Zeit, Stuttgart 1970.
	Translation	*George Adams—Ein Geistsucher unserer Zeit.* Biography and an article by Adams, Dornach 1973.
		George Adams—Interpreter of Rudolf Steiner, Biography and an article by Adams, East Grinstead, 1977.
		The Significance of the Idea of Counterspace, in: *Main Currents in Modern Thought*, New York, 1974.
Wilder, Raymond		*Evolution of Mathematical Concepts*, New York/London 1986.
Wilmar, Frits		*Vorgeburtliche Menschenwerdung*, Stuttgart 1979.
Ziegler, Renatus,		*Synthetische Liniengeometrie*, Dornach 1981.
		Geschichte der geometrischen Mechanik im 19. Jahrhundert, Stuttgart 1983.

Acknowledgements: Figures

The geometrical drawings are with a few exceptions taken from earlier works of George Adams and Olive Whicher, particularly from Strahlende Weltgestaltung *(see Bibliography); these drawings were prepared for print by the late Louis Loynes, London.*

(a) Rudolf Steiner: Foto Rietmann, Verlag am Goetheanum, Dornach. (b) George Adams, (c) Louis Locher-Ernst, (d) Georg Unger: Verlag am Goetheanum, Dornach, (e) Blake's "Newton": Tate Gallery, London. Figs. 11, 68: National Gallery, London. Fig. 19: photo Theodor Schwenk. Figs. 47, 49, 50, 52, 53, 57, 61: Author's archives. Figure 43: Cara Groot, *Marie Savitch*, Dornach 1989. Fig. 45: Weleda Calendar, Arlesheim 1963, photo Theodor Schwenk. Fig. 46: Lennart Nilsson, *Ein Kind entsteht*. Fig. 48: from Rudolf Steiner: *Die Bedeutung der Anthroposophie im Geistesleben der Gegenwart, GA 82, Dornach 1957, S 153. Fig. 51: Musäum Hermeticum, 1625. Figs. 54, 55, 58b: Andreas Vesalius, The Anatomical Drawings of Andreas Vesalius*, New York 1982. Fig. 56: drawing taken by Olive Whicher from an old anatomical textbook. Fig. 60: from *Moving and Growing*, Mrs. E. Tudor Hart, 1952. Fig. 62: photo H.-J. Heitmann. Figs. 63, 65: Lawrence Edwards, *Geometrie des Lebendigen, Stuttgart 1986. Fig. 64: photo John Wilkes. Fig. 66: Hans Ulrich Schmutz, Die Tetraederstruktur der Erde.* Verlag Freies Geistesleben, Stuttgart 1986. Fig. 58a, 59: from Prof. Dr. Fr. Kopsch, *Rauber's Lehrbuch der Anatomie des Menschen, 11. Aufl. Leipzig 1919. Fig. 67, 69, 72, 74: Bildarchiv Foto Marburg, Marburg. Fig. 70: Verrié Editor, Barcelona, Museum d'Art de Catalynya. Fig. 71: Buchkunstverlag Ettal Oby. Fig 73: A.C.L., Brüssel. Fig. 75: Staatl. Museum, Berlin. Fig. 76: Casa Editrice Giusti di S. Becocci. Museo S. Marco, Florence. Fig. 77: Jakob Streit, Sonne und Kreuz,* 2. Aufl. Stuttgart 1986. Fig. 78: Frank Teichmann, *Der Mensch und sein Tempel*, Bd. 3: *Megalithkultur in Ireland, England und der Bretagne*, Stuttgart 1983. Fig. 79: drawing by Axel Ewald. Fig. 80: drawing by Olive Whicher, after Rudolf Steiner. Fig. 82: after Rudolf Steiner. Dodecahedron in a Sun Space: Karl Kemper, *Der Bau* Stuttgart 1966.

Plates

Plates I, II: drawings by George Adams/Olive Whicher. Plate III: drawing by George Adams/Lawrence Edwards. Plate IV: photo W. Schaumann. Plate V: Child's drawing, Ecole Perceval, Chatou (France). Plate VI: author's archives. Plate VII: Fritz William Museum, Cambridge. Plates VIII, X, XII: Archiv für Kunst und Geschichte, Berlin. Plates IX, XI: National Gallery, London. Plate XIII: Stichting Magenta, Driebergen, (Holland). Plate XIV: Gideon Spicker Verlag, Dornach. Plate XV: Tate Gallery, London. Plate XVI: Elisabeth Koch/Gerard Wagner, *Die Individualität der Farbe.* 2. Aufl. Stuttgart 1982.

A deep debt of gratitude is owed to all those who contributed warm gift money to the financing of the book.

INDEX

Absolute 44 et seq.
Adler, Claire Fischer 128
Agriculture xx, 79, 98, 119
Ahriman 67, 98f, 104, 111
Alchemists 62f
Alice in Wonderland 29
Allen, Paul Marshall 34f
All-relating point 58
Aloneness (solitude) 109
Ambrogio, S 89
Amnion-sack (sheath) 53
Analytical method (mode) 6, 24, 31, 46
Analytical Geometry 15, 25
Anatomy 42
Angelico, Fra Beata xii, 96
Angelus Silesius 32
Anharmonic ration, see Cross-ratio
Animal kingdom 60, 62, 64, 67
Annunciation 94
Anthroposophical Society 116f, 119f, 124
Anthroposophy 117
Anti-gravitational force (law) 50f, 121
Anti-gravitational space 69, 103
Anti-space 13, 44
Aquinas, Thomas xv, 35
Archangel (Time-Spirit) 109
Archangel Michaël 37, 50, 109
Archangel Gabriel 94
Archetypal phenomenon 58, 66
Archetypal plant (Urpflanze) 6, 57
Architecture 105 et seq.
Aristotle xvi, 35
Art of Painting 106
Art Therapy 73
Assensa, Beppe ix, 97, 106
Astral body 6f, 50
Astronomy xv
Astro-physics xv
Atlas 64
Atom, (atomic) 6, 13, 36, 70
Atomic fission 31
Autopsy 62

Backbone, spine 63
Bacon 104
Balance 11, 29, 46, 62 et seq., 66f, 93, 98, 108

Balance, organ of 64
Baptism, Baptist 89, 94f
Barfield, Owen xvi
Bees, hive, keeper 32, 68
Being(s) 54, 66, 69, 83, 107
Being Divine 90f
Bernhard, Arnold 128
Bernoulli Lemniscate (Cassini curves) 28, 46, 120
Biology xviii, 6, 28, 52, 64 et seq., 79
Bio-dynamic Agriculture xx, 73f, 121
Birds 68
Blake, William x, 13, 105
Blattmann, Georg, 123
Blood 92
Blossom, flower 4, 29, 67, 107
Bock, Emil 123
Bockemühl, Jochen 123, 128
Body of formative forces 39, 41, 47
Body of light 50
Body of darkness 50
Boehme, Jacob 34 et seq.
Bohm, David 81, 123, 128
Bothmer 120, 128
Bothmer Gymnastics 121
Bolyai, W 12
Brianchon, Charles 26
Briggs, J and Peat, 128
Bruno, Geordano 35f
Bud 77f, 102
Buddha 90
Butterfly 68

Caduceus, Mercury Staff 63
Calyx 69
Cambridge, England 13, 31f, 90
Cancer research 73
Cancer remedies, Production of 73
Cajori, F 120
Capillary Dynamolysis 74
Capra F 123
Cartesian Axes, coordinates 23f
Cartesian Space, conception of 14, 38, 43f, 49
Caterpillar 29, 67
Caterpillar, transformation of 67 et seq.

133

Cathedrals 105f, 107
Cayley, Arthus 13, 45
Cell, germ, ovum 5f, 47, 61, 79, 103
Celtic 95, 109
Centre and periphery 27 et seq.
Centric and peripheral space 47, 108
Centifugal and centripetal 47, 57
Cerebro-spinal fluid 63
Chagall, Marc 96
Chaos and Cosmos 58f, 69, 92
Chartres 106
Chemistry 9, 32, 69, 74
Chernobyl 55
Christ 93, 109
Christ Being 9, 87, 91
Christ Birth 91f
Christ Event 111
Christ Impulse 92
Christ Jesus 91
Christ Risen 9, 56, 95
Christianity 39, 111
Christmas Foundation Meeting 111
Chromosomes (Transporation) 79
Chrysalis 67f
Clairvoyance 43, 54
Cochlea 64
Coleridge, Samuel Taylor xiv
College of Teachers 55
Collineation and Correlation 29
Collot d'Herbois, Liane ix, 96, 106
Colour and light 4, 23, 32, 50, 53, 66, 91, 96, 106
Colour and tone 38, 43, 48, 53, 65
Colours (complementary) 46, 106f
Community, a new consciousness 54
Compte, August 9, 11
Concave and convex 28, 46, 57f, 94, 107
Cone, counterspatial 48
Cone, in plant growth 59
Conic 21, 26f
Consciousness xiii, 66
Consciousness evolving xiii, 45, 67, 104
Consciousness soul 25, 35, 89, 94
Consciousness, states of 48, 54
Continuum 52
Cook Theodor A 120
Copernican conception of space 52
Copernican way of thinking 23
Copernican world conception 35
Corpse 62, 93
Cosmic and earthly 51f, 63
Counterspace vi, xviii, 8, 12, 95, 113

Coxeter, H. S. M. 127
Cranach, Lucas ix, 84
Cromlech, dolmen 70, 100, 106, 109
Cross 55, 92, 97, 99 et seq.
Cross-ratio 20
Crucifixion 91, 96
Cube 20 et seq., 111
Cubic net 20
Culpepper 78
Curves, curvature 19, 22, 27
Curves and surfaces 21
Crystallisation test method 74
Crystal-weaving (geometrical) 19 et seq.
Cusa, Cardinal Nicolas of 34 et seq.
Cytology 79

Davy, John 81f, 84, 127
David, Gerhard xii
Desargues, Girard 23 et seq., 104, 120
Descartes, René 7, 12, 16, 24f, 35, 62, 104, 120
Dewdrops, droplets 52 et seq., 59
Dimensions, positive 22-24
Dimensions, negative 43
Drop-picture test method 74
Drop-form 51
Druids 70, 95, 100f, 124
Druid circles 100, 110
Duality, Principle of 15, 25f
Dunlop, Daniel N 2, 79, 123
Dynamics, polar dynamics 58

Earth 8, 47, 79, 102
Earth spaces 8, 20, 24, 31, 39, 59, 61f, 107, 109f
Earth geometry 29
Earthquake 93
Easter 97
Eckhart, Meister 10, 34
Ecliptic 49
Ecology 78f
Economics 39, 87, 97, 111
Eddington, Arthur 33f
Edmunds, Francis 92, 129
Edwards, Lawrence ix, 75 et seq., 120, 122f, 129
Egg, germ-cell 67f
Egg-shaped curves 77, 120
Ego 6f, 50 et seq., 62
Egypt 23, 87
Einstein, Albert xv, 72
Electricity, electron 33
Elements 52, 69, 95, 121

Elemental Beings 54, 68, 93
Ellipse 17
Ellipse parabola, hyperbola 21
Embryology 53
Emerson College 76, 122
Emptiness (Leere) xiv, 8, 56, 65, 93
"Empty" consciousness 54
Empty space 54, 58, 68 et seq., 86f
"Encircling Round" ("Umkreis") 19, 46, 91
Enhancement (Goethe's theory) 69
Envelope 27f
Environment 79, 88
Esotericism 124
Ethereal (etheric) Being 83, 93
Ethereal body 7, 40, 50 et seq., 61, 93
Ethereal earth 9
Ethereal force-field, forces 74, 103, 105
Ethereal formation 42
Ethereal formative forces, principles 52, 59, 61
Ethereal space 7, 8, 44ff, 50 et seq., 87, 92, 105, 113
Ethereal world, realm 6, 9, 37
Ether 57, 69, 97, 121
Ethers (four) 50, 52, 121
Euclid 7, 23ff
Euclidean thought-forms 12
Euclidean field 18
Euclidean forms 28
Euclidean geometry 15 et seq., 55
Eurythmy 41, 48, 50, 91, 108, 120f
Ewald, Axel xii
Expansion and contraction 28, 49
Experimentation 57, 72, 74, 78, 113
Extensive and intensive 28, 49
Eye 8, 52, 64, 92, 114

Faraday, Michael 100
Fire, burning of the Goetheanum 109f
Floride, Athys 122, 127
Flower, flower-bud 29, 45, 77
Flow-forms 76f
Forces, centric and peripheral 47, 64
Forces in surfaces 40
Forces, cosmic 75
Formative forces body (ethereal) 6, 39f, 78, 92
Form-creating process 15, 18
Form, language of (script) 63, 65
Foundation, see Ground-plan
Foundation Stone 111

Foundation Stone Meditation 111, 115 et seq., 122
Fouquet, Jean xii
Fourfold human being 50
Fourth dimension 39, 43
Francke, Meister 90
Freedom 10f, 24, 34, 61, 67, 82, 104, 109
Freedom, Equality, Fraternity 11
Fritzsch, Charlotte 129
Fry, Christopher 1
Functional (inner) infinitude 45, 63, 78
Fyfe, Agnes 123, 129

Galileo Galilei 16, 23f
Gauss, Karl Frederick 12
Gegenraum (Counterspace) 7f, 12, 63
Genetics, genes 79
Genetic engineering 54, 80
Genetic mobility 79
Geology 84
Geometry 10
Geometry non-Euclidean 12
Geometry in a point 45f
Geotropism, heliotropism 67
Germ, germ-cell 58, 115
Germination 101
Gertgen, tot sind Jans ix
Gesture of form 22, 54
Giotto 96
Goethe vi, 4 et seq., 7, 32, 44ff, 53, 57, 61, 66, 91, 104, 120, 129
Goethean phenomenology 66f
Goethean theory of colour and light 73, 106
Goethean Science Foundation 73
Goetheanum 52, 57, 83, 96, 101, 105f, 110, 119, 124
Goetheanum forms 106 et seq.
Goetheanum Impulse 111
Goetheanum, Mathematical-Astronomical Section at the xx, 76
Gold 55, 67
Golden Star 87
Gospels 88
Gravity xiii, 6, 41f, 49, 55, 58f, 105, 120f
Gravitational experience 41, 64
Gravitational field 73, 103
Gravitational force 50, 69
Greece, Greeks 23, 63, 88
Green and "Peach-blossom" 46

Grigor, Meister 96
Grosse, Rudolf 129
Ground-plan of the First Goetheanum 110f
Growing-point, shoot 8, 60 et seq., 74, 77
Growth Measure 21, 49, 63 et seq., 69, 78, 122
Grünewald, Matthias 96
Gschwind, Peter 76, 121, 129

Hardy, G. H. 13
Harmonic Net (quadrangle) 18 et seq.
Harmony of the Spheres 91
Hausbuches, Meister des xii, 96
Hauschka, Margarethe 120, 129
Hauschka, Rudolf 123, 129
Healing xvii, 8
Heart 65, 77
Heart and lung 46, 63
Heart, Sun as 8
Hexagon Net 19
Hexagrammum Mysticum 26
Hiscia Laboratory 103
Histology 5
Hobbena Avenue x
Hollow, hollowed-out form 58, 62 et seq.
Hollow space 28, 58 et seq., 68f, 87, 95f, 101
Homeopathy 73, 75
Horizon 49, 61
Horizon-line 18
Human form 60 et seq., 91, 107
Hybernian Mysteries 124
Hydrodynamics 51

"Ideal" (geometrical) elements 27
Ideal point at infinity 16f
"Imaginary" elements in mathematics 3, 27, 44, 77, 109, 120
Imagination 30, 40, 52, 56, 68
Imagination, Inspiration, Intuition 11, 66, 87, 114
Imaginative perception, cognition 39f
Infinitesimal 35
Infinitude within 58
Infinitely distant elements 16
Infinite, Infinity 15 et seq., 64
Innermost point at infinity 22
Innermost infinitude 31, 45, 58, 98
Innermost line (of light) 49, 61
Initiation, Way of xx
Initiation, Sun 102, 123
Insect 29, 32, 67 et seq.

Insect metamorphosis 67 to 70
Inner column, axis, of Light 48 et seq., 61, 69, 78
Inner column, axis, of Tone 48
Inner Sun 123
Institute for Research into Streaming Media, Black Forest 73
Intensive experience 41
Intensive point or line within 58, 61
Intensive organs 8
Intensive space 69
Invariance, Principle of 26
Invariant 45, 77
Involution 22
Inward hollow 29

de Jaager, Isabella 121
Jammer, Max 129
Jesus Children 88 et seq.
Jesus of Nazareth 91f
Jewish people 90
Johnson, Samuel xiv

Karma and Reincarnation 70, 83
Keller, Evelyn Fox 121
Kemper, Karl xii, 129
Kepler, Johannes 16, 35
Klein, Felix 73
Knowledge, Path of (led by the Sun) 123
Koepf, Herbert 129
Kolisko, Eugen 123
Koliski, Lili 74, 123
Kranich, Ernst-Michael 127
Krause-Zimmer, Hella 89, 121, 127

Lambda 78
Last Supper 96
Lehrs, Ernst 58, 127
Lemniscate of Bernoulli 28, 46, 120
Lemniscatory formation 77, 120
Lemniscatory space 28, 47, 58, 82, 88, 107, 120
Lemniscatory surfaces 73f, 98, 120f
Leonardo da Vinci xi, 94
Leroi, Alexandre 73, 75
Leroi, Rita 73, 129
Levity 41, 120f
Levitational force 42, 51, 120f
Leyden, Lukas van xi
Light, 55, 60, 107
Light and darkness 66, 82, 96
Light, Column of 48
Light-forces 64

Light, Love and Life 93
Lie, Sophus 73
Line 10, 16
Line at infinity 19 (within) 61
Line-line polarity 49f
Line of planes 16, 49f
Line-woven forms 17
Linnaeus 6
Lobaschewski 12
Locher-Ernst, Louis xx, 3, 31, 120, 129
Lochner, Stephan ix
Logarithmic (growth) measure 21
Lombardy Poplar 59
Luini, Bernadino 94
Lukas Clinic 73, 103
Lucifer and Ahriman 66, 98f, 122, 124

Magic 60
Maize 58
Marionettes 61
Mary and Joseph 90
Materialism xiv, xix, 11f, 17, 33, 36f, 46, 65, 104, 110f
Mathematics xv, xix et seq., 3ff, 10ff, 33ff, 37, 46, 61, 64, 76, 82, 105, 113, 124
Mathematics latent in the human being 12, 64
Mathematical reasoning 13, 66, 81
"Mathematising", Process of 38, 43, 64
Matrix, materia 58
Matter xiv, 8, 33, 39 46, 70, 92
McClintock, B 79f, 123
Measure 15, 18, 63
Measure relationships 15, 18
Measure, number and weight 13, 20f
Median plane 49
Medicine xvii, 8, 35, 62, 73f, 98, 119
Medieval Guilds 106
Meditative practice 54, 81, 111
Membranes, permeable, sensitive 52
Memling, H. 90
Mercury Staff (Caduceus) 63
Metabolic-limb system 50
Metamorphosis 4, 28f, 50, 63 et seq., 66 et seq., 70, 107
Meyer, Thomas xxi, 123, 129
Michaël Age 109f, 123
Michaël Mystery 123
Michaelmas Daisy 32
Microscope and telescope 72, 79
Mobius strip 121
Models of Path-curve Surfaces 75f

Molecular biology 58, 79 et seq.
Molecular physics 81
Morphology 6, 7, 9, 15 et seq., 21 et seq., 29, 51 et seq., 61, 75
Morphogenetic fields 81
Movement 15, 31f, 41, 43, 48, 50, 58f, 73, 78, 102
Movement, Sense of 64
Mueller, Bertha 120
Muscle layers 62
Mother and Child 89
Mystery Drama 23
Mystery Temple 36, 55
Mystery of Golgotha 70, 88, 91, 95, 99, 102
Mysteries of the Future (Sun) 8f, 88, 100, 111
Mysticism, mystic 34f
Mysticism and Mathematics 34

Natura 33f, 36
Natural science xiii, 34, 43, 102, 113f
Natural laws 33, 79
Negative dimensions 43
Negative space xx, 7, 39, 41, 74f, 86
Nerves-senses system 50, 68 et seq.
Newton, Isaac 13, 24, 32, 79
Nilsson, Leonard 121
Non-Euclidean geometry 12, 44
"Not I" 54
Nought, nothingness 46, 56, 69, 92, 104, 110
Novalis 78

Observation and thinking 67
Octahedron 30, 52
Origin of the universe 81
Optics 23
Osiris 87
Ovum 47, 53

Painting, new art of 106
Pappos's Theorem 12, 15, 25f
Paracelcus 36, 78
Pascal, Blaise (theorem) 23 et seq., 120
Path-curves 74
Path-curve surfaces 74
Paul, St 96
Pendulum 39
Pennmaenmawr 100
Pentagon Dodecahedron 30, 52, 111
Pentagram curve 81
Peripheral (formative) forces 47, 50, 58, 64, 106

Peripheral formation 18, 20, 53
Peripheral space 47
Perspective transformation 15, 18 et seq., 25, 28, 106
Pettigrew, J. Bell 122
Pfeiffer, Ehrenfried 74, 123
Philadelphia 50
Philosophy of Spiritual Activity (Freedom) 10f, 34, 119
Philosophy of science 13
Photo-synthesis 59
Phyllotaxis 61
Physical and ethereal spaces 3, 31, 44
Physical body 6, 50, 52, 54

Physical space 38, 44f
Physics 9, 12, 28, 33f, 36, 39, 43, 64, 73f
Physicists 31, 70
Physiology 6
Planar space 42, 49, 61, 120
Planar forms 60
Planar line 16, 49f
Planar point 16
Planck, Max 71
Plane 16ff
Plane at infinity 23
Planes and surfaces 19, 43, 51, 96, 106
Planes of force 40f
Planet 7f
Plant 8, 9, 29, 32, 44, 53, 56 et seq., 61, 60 et seq., 66, 120 et seq.
Plate tectonics 83
Plato 13, 52, 111
Platonic forms 30, 53
Point at infinity 31, 40
Point at infinity within 31, 45
Point line and plane 16
Point of lines and point of planes 28, 31, 45f
Polarity xxi, 26, 48, 51, 60 et seq., 108
Polar Euclidean space 13f, 31, 41, 45f, 58, 86
Pole and polar (theorem) 27 et seq.
Polar forces (dynamics) xx, 3, 7, 30f
Polar spaces xx, 3, 7, 32, 69f
Polar reciprocal transformation 25 et seq., 29, 46, 49
Polar reciprocal dynamic process 29, 61
Polar-reciprocation of curves 27, 29, 41, 83, 109f
Poncelet, Charles 26
Positivity 56, 66
Principle of Polarity, (Duality) 25 et seq.

Projective Growth Measure 63, 78
Projective morphology 16, 23
Projective plane 17,
Projective space 20, 45
Projective transformation (perspective) 15
Projective Synthetic Geometry xiv et seq., 2, 10, 12, 15, 23, 25f, 30 et seq., 42, 46, 119
Prometheus 12
Proportion 20
Pupa 67
Pythagoras 11

Quadrangle 18 et seq.
Qualities 38f
Quantum theory 33
Quinta-essentia 52, 111
Qumran texts 89
Rainbow colours 52, 107
Raphael 94
"Raying Formation of Worlds" (Strahlende Weltgestaltung) 20
Raum und Gegenraum (Space and Counterspace) 31, 44
Reality principle xiii et seq.
Red Admiral 32, 68
Reincarnation 65, 70
Relationships (social) 18, 20, 79
Rembrandt ix, 95
Reredos 106
Resurrection 55, 68, 96
Resurrection Body 93
Rhythm 8, 43, 46, 61, 65, 75
Rhythmic system 50, 62f
Rohen, J. W. 123
Root, shoot (leaf) and flower 57, 59 et seq.
Rosenkreutz, Christian 124
Rosecrucian School 56, 62, 124
Rudolf Steiner House, London 1
Russell, Bertrand 13, 33

Sacrifice 54
Saturn, Sun, Moon 63, 68f
Savitch, Marie 121
Schaumann, Wolfgang ix, 121
Schiller, Friedrich von 8
Schmutz, Hans Ulrich 84, 123, 129
Schuberth, Ernst 130
Schultz, Joachim 130
Schwann, Theodor 5
Schwenk, Theodor 52, 73f, 130
Science, art and religion 9
Science, Materialistic 6, 33, 89

Science, Natural xiii, 8f, 12, 34, 38, 43, 62, 65, 67, 72, 113
Science, Spiritual 9, 31, 104, 110, 114
Sculpture (sculptor) 39, 41, 47, 63, 108, 120
"Seal-forms" 109
Seed(s) 8, 31, 53, 56, 58ff, 68, 70, 74, 93, 97, 99, 111, 114
Selawry, Alla 123, 130
Sense-free thinking 30f
Sensitive membranes 51 et seq.
Sensitive surfaces 54, 74
Sentient soul 35
Sense perception 11, 60, 64
Sheathes 74f, 90, 92
Sheathing process (skin) 47
Sheathing membranes 54
Shakespeare, William 92, 104
Sheldrake, Rupert 123, 130
Shoot 45, 53, 58
Silesius, Angelus 32, 36, 56
Sion, in Switzerland ix, 90
Skeleton 50, 62
Skin, epithelium 52, 85
Skull 64
Smit, Jörgen 122, 128
Sociology 55
Social organism 55
Solar physics 86
Soul forces (higher) 66
Space and Counterspace 3, 44, 57, 76
Space, Conception of (see under Copernican)
Space, Experience (consciousness) of 37 et seq., 68
Space, hollowed out 101
Space, Idea of 69, 110
Space, Perception of 39
Space, Negative, "other kind" of, 41, 74, 77
Sphere, spheroid 52, 57, 77
Spine 63
Spinoza 12
Spiral 21, 121
Spiral Archemedian 100
Spiral Logarithmic 77, 100
Spiral process 61
Spiral surface 51, 59
"Spiritual Staff" 61, 91, 97
Spiritual (consciousness) soul 25, 35, 89, 94, 102, 119
Spring, source 51
Standing Stones 100

Starry sky 31, 40, 45f
Starry canopy 41
Star-centre 28
Star-point 28, 44 et seq., 49
Staudt, Christian von 45
Stein, Walter Johannes 1f
Steiner, Marie 9, 105
Step measure (geometric progression) 21, 39, 63, 95, 107, 109
Stockton, Anne 106
Stone circles, crosses 70, 100
Streaming media 73
Streit, Jacob 130
Struik, Dirk J. 130
Substance 41, 59, 78
"Suctional" force 41, 58, 86
Sugar Maple 19
Sun 56, 63, 65, 85f, 123
Sun and Earth 60f, 123
Sun forces 70
Sun space 44, 53, 63, 68 et seq., 77, 87, 107, 109
Sun, The Being of 70, 85, 87, 91, 93, 100
Sun-seal 109
Supersensible (perception) 7, 37f
Supersensible body, 40 42f, 44, 54
Supersensible cognition 80
Supersensible research 114
Surface(s) 51 et seq., 74, 96f, 107, 121
Surface forces (suctional) 40f
Surface tension 51f
Symmetry 18, 109
Symmetry exercises 109
Sympathy and antipathy 54 et seq.
Synthesis 25, 77, 81
Synthetic geometry, see Projective

Tarling, D. H. and M. P. 123
Technology 51, 53
Teichmann, Frank 130
Technology 58, 79, 104
Temple (buildings) 65, 91, 100, 105f, 107
Temple Mystery 55
Temptation of Christ 98
Terminology 17, 119
Tetrahedral Structure of the Earth 53, 83f
Tetrahedron 30, 52
Thinking, Feeling, Willing 11, 22, 50, 61, 64, 98, 121
Thinking (thought-forces) 9, 55, 62, 65, 72, 123f
Thinking, Ways of xix, 78

Thinking, Transformed, enhanced 55, 67, 80f, 123f
Thinking, Mathematical 66
Thompson, D'Arcy 122
Three-dimensional space 8, 37f, 63, 99
Threefold Commonwealth (Social Order) 55, 111
Threefold nature of Man 50, 60, 65, 121, 123
Threefold organ 64
Threefold plant 60, 107
Threefold Sun 88
Threshold 36f, 55, 61, 67, 106f
Tibet 80
Time 10, 44, 46
Time-space 45
Time, Turning-point of 70, 99, 102
Tintagel 95
Togetherness 109
Tone 48, 64f
Tour, Georges de la 95
Transformation, perspective 15, 18, 21, 23, 25, 78
Transformation, polar reciprocal 25 et seq.
Tree 60
Trinity 111
Truth 36, 71
Turbulence 74
Turner ix, 96
Twice-curved surface 57f, 94, 121

Unger, Georg xx, 73f, 77, 130
Universal forces 45, 59, 64, 76f, 121
Upright (erect) stature 37f, 48f, 60, 64, 91, 94
Up-thrust 66
Ur-plant (archetypal) 6, 57
Umkreis, see "Encircling Round"
Uterus 77

Vacuum 39, 69, 92
Vanessa 67
Vanishing line 18 et seq.
Vanishing point 106
Verses and Meditations (Wahrspruchworte) 126
Vertebrae 64

Vertebral column (spine) 63 et seq., 120
Verticality 94
"Verticon" 91, 97, 109
"Verticon" and Horizon ("Encircling Round") 61
Vesalius, Andreas 62, 121
Voith, Hanns 73
Vortices 59
Vortical flow 74, 77
Vreede, Elisabeth 73, 130
Volcano 83

Wachsmith, Guenther 73, 84
Wagner, Gerard ix, 97, 106
Water 50 et seq., 59, 63, 73
Water-drop 52, 74
Water purification 74
Wave-mechanics 33
Wave-motions 64
Wegman, Ita 42, 73, 118, 128
Wegman Clinic 73
Werbeck-Sverdstrom, Walborg 48, 121
Whicher, Olive 128, 130
Whitehead, A. N. 119
Whole 46, 91, 102, 106
Wholism 79, 81
Wholeness 45, 81, 88
Wilder, Raymond 130
Wilkes, A. John 75f, 122
Wilmar, Frits 53, 121, 123, 130
Wilson, Michael 73, 130
Wings 42, 68, 95
Wirbela Flow Design Research Institute 122
Wisdom and Love 88 et seq.
Woloschina, Margarita 96
Womb 65
Word 107
World Economy 97
World Power Conference 79

Yoga of Breathing 11
Yoga of the Light 11

Zarathustra 87, 89f
Ziegler, Renatus 76, 130

BLACK AND WHITE ILLUSTRATIONS

INTRODUCTION
Photographs (a) Rudolf Steiner   (b) George Adams Kaufmann   (c) Louis Locher-Ernst   (d) Blake's "Newton"

CHAPTER IV
Figure
1. Theorem of Pappos
2. Line of Points and Line of Planes
3. Plane of Lines and Points
4. Point of Lines and Planes
5. Finite Euclidean Forms
6. Triangle in a Projective Plane
7. Lines of a Point in relation to Points of a Line
8. The Harmonic Quadrangle
9. Transformation of the Quadrangle through the Infinite
10. Projective Net of Quadrangles in Step-Measure
11. Hobbema's Avenue
12. Regular Net of Quadrangles in Step-Measure
13. Planes in a Line and Planes and Lines in a Point
14a. Cubic Form projected from a "Vanishing Plane"
14b. Cubic Forms woven side-by-side (Step-Measure)
15. Quartz Crystal light-woven from a Projective Plane
16. Projective Transformation of Circle into Ellipse
17. Projective Transformation of Circle into Parabola
18. Projective Transformation of Circle into Hyperbola
19. Forms convex and concave
20. Step-Measure and Growth-Measure
21. Projective Net of Quadrangles in Growth-Measure
22. Regular Net of Quadrangles in Growth-Measure
23. Logarithmic Spirals (Growth-Measure and Circling Measure)
24. Projective Net of Cube and Octahedron giving Growth-Measure
25. Circle-Curves in Growth Measure
26. Circle-Curves in oblique perspective
27. Family of Circle-Curves touching two fixed points and two fixed lines
28. Theorem of Pappos showing the Principle of Duality
29. The Dual Theorems of Pascal and Brianchon
30. Points and Lines and the Circle-curve
31. Pole and Polar with respect to

32. an Ellipse (Circling Measure)
32. As the Pole moves out, the Polar moves in, and vice versa
33. Pointwise and Linewise Circles
34a. Poles within answer to Polars without
34b. Polar Families of Circles in Growth-Measure
35. Creation of Lemniscate and Cassini Curves
36. Polar reciprocal Curves
37. Polar Reciprocation between Centre and Infinite Periphery
38. Pole and Polar with respect to the Sphere
39. Polar Transformation (Metamorphosis) Cube and Octahedron
40. Cube Contracting, Octahedron Expanding
41. Self-polar Tetrahedron
42. Icosahedron and Pentagon-Dodecahedron

CHAPTER VI
Figure
43. Eurythmists
44. Polarity of Circles in a Plane and Cones in a Point
45. Flowing Movement in Water and Plant (Schwenk)
46. Cosmic Space for the Development of a Life (Nilsson)
47. Field Hamster feeling towards Human Verticality
48. Sketch: Plant between Earth and Cosmos (Steiner)
49. The tiny Hollow in the Heart of a Seed
50. Germinating Seeds—Polarity of Centric and Peripheral Gestures
51. The Well, an inner, living space
52. The Tree's Unfolding Growth and Plastic Outline
53. Two kinds of Force and the Horizontal Plane
54. The Sheath of Muscles (Vesalius)
55. The Man of Bone (Vesalius)—Finished Form
56. Heart and Lung (Rauber Kopsch)—Leaf and Bud
57. Study of a Nude Youth (Michelangelo)
58a. Growth-measure revealed in the Human Hand (Rauber Kopsch)
58b. The Spinal Column (Vesalius) pictures a projective Growth Measure
59. Bones of the Vertebral Column (Rauber Kopsch)—Lemniscatory Formation
60. Experiment on Foot
61. Plant and Insect Metamorphosis

CHAPTER VII
Figure
62. Christ in the Mandala (Veselay, France)
63. Path-Curves (Edwards)
64. Models of parts of Path-curve Surfaces
65. Path-curves in Plant Buds (Edwards)
66. The Tetrahedral Structure of the Earth

CHAPTER VIII
Figure
67. Twelve-year-old Jesus in the Temple
68. The Virgin and the Child (Leonardo da Vinci, 1452—1519)
69. Madonna di Terranova (Raphael, 1483—1520)
70. Mestre de Sant Joan de Boi (End of the 11th century)
71. The Annunciation (Lukas van Leyden, 15th century)
72. The Nativity (Meister Francke 14th—15th century)

73. The Baptism (Gerhard David, around 1460—1523)
74. The Enthronement of the Virgin (Jean Fouquet, around 1415—1460)
75. The Last Supper (Meister des Hausbuches, end of the 15th century)
76. The Resurrection (Fra Beato Angelico, 1387—1455)

Unnumbered—
Dodecahedron in the Sun Space (sketch by Karl Kemper 1881—1957)

CHAPTER IX
Figure
77. Irish Sun Cross
78. A Dolmen (south of Penmaenmawr, Caernarvon, N. Wales)
79. The First Goetheanum (drawing by Axel Ewald, from a photograph)
80. Freely drawn symmetry exercises for children (after Steiner)
81. Polar curves with respect to an imaginary circle
82. Sun Seal (after Steiner)

Karl Kemper

PLATES

I   Ethereal Space of Plant Growth (From *The Plant between Sun and Earth*)
  The planar cones reveal the gesture at the growing point

II   Lemniscatory Space (From *The Plant between Sun and Earth* first edition)
  The curves illustrate the interpenetration of cosmic and earthly spaces

III   Ethereal Space of Path-curve Surfaces (George Adams and Lawrence Edwards)
  Path-curve surfaces are of a higher mathematical order than lemniscatory surfaces; they solve more elegently the mathematical problem of depicting the nature of an ethereal space

IV   Germination in an Ethereal Space (Photographs by W. Schaumann)
  In the hidden, "empty" realms of the growing-points, substance is born anew

V   Descent of the Sun-Being (Ecole Perceval, Chatou, Paris)
  A child's Imagination: the Sun is not just a fiery ball in the sky, but an all-embracing presence

VI   Adoration of the Shepherds and Kings (Mural at Sion, in the Alps; unknown master, probably about the end of the 15th century)
  The two Families; one in the snowy cold of winter, the other in the sunlit world of the eastern potentates

VII   Adoration of the Shepherds, Adoration of the Kings (Flemish School, early 16th century)
  The two Families; one Child, erect and active, is revered by the Kings, while the other lies on the ground and the wingéd angels hover over him and sing

VIII   Betrothal of St. Catherine. (Lukas Cranach the Elder, 1472—1553)
  The Child, intensely aware, observes natural phenomena

IX   Nativity (Geertgen tot sint Jans, about 1465—1495)
  Descended to the three dimensions of the earth.

X   Presentation of the Jesus-Child in the Temple (Stephan Lochner, about 1410—1451)
  In a Human Circle there appears the Seed of New Life

XI   The Adoration of the Shepherds (Rembrandt van Rijn, 1606—1669)
  Human beings form a Sun Space on earth

XII   The Pilgrims at Emmaus (Rembrandt van Rijn)
  Conversation between Heaven and Earth

XIII   "Nole me tangere" (Liane Collot d'Herbois, born in Tintagel in 1907)
  The Resurrection-Body, still standing on the Earth

XIV   "Easter" (Beppe Assensa, 1805—1987)
  Redemption of the Cross of Matter

XV   "Light and Darkness"—Goethe's Theory—The morning after the Deluge—Moses writing the Book of Genesis (J.M.W. Turner, 1775—1851.)
  Space for the birth of new matter

XVI   "Plant Growth" (Gerard Wagner, born in 1906)

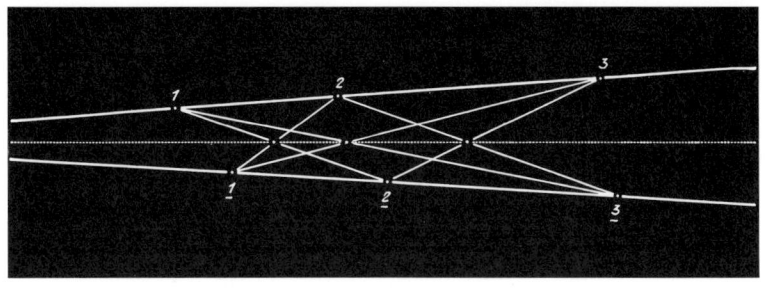

1

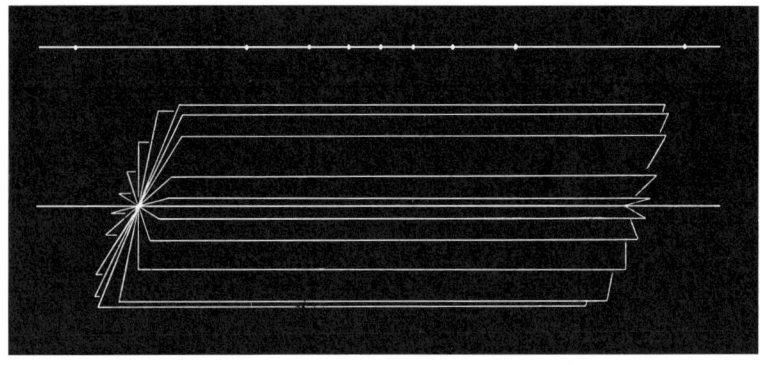

2

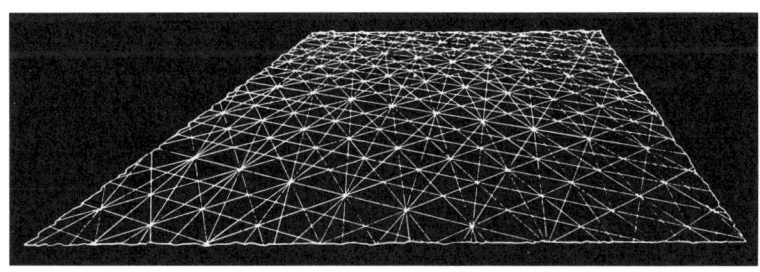

3

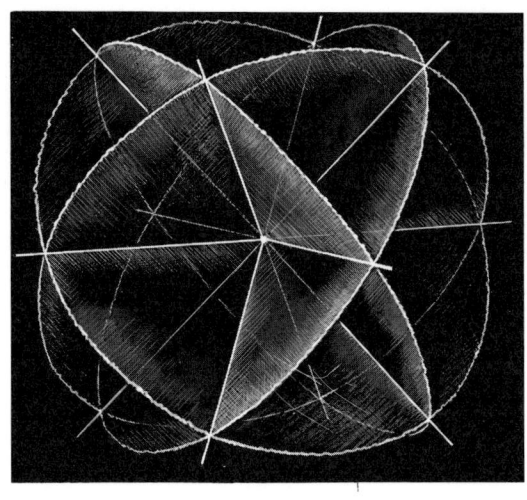

4

 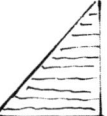

5

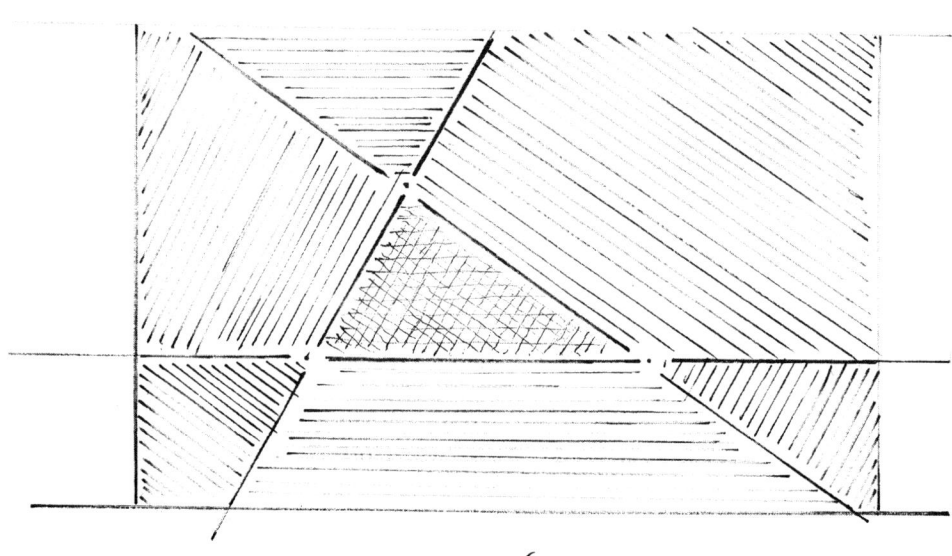

6

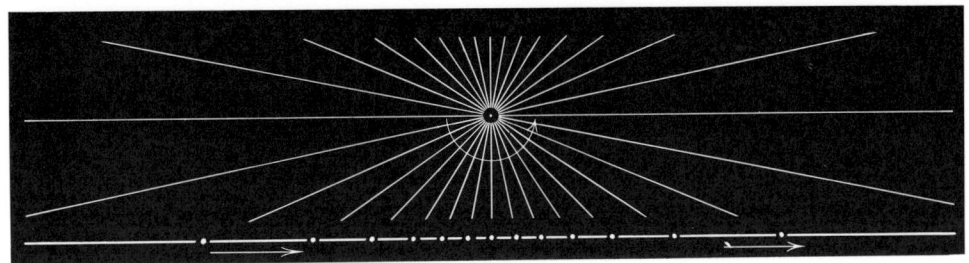

7

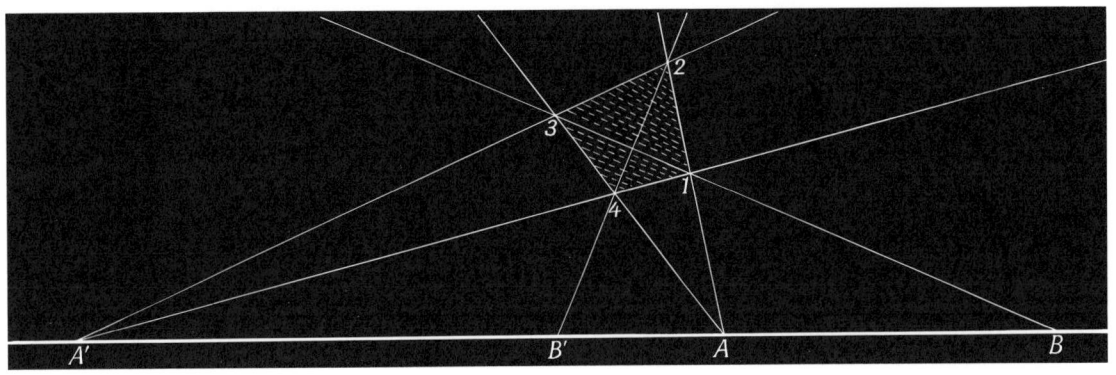

8

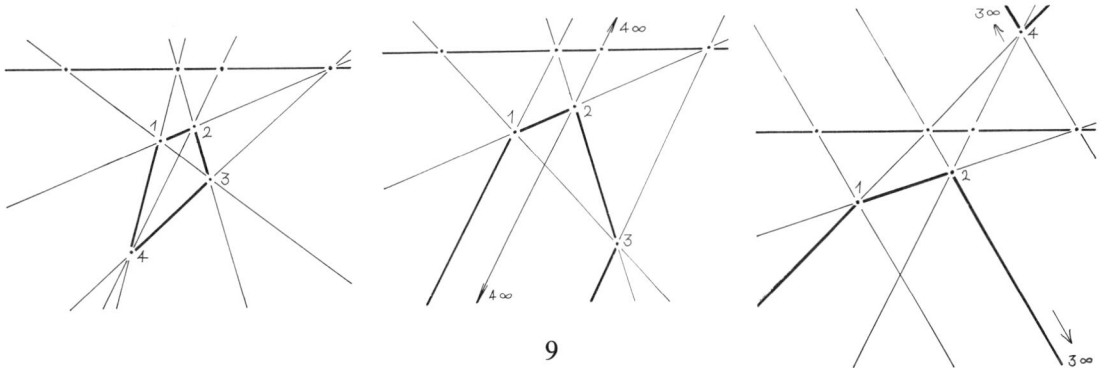

9

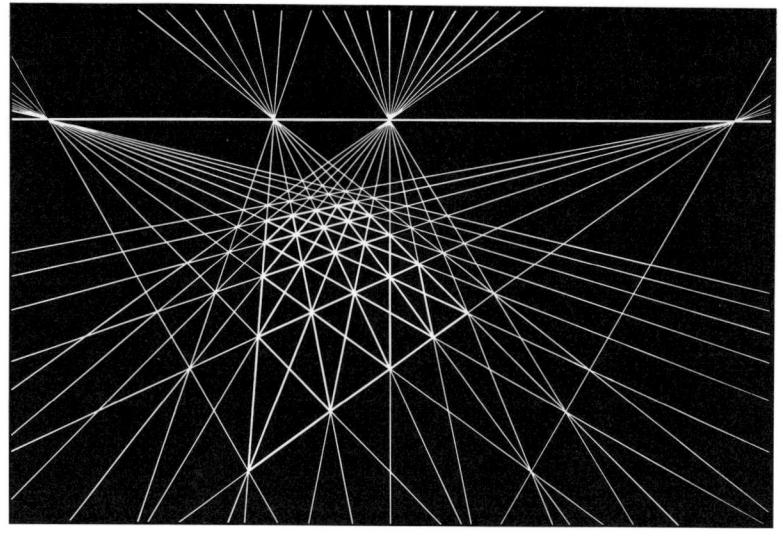

10

11

12

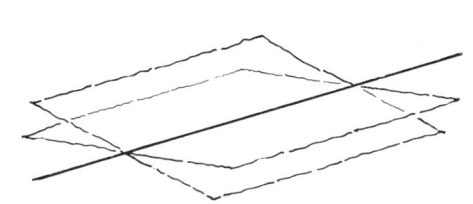 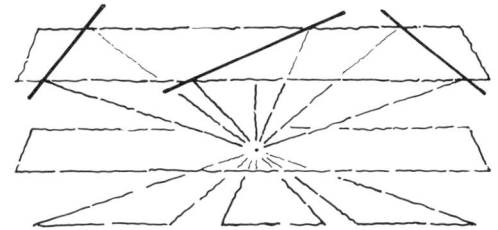

13

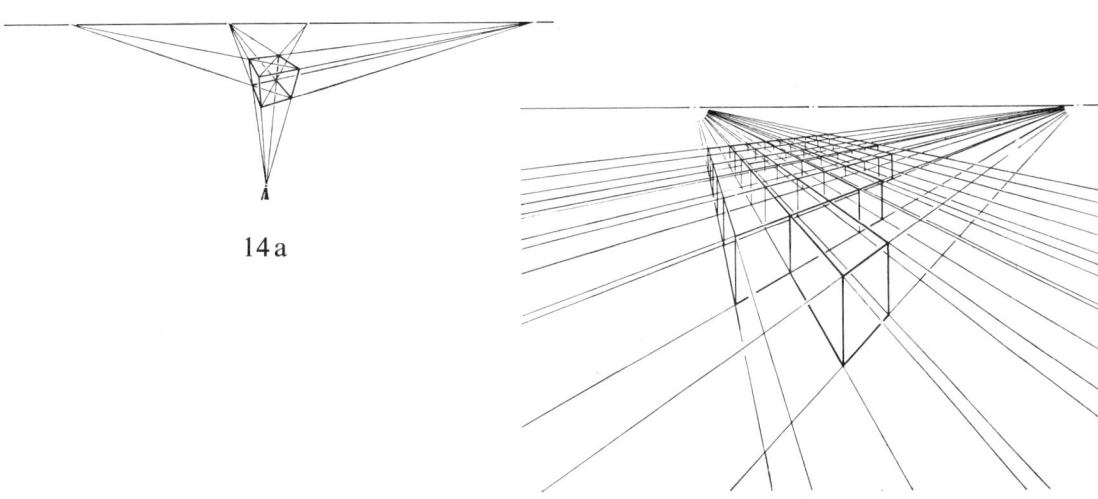

14a

14b

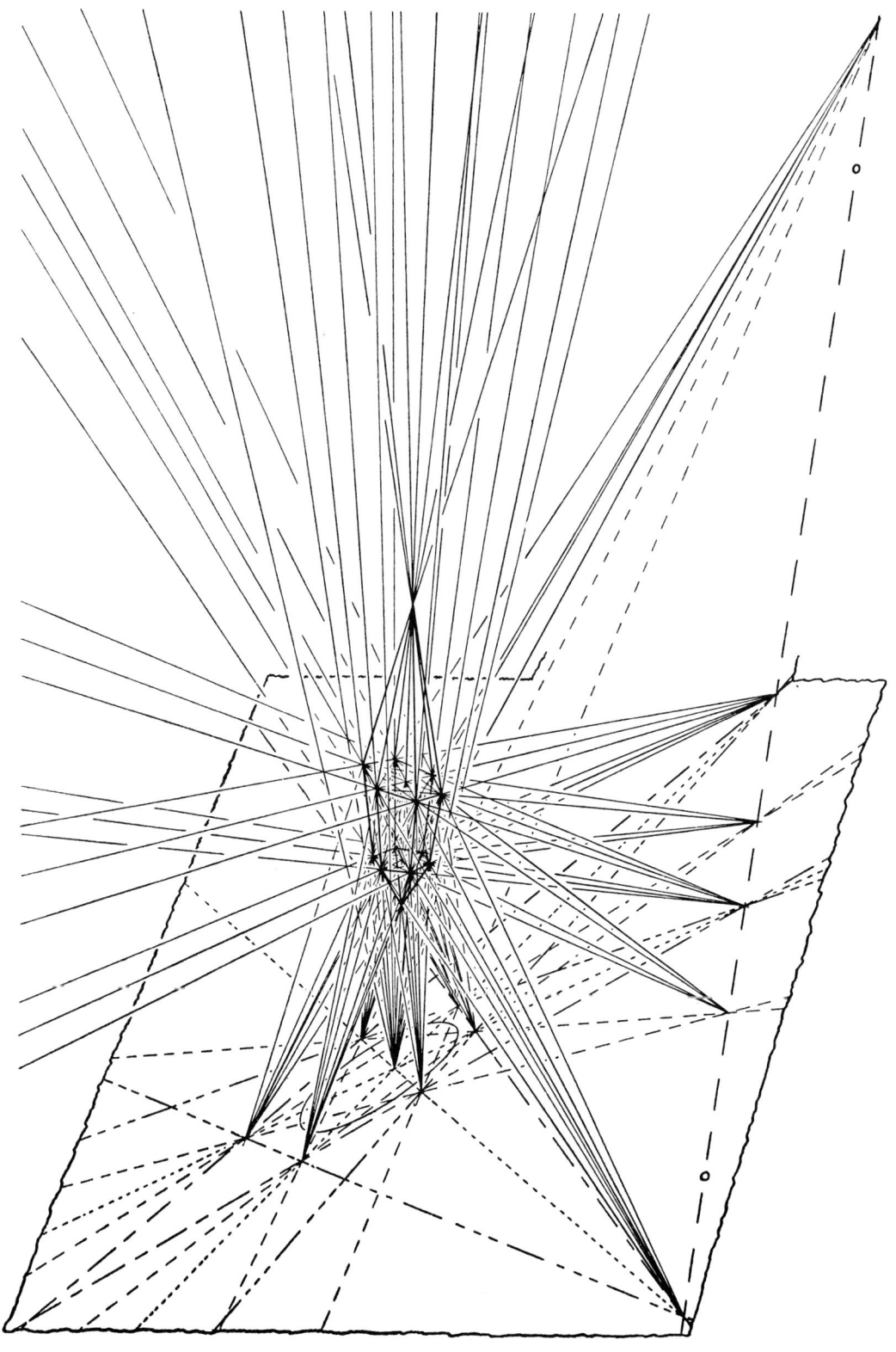

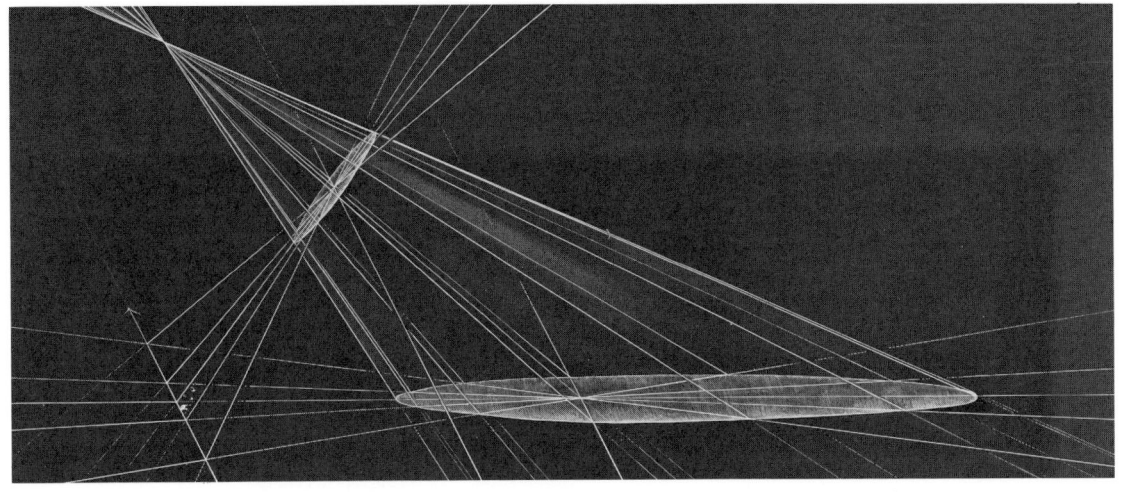

16

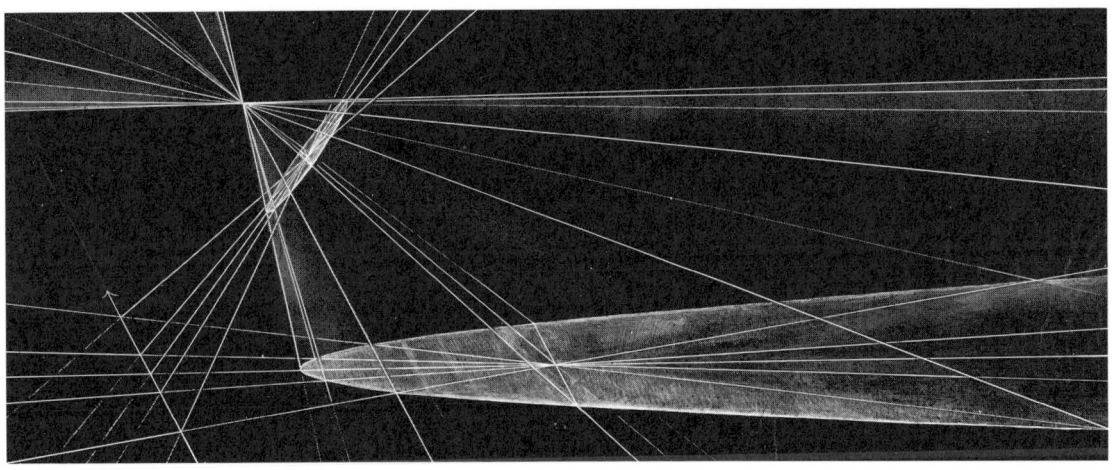

17

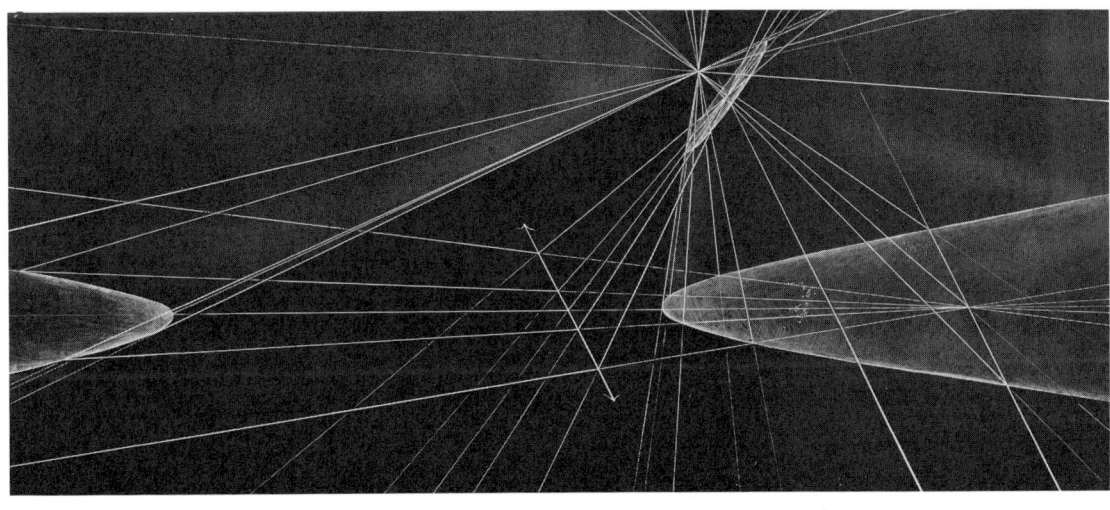

18

19

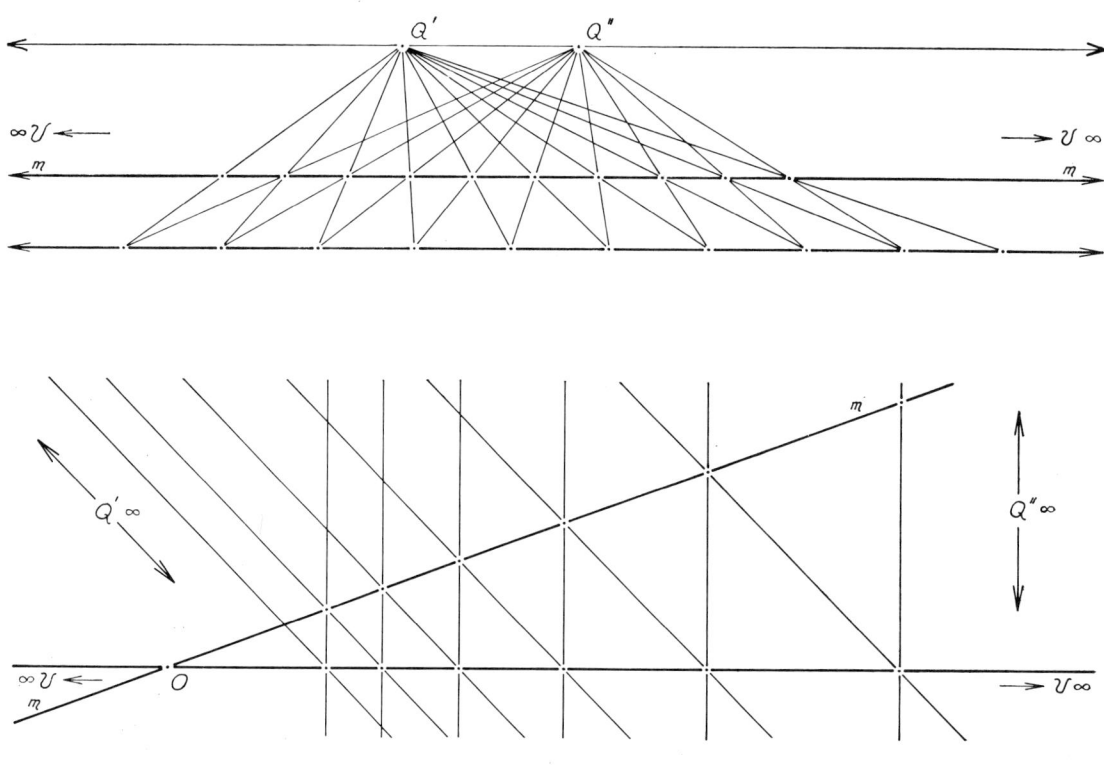

20

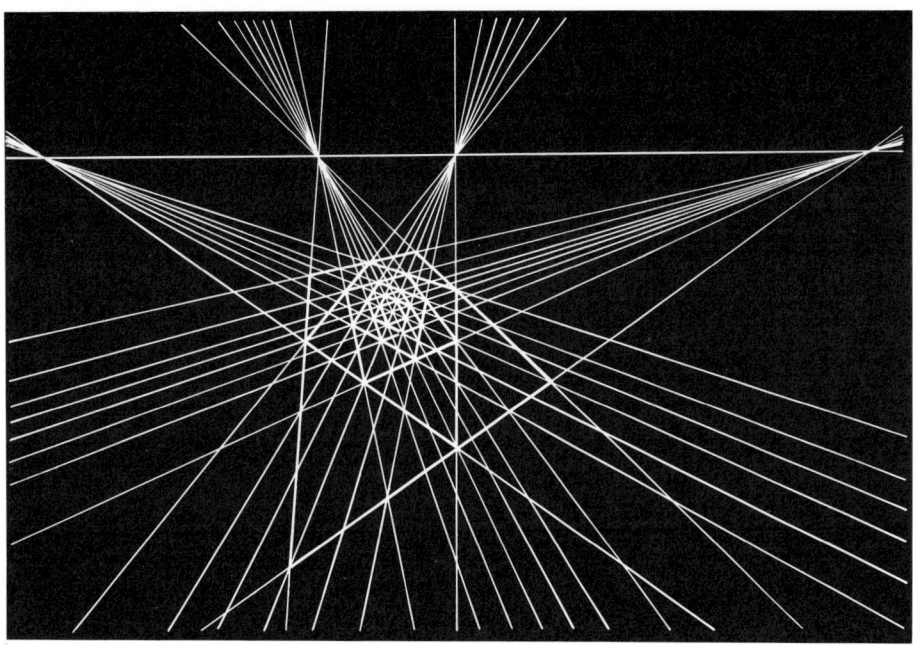

21

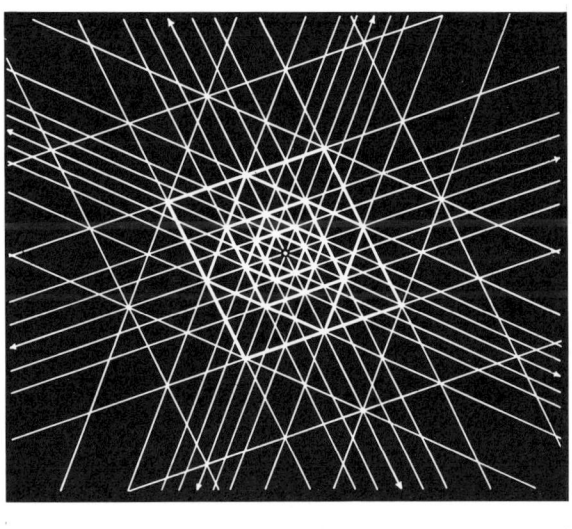

22

23

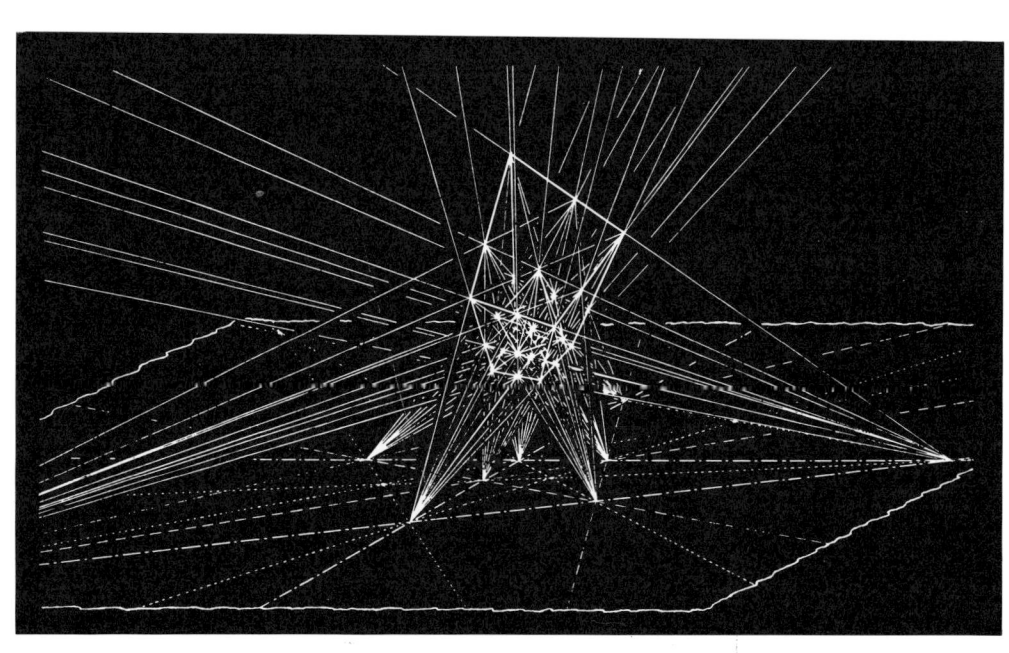

24

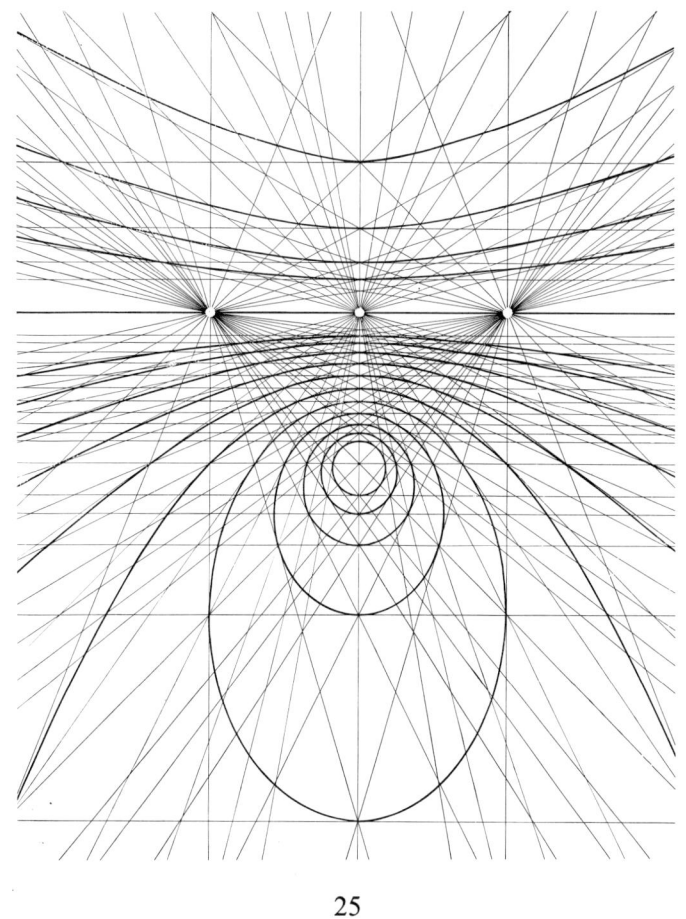

25

26

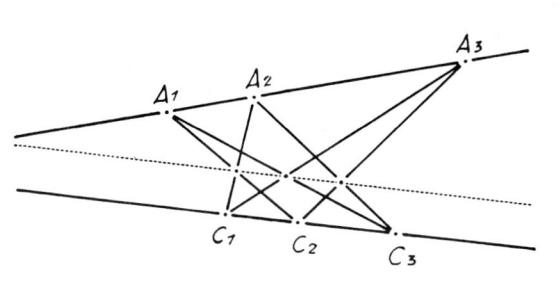 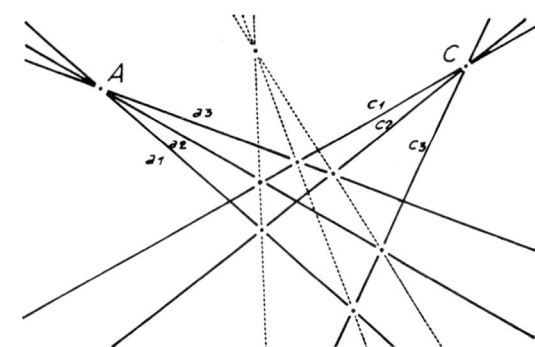

28

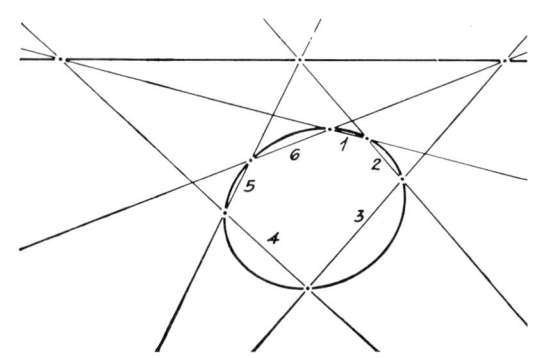 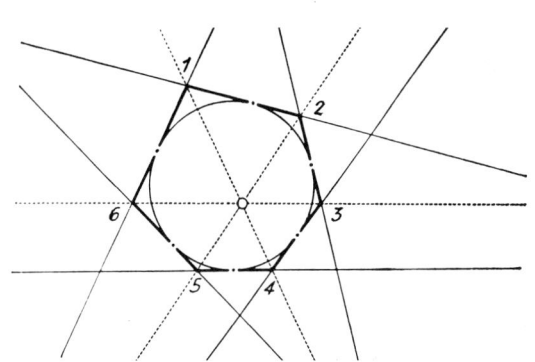

29

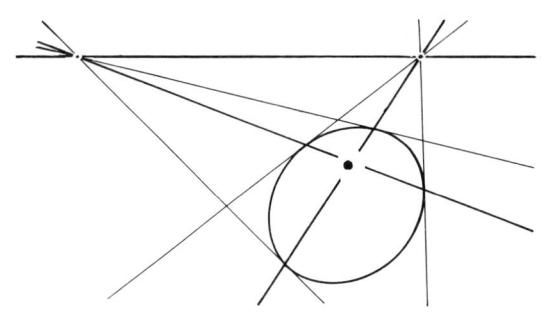 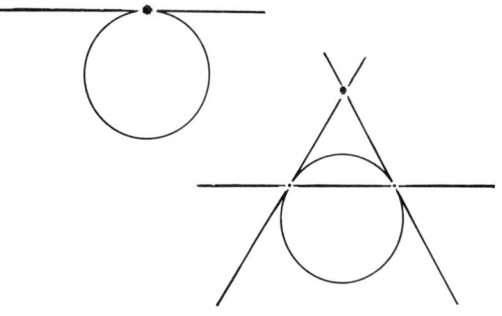

30

31

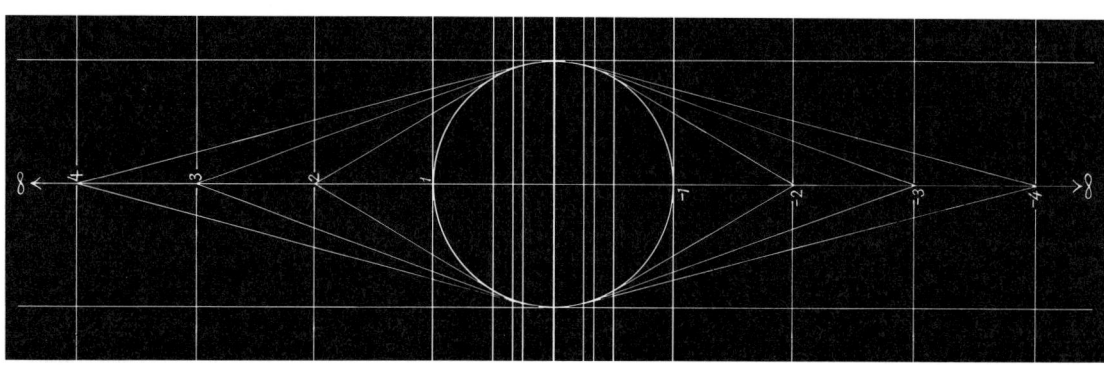

32

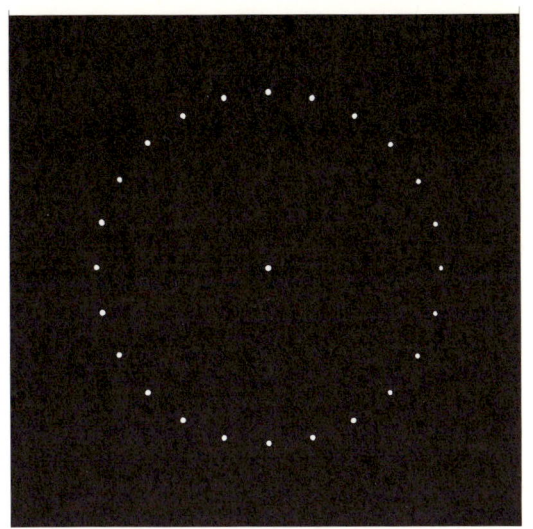

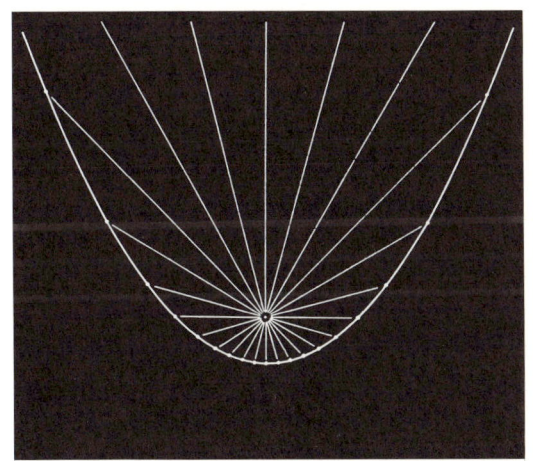
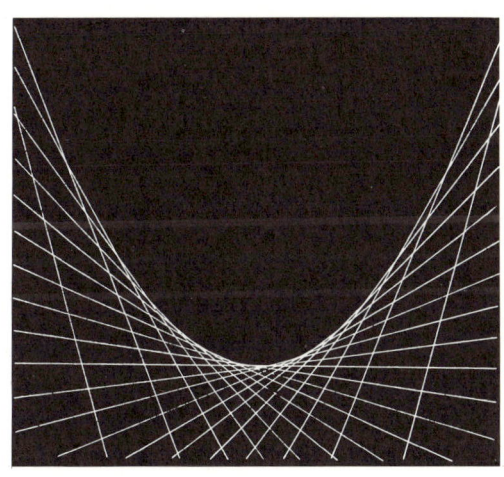

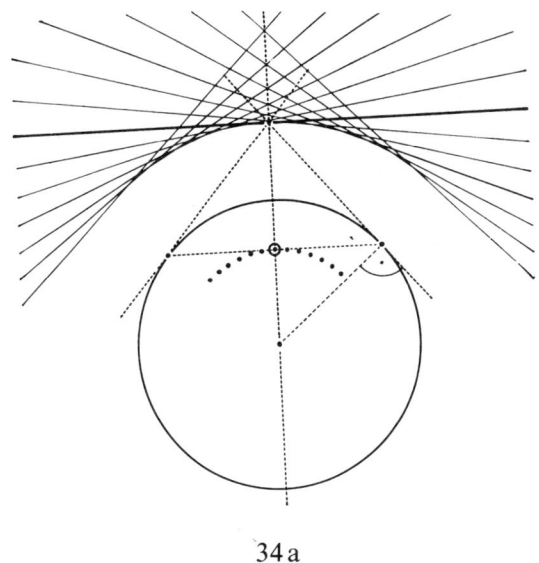

34 a

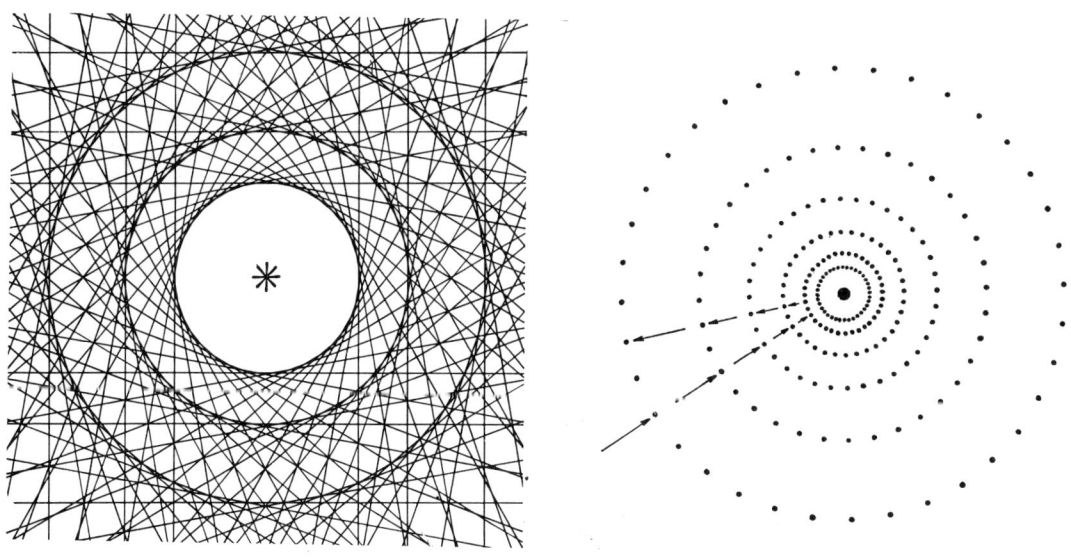

34 b

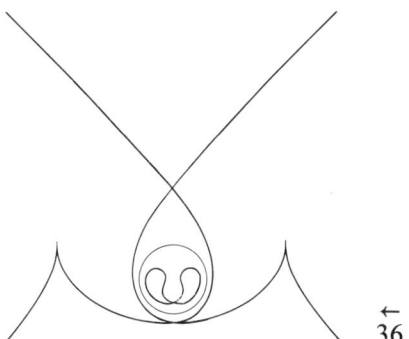

← 36

37 ↑   38 ↓

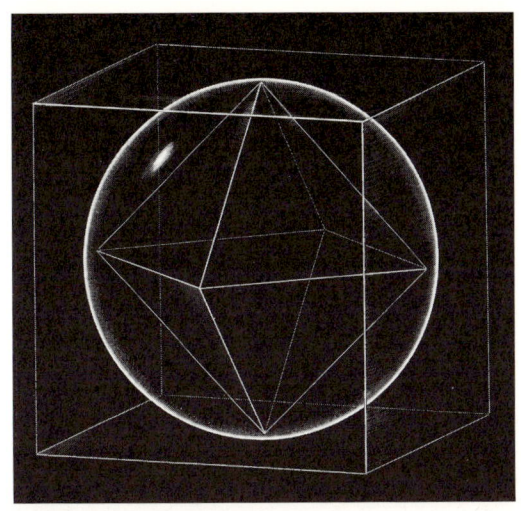

39 →

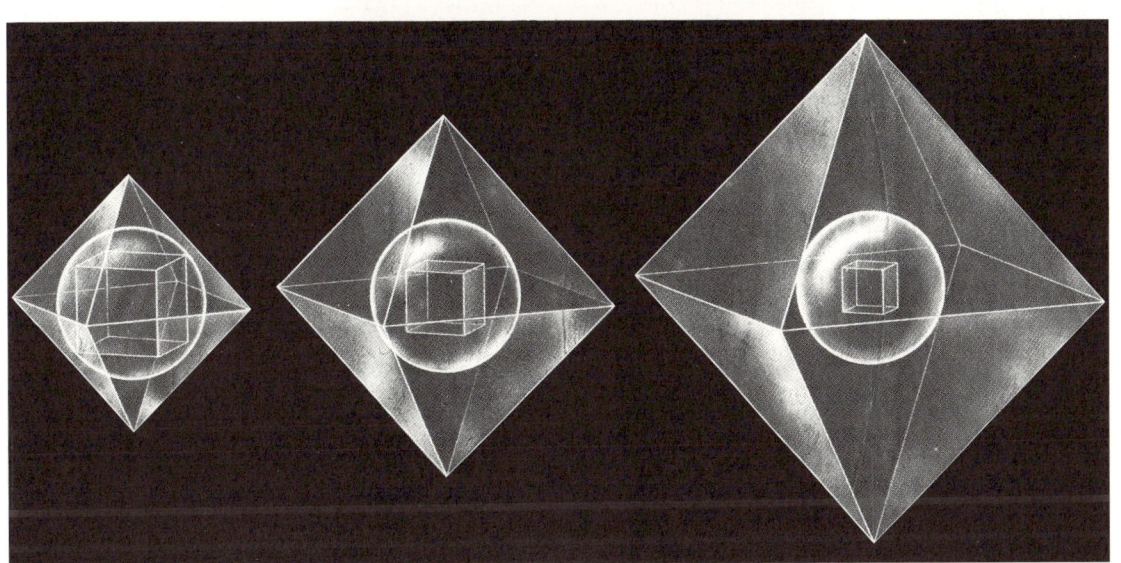

40 ↓

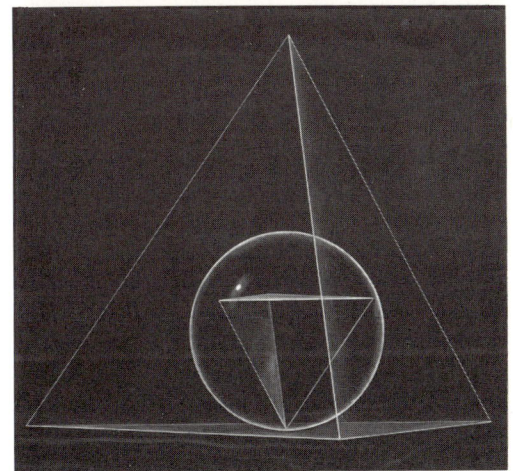

41 ←

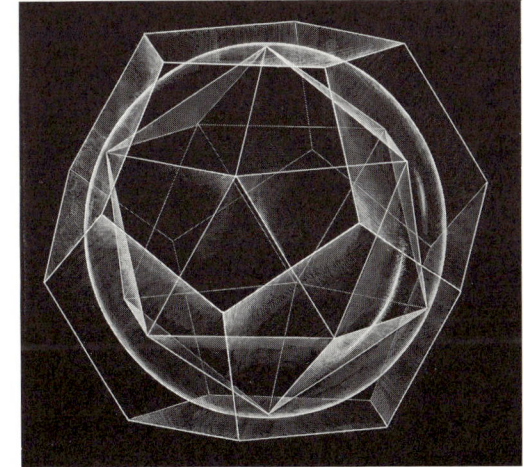

42 →

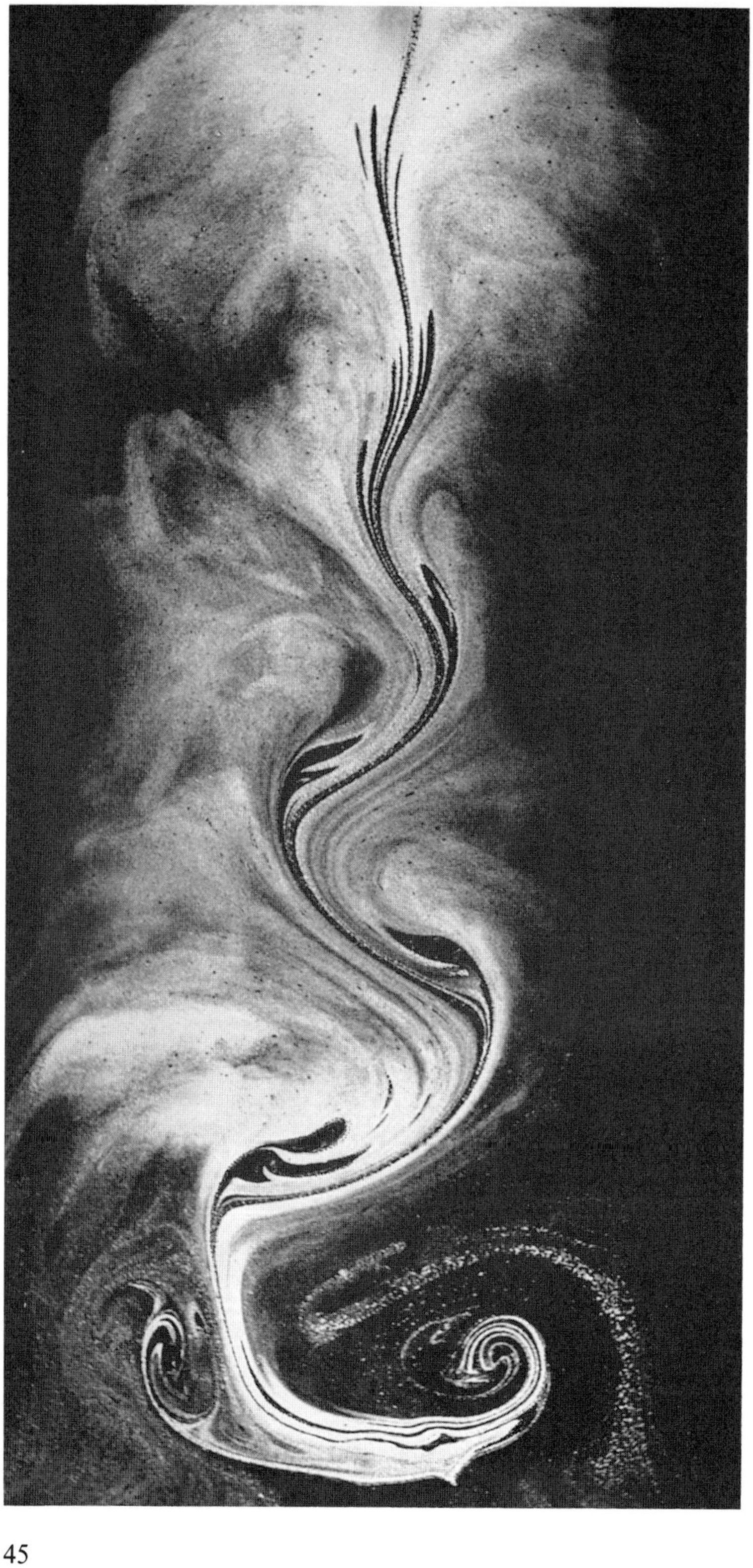

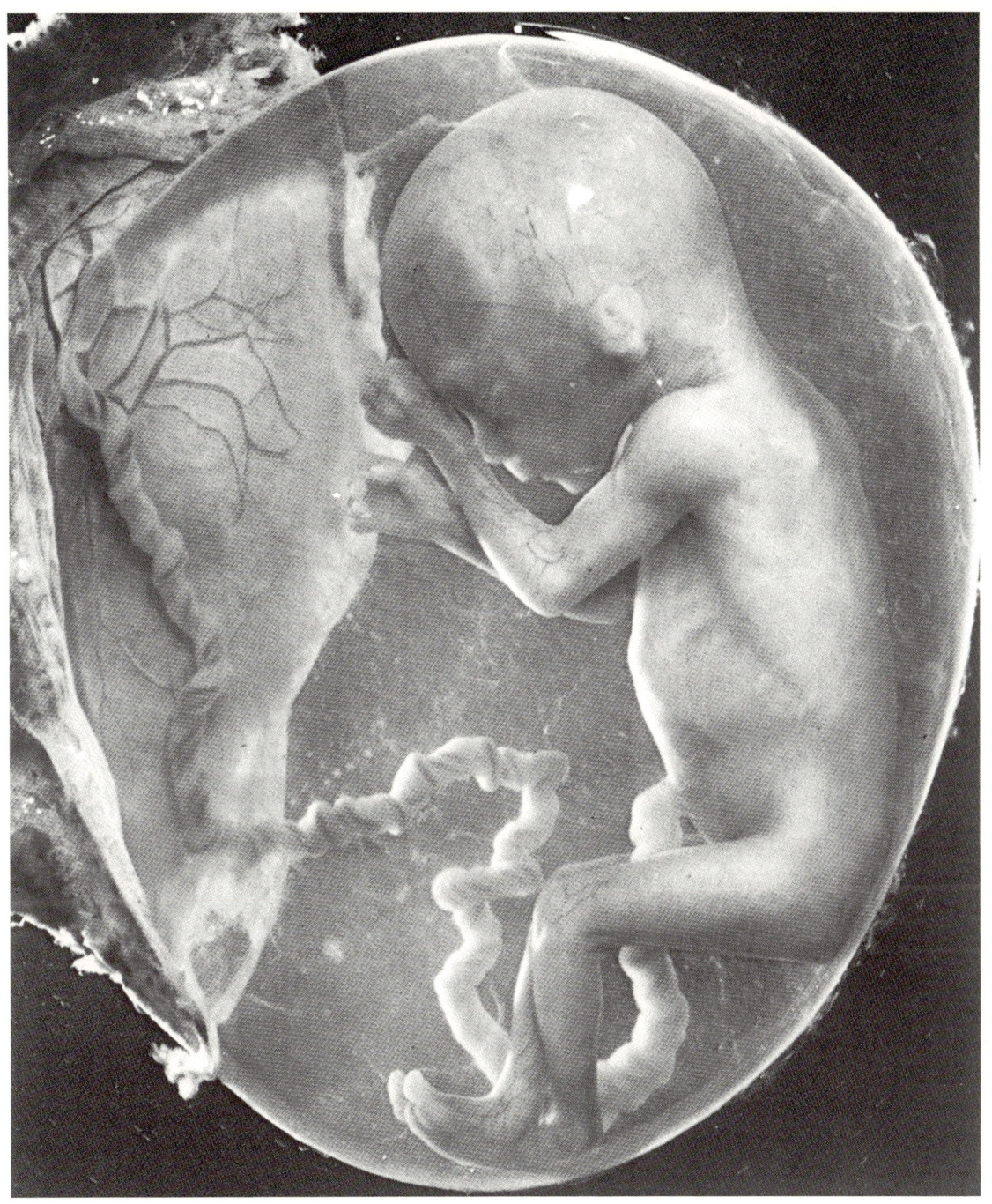

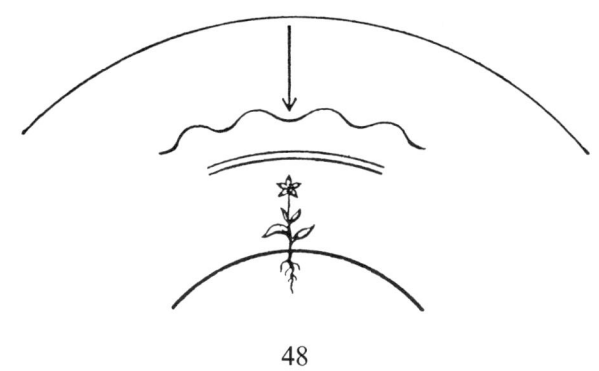

48

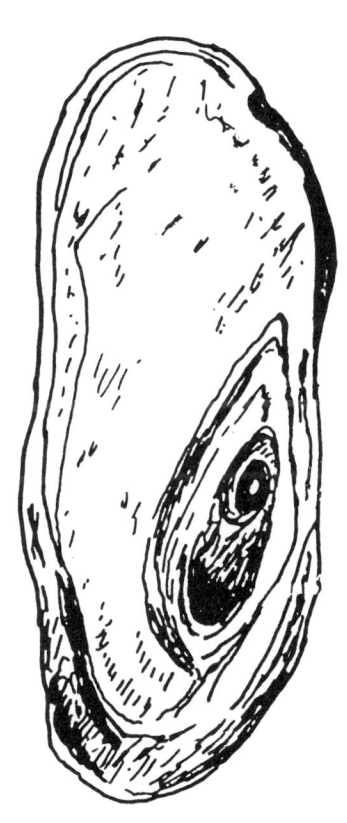

49

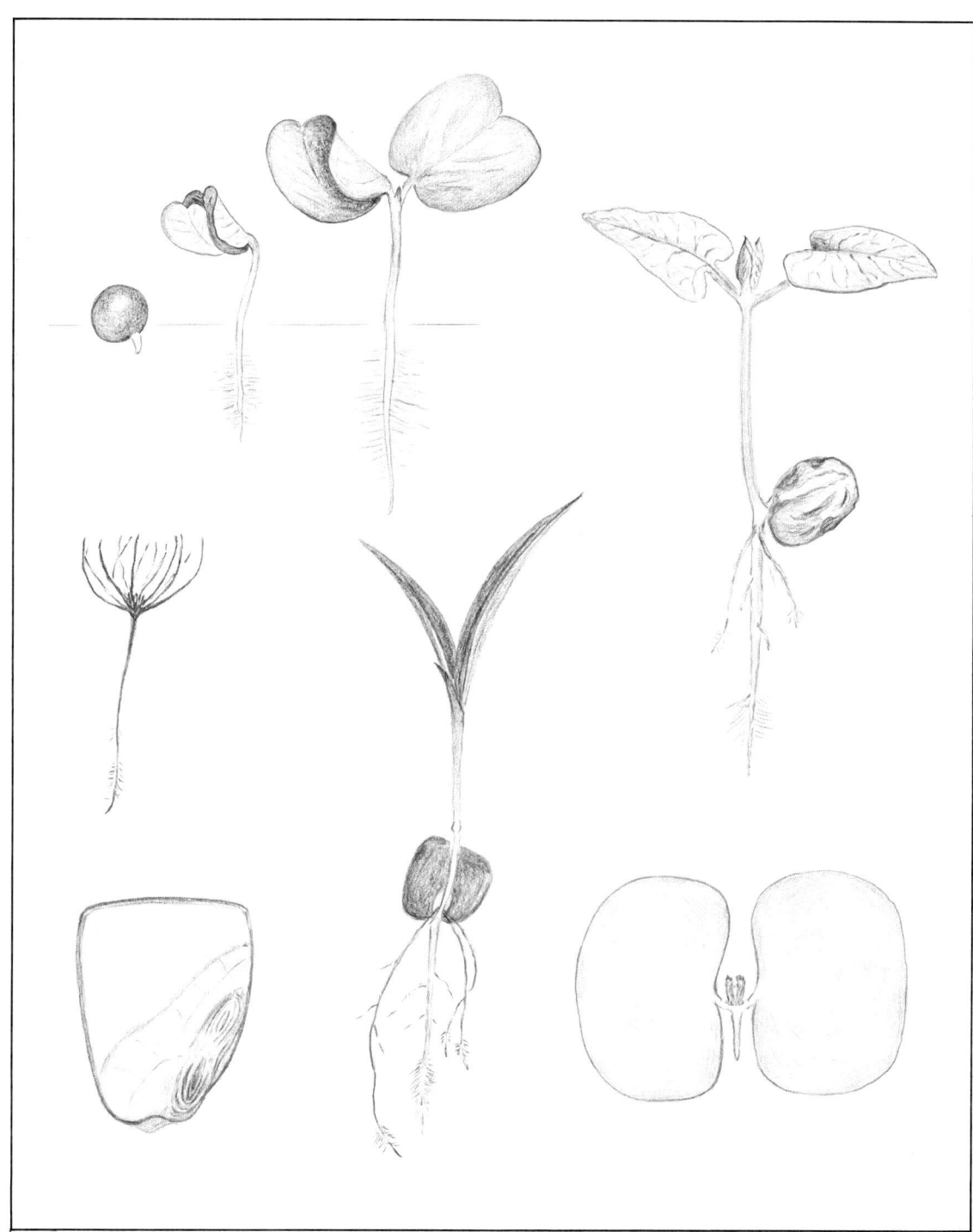

50

Quæ sunt in superis, hæc inferioribus insunt:
 Quod monstrat cœlum, id terra frequenter habet.
Ignis, Aqua et fluitans duo sunt contraria: felix,
 Talia si jungis: sit tibi scire satis!

D. M. à C. B. P. L. C.

52

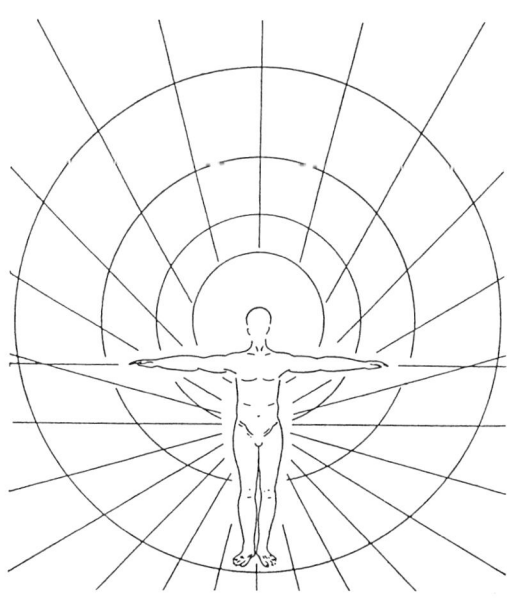 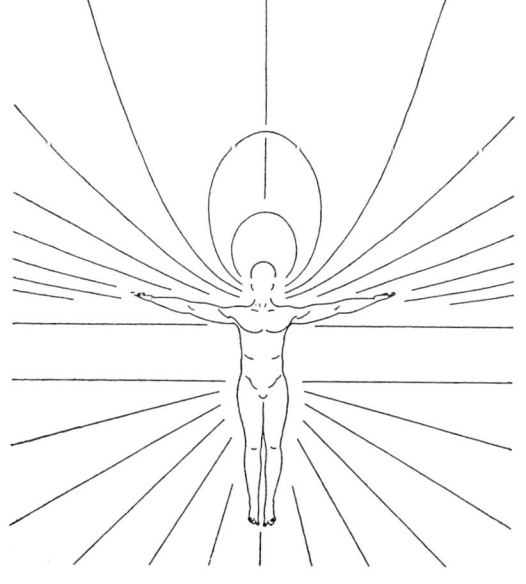

53

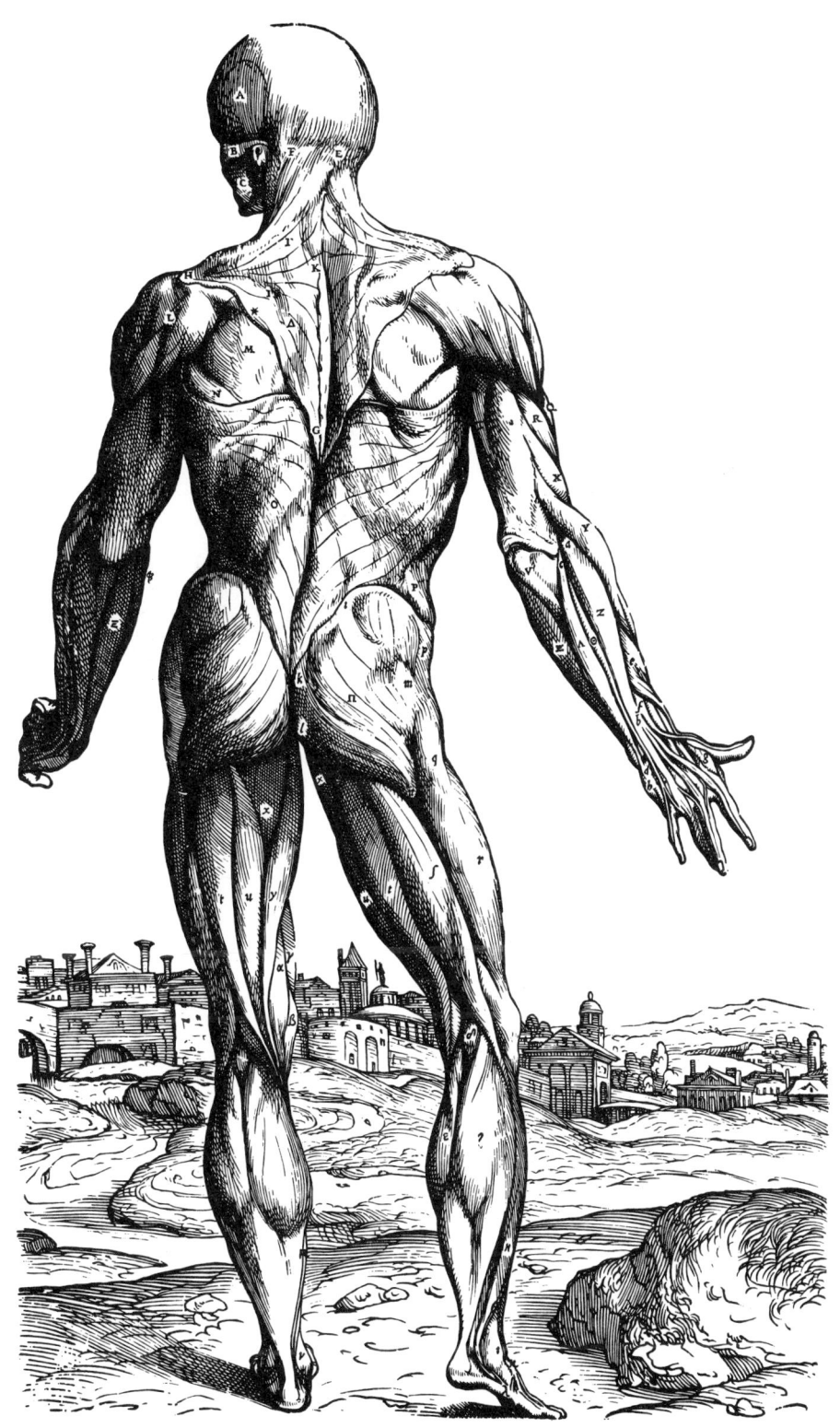

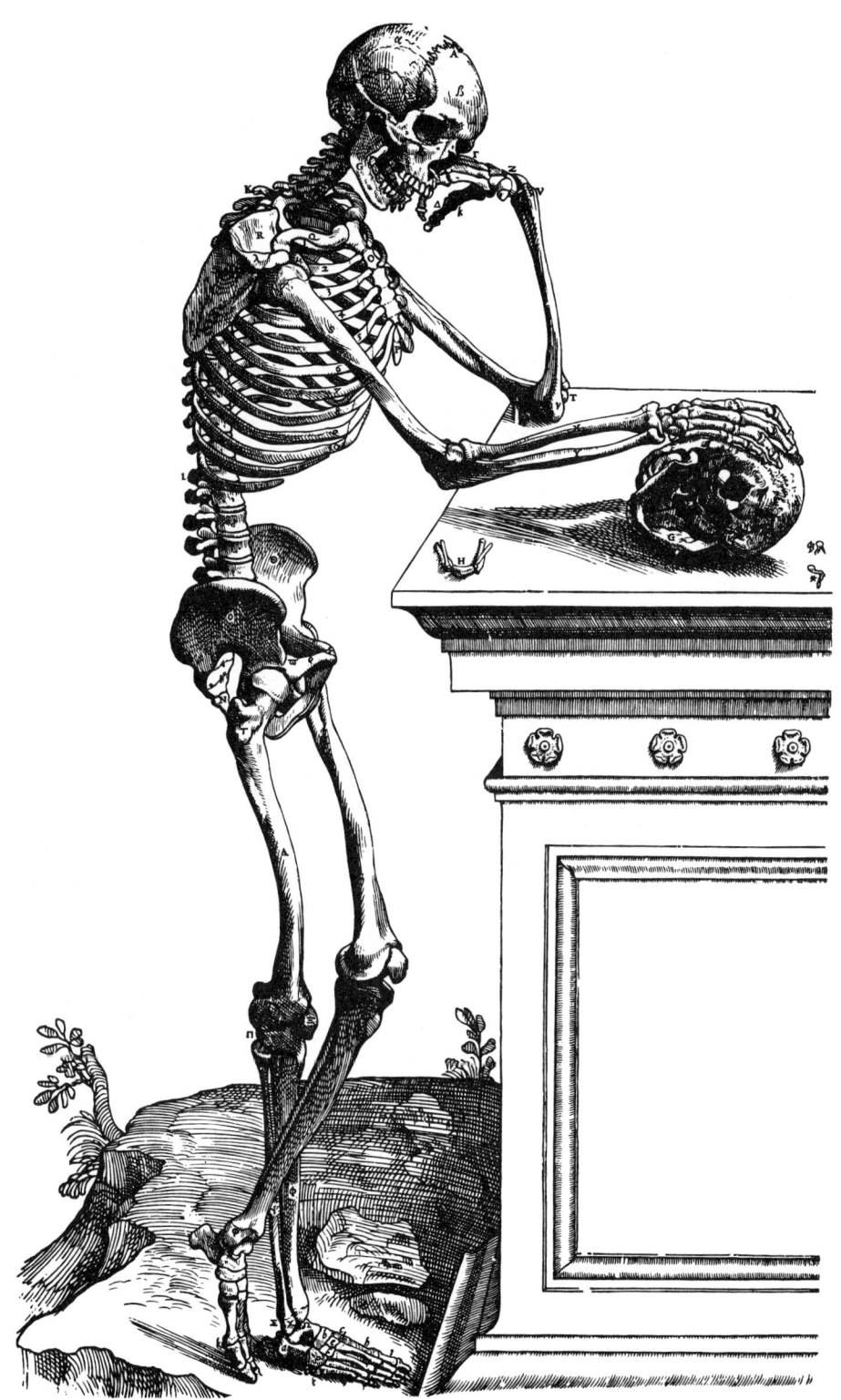

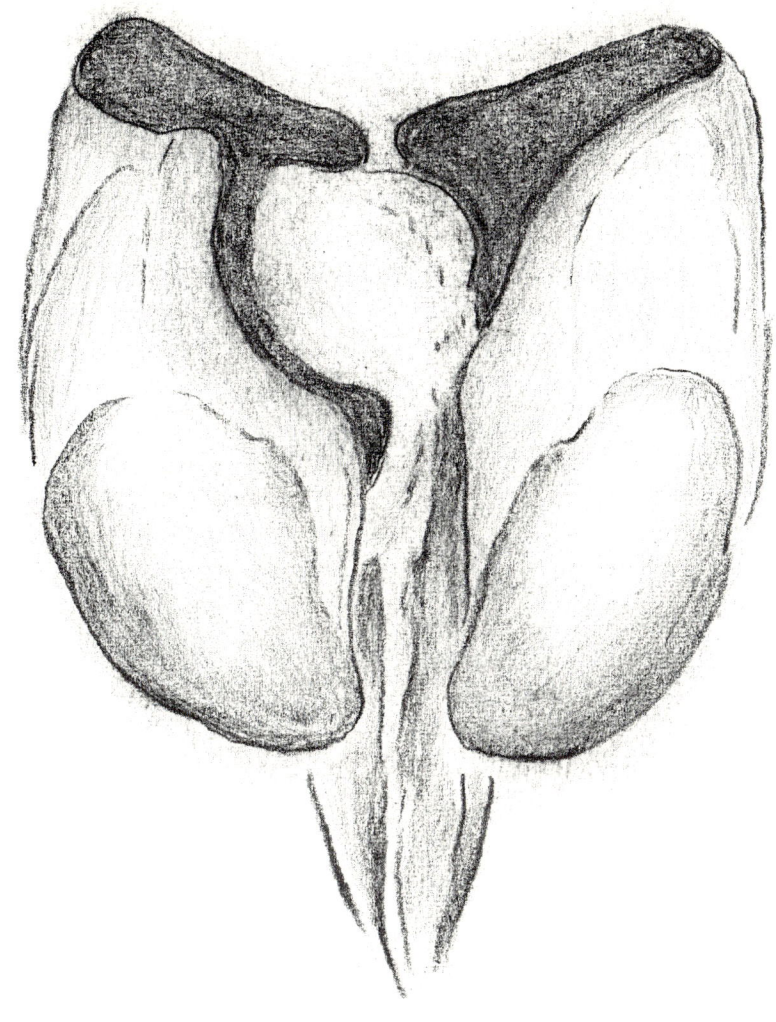

56

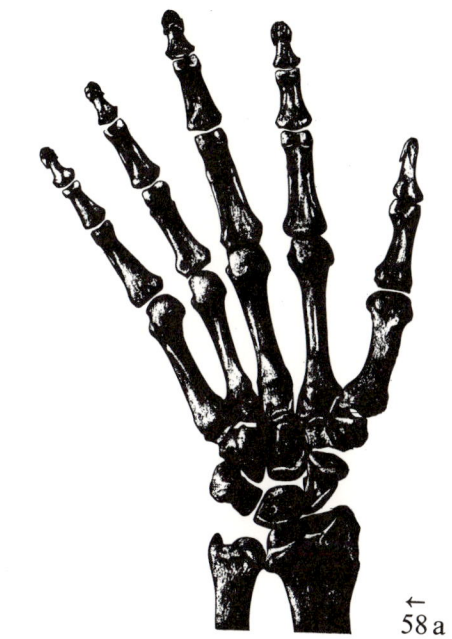

← 58 a

↓ 58 b

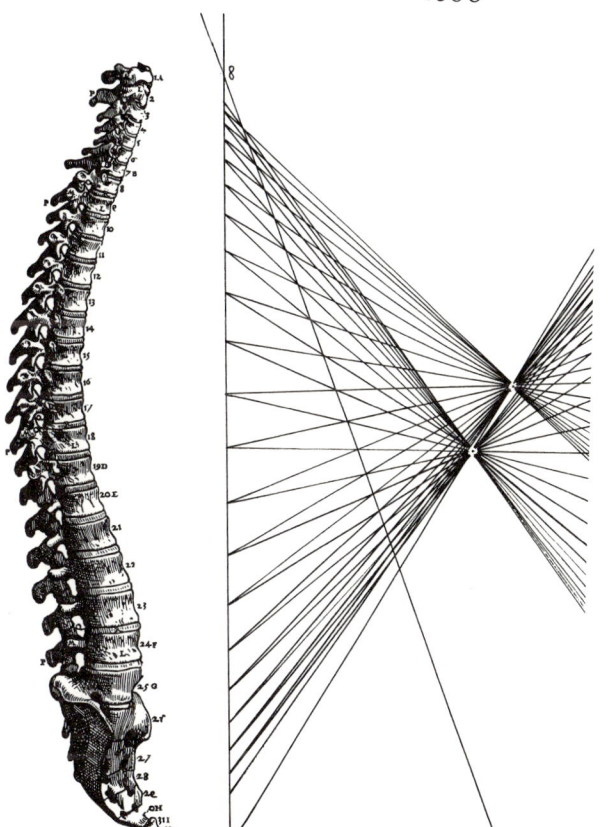

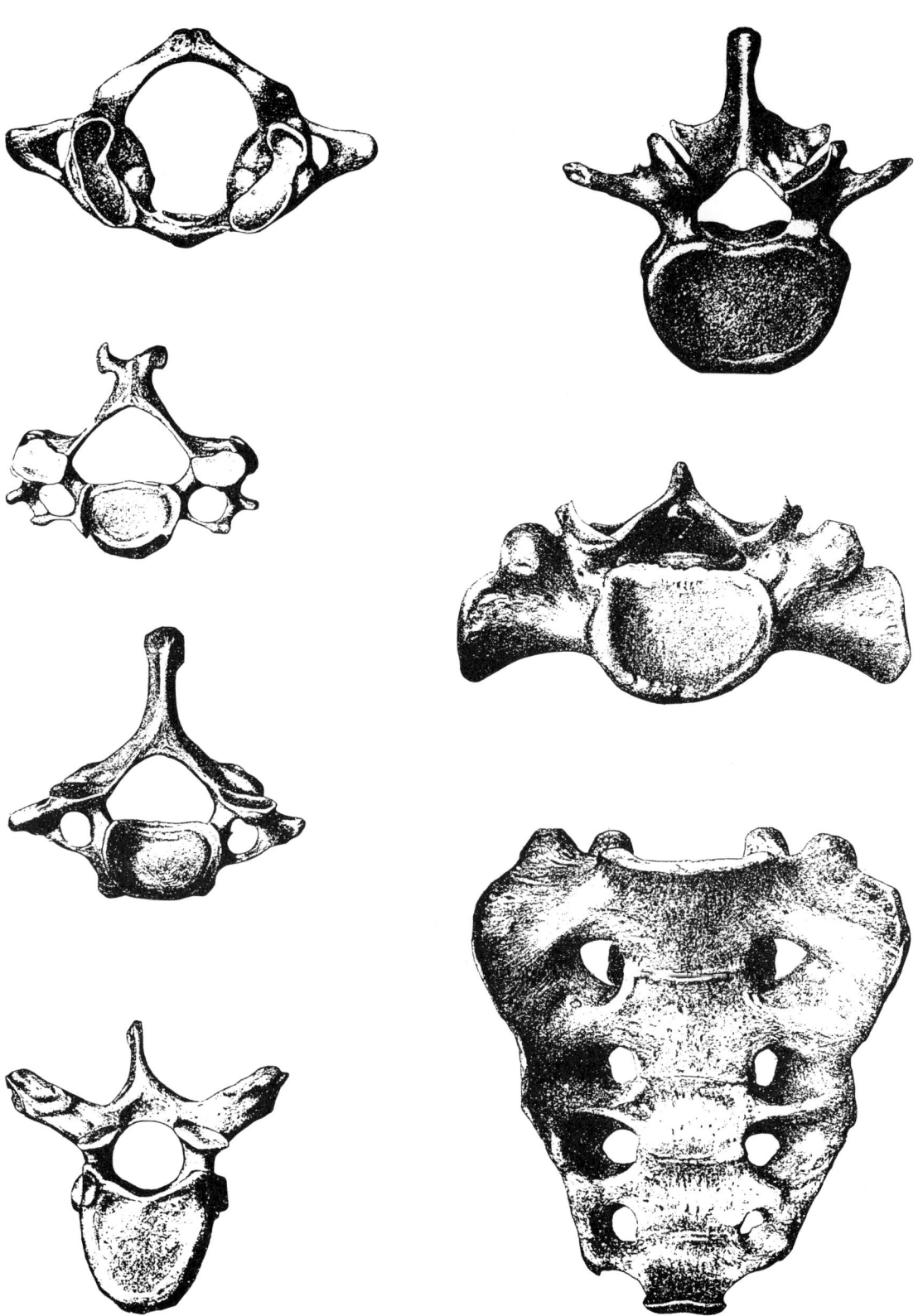

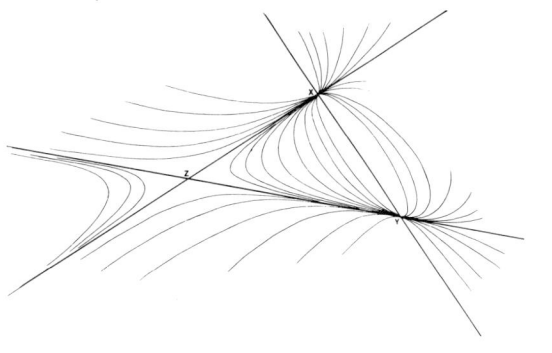
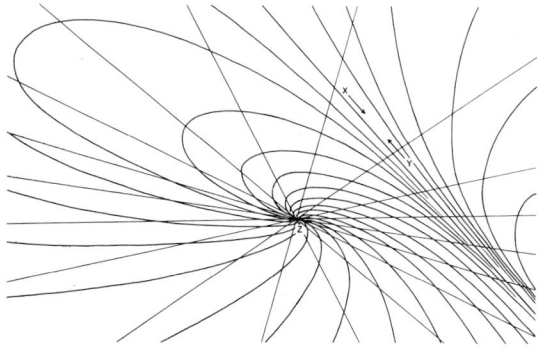

63

64 a

64 b

   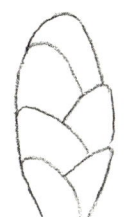 

65

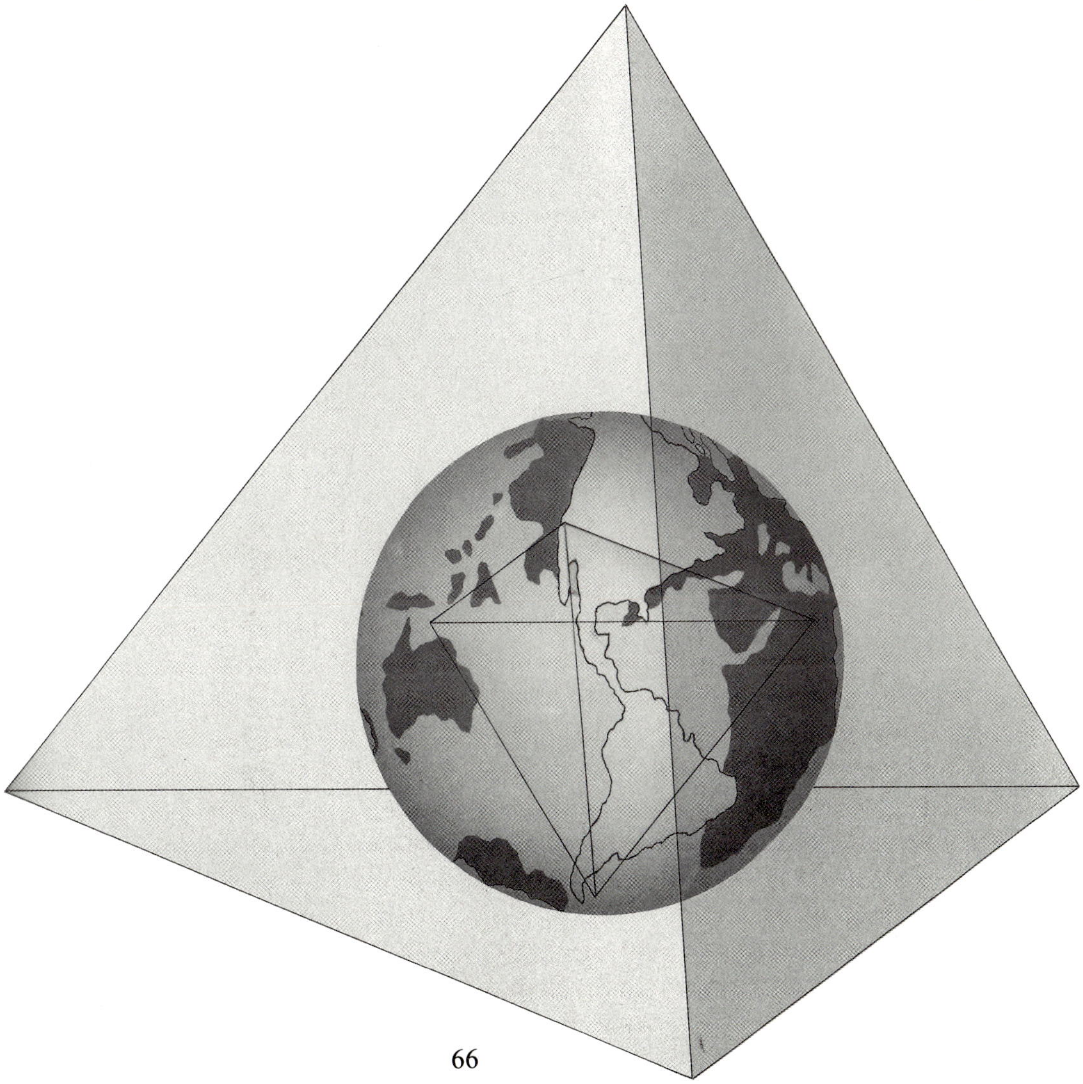

66

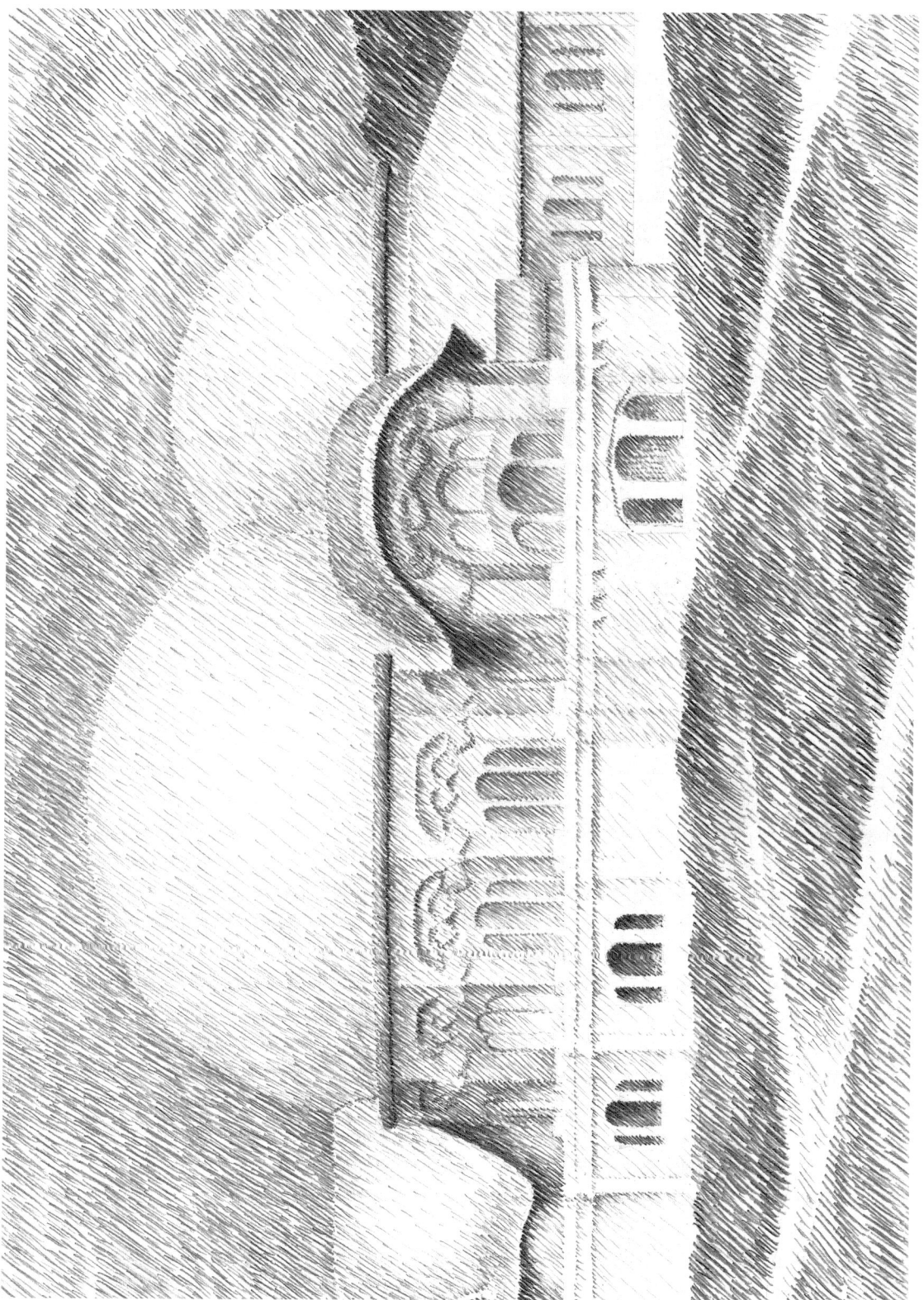

80

81

82

I

II

III

IV

V

VI

VII

VIII

X

XII

XIII

XIV

XVI